UNDER
SIEGE

UNDER SIEGE

Literary Life in London 1939–1945

Robert Hewison

WEIDENFELD AND NICOLSON
LONDON

Contents

List of Illustrations

Foreword

'The war marked the end of literary society.' J.B. Priestley in an interview with the author. 'I would rather have been in London under siege between 1940 and 1945 than anywhere else, except perhaps Troy in the time that Homer celebrated.' John Lehmann in his autobiography. This book tries to show how these are complementary rather than contradictory statements. I was born in 1943, so this is an account written from the outside. It is a survey which attempts to establish the geography and demography of literary life in London during a period defined by external factors – the Second World War as it affected the United Kingdom between 1939 and 1945.

Both 'literary life' and 'London' have been used as fairly loose frames of reference: the literary life is only one part of a nation's culture, London is only its titular head. Yet between 1939 and 1945 there was little literary life outside London, and the events of those years imposed distinctive conditions upon it. The particular study of this book is the relationship between the external conditions and the work that was produced during those years. As far as possible the evidence is taken from what was written within the enclosing dates. Above all, I must stress that this is a survey, as far as I know the first of its kind. The themes that emerge are those which were common concerns at the time, in so far as an outsider can detect them. I hope that the details that have been omitted – or missed – will be the subject of a great deal of further research.

My own research has been much helped by insiders who in every case gave me not only information not otherwise accessible, but encouragement to continue my investigations: G.S. Fraser, John Heath-Stubbs, Philip Hope-Wallace, Rayner Heppenstall, John Lehmann,

Jack Lindsay, J.B. Priestley, Alan Ross, John Sommerfield, and William Sansom. Each gave me personal interviews from which I have drawn both directly and indirectly in this book, and I am very grateful to all of them.

Besides these I would like to thank Amy Capon for access to Paul Capon's papers, and for the interest she has shown in the project, Cornelia Cook for information on Joyce Cary, and Francis Crowdy for information on Victor Cazalet's Anti-Aircraft Battery. Both Dorian Cooke and Bill Crozier have contributed to my knowledge of the period, and Robert Radford most generously allowed me to consult his thesis for the University of East Anglia on the Artists' International Association.

Jonathan Barker, the Librarian of the Arts Council Poetry Library, has been a great help both in his professional capacity and as an enthusiast for the study of modern poetry, and I wish to name him among those personal friends who have helped me greatly: Michael Palin, Neil and Helen Taylor, Nigel Walmsley and David Britt. Finally, it would have been difficult to have done anything at all without the help of my sister, Anthea Ridett.

A NOTE ON THE REFERENCES

Rather than spatter the page with footnotes I have written a running commentary on the sources quoted in the notes (from p. 187). Details of contexts, dates and publishers will be found there, except where the reference is obvious in the text itself.

Enemies of Promise

> *'1939 was not a year in which*
> *to start a literary career.'*
>
> E.M. Forster

'This is the time of year when wars break out and when a broken glass betrays the woodland to the vindictive sun.' After lunch on a sultry day in the South of France in the summer of 1937, Cyril Connolly settled down at a table in the shade of a plane tree and asked himself a series of questions. What was going to happen to the world in the next ten years? To himself, to his friends, to the books they wrote? Especially to the books. As the cinders of forest fires drifted across the garden he confronted a dangerous future. 'I have one ambition – to write a book that will hold good for ten years afterwards.' The result was published in September 1938. It was the same week as the Munich crisis, and war very nearly did break out.

Connolly achieved his ambition; his book held good until 1948, and beyond. But its survival comes from the discussion of literary failure, not success. *Enemies of Promise* is remembered not for the demonstration of how books should be written, but for the explanation of how they come not to be written at all. Connolly was looking back over what W.H. Auden called 'a low dishonest decade'; the next ten years were to be worse. Drink, talk, day-dreams, journalism, worldly success, duty and domesticity, sex – these enemies of literary promise listed by Connolly were to be even more subversive during the war years than they had been in the Thirties. But the greatest enemy of all was politics. 'My own predicament is –' Connolly stated,

1

'how to live another ten years.' And that, he concluded, was a political problem: how not to get killed.

Politics were unavoidable for anyone in 1938. For a moment it looked as though Britain's Conservative coalition government was about to go to war to prevent Hitler's annexation of Czechoslovakia; on another front Germany and Italy were helping right-wing Spanish forces to squeeze the life out of the legitimate Spanish Republican government. Connolly knew what a writer must do:

> He has to be political to integrate himself and he must go on being political to protect himself. Today the forces of life and progress are ranging on one side, those of reaction and death on the other. We are having to choose between democracy and fascism, and fascism is the enemy of art. It is not a question of relative freedom; there are no artists in Fascist countries.

But the dramatic contrast was weakened by the observable fact that the stagnation and demoralization of capitalist countries such as Britain were equally stifling to a writer. And there was a snare. Political commitment might be necessary to a writer for self-preservation, but: 'being political is apt to become a whole time job'.

1938 was the penultimate year of what quickly became known in retrospect as The Pink Decade. The Depression, the collapse of the Labour Party at the general election of 1931, the rise of Fascism and Communism were the external factors shaping a generation of English writers whose concerns were chiefly political. That is a generalization – but it seemed confirmed by the Spanish Civil War. And 'Spain', too, is now a generalization. The majority of Englishmen who fought in Spain were working-class, and were not writers or intellectuals, but intellectual or not, those whose view of the world was formed by the events of the early Thirties saw in Spain what seemed to be another chance of revolution, another 1848. The idea of being able to oppose Fascism physically as well as morally had an emotional appeal, but 'Spain' was a defeat, external and internal. The capitalist democracies did nothing to help the Republican government from the outside, while the consequence of help from Communist Russia was the suppression of democratic principles.

Writing *Enemies of Promise* without benefit of hindsight in 1937, when Madrid and Barcelona were still in Republican hands, Connolly unconsciously conveys the paradox. On the one hand he genuinely believes in the 'mystical feeling of release and emancipation' which writers felt in Spain. On the other he warns that 'another effect of becoming too political is that such activity leads to disillusion'. By 1939, with Republican resistance collapsing and the truth about the Communists' suppression of their rivals filtering out, release and emancipation were succeeded by despair.

The contemporary literature of the Spanish Civil War is a minefield in which one rarely stumbles on the truth. George Orwell's *Homage to Catalonia* (1938) was an attempt to tell it, but it had little immediate impact because it was cold-shouldered by the English Left who feared any break in the ranks against Fascism. Franz Borkenau's *Spanish Cockpit* (1937) had received the same treatment. It was in a conscious effort to cut through 'the farrago of nonsense' that had been written during and immediately after the war that a virtually unknown former Communist, Jason Gurney, set out to record his memories thirty-six years later, and even then he could not suppress his emotions:

There is no longer any point in trying to untangle the web of lies and confusions which lay behind that ghastly Civil War. It arose out of total confusion and chaos. There were individuals on both sides who committed every possible form of cruelty and beastliness. And nobody, from either side, came out of it with clean hands. We, of the International Brigades, had wilfully deluded ourselves into the belief that we were fighting a noble Crusade because we needed a crusade – the opportunity to fight against the manifest evils of Fascism, in one form or another, which seemed then as if it would overwhelm every value of Western civilization. We were wrong, we deceived ourselves and were deceived by others: but even then, the whole thing was not in vain.

In 1939 it seemed as though it had been in vain, and deception, self-deception and the washing of unclean hands were the occupations of the day. Julian Symons recalls: 'After Spain, and indeed before the end came in Spain, there was little left of the Thirties movement but a feeling of resignation and a sense of guilt.' Cyril Connolly had already identified the fate of writers who became disheartened by politicians: 'Defeatism is their occupational disease.'

Worse defeats were to come.

> To-day was a beautiful day, the sky was a brilliant
> Blue for the first time for weeks and weeks
> But posters flapping on the railings tell the fluttered
> World that Hitler speaks, that Hitler speaks

Spain did nothing to stop the onward march of totalitarianism, the Munich crisis ended in the acceptance by France and Britain of Hitler's takeover in Czechoslovakia.

In the darkening atmosphere George Orwell began a series of essays later published as *Inside the Whale*. Before the book was finished war had broken out, and totalitarianism seemed unstoppable. 'The autonomous individual is going to be stamped out of existence. . . . The literature of liberalism is coming to an end and the literature of totalitarianism has not yet appeared and is barely imaginable. As for the writer, he is sitting on a melting iceberg; he is merely an anachronism, a hangover from the bourgeois age, as surely doomed as the hippopotamus ... from now onwards the all-important fact for the creative writer is going to be that this is not a writer's world.'

CHAPTER ONE

Barbarians at the Gate

'Glory to God for Munich.
And stocks go up and wrecks
Are salved and politicians' reputations
Go up like Jack-on-the-Beanstalk; only the Czechs
Go down and without fighting.'

Louis MacNeice

The crisis of September 1938 was useful only as a dress rehearsal. The mobilization of the French Army and the British Fleet, the digging of air-raid trenches in London's parks, the distribution of thirty-eight million gas-masks and the full deployment of the Air Raid Precaution services were all in vain. Chamberlain and the French Prime Minister Daladier agreed to Hitler's demand for the annexation of Sudeten-Czechoslovakia. The complete occupation of Czechoslovakia in March 1939 seemed only a formality.

As a dress-rehearsal, it went very badly for the British participants. It was now only a matter of time before the performance, and there was a general feeling of crisis and suspense. H.G. Wells, the once optimistic prophet of a scientifically ordered new world, mourned *The Fate of Homo Sapiens* (1939):

At any time, by night or day, with less than an hour's notice, the sirens may be screaming and the high explosive and incendiary bombs may be bursting about us. . . . Almost every intelligent human being and every township and community in Eur-Asia is in a state of mental tension which is rapidly approaching the breaking-point.

Wells predicted that this inevitable holocaust would be followed by a

5

planetary war, the destruction of resources and populations followed by a punitive peace, itself only the prelude to further conflict and chaos, ending in a new Dark Ages during which man could well slip into extinction.

The crisis of feeling was profound. T.S. Eliot states in *The Idea of a Christian Society* (also published in 1939):

> I believe that there must be many persons who, like myself, were deeply shaken by the events of September 1938, in a way from which one does not recover; persons to whom that month brought a profounder realization of a general plight. . . . The feeling which was new and unexpected was a feeling of humiliation, which seemed to demand an act of personal contrition, of humility, repentance and amendment; what had happened was something in which one was deeply implicated and responsible. It was not, I repeat, a criticism of the government, but a doubt of the validity of a civilization.

Virginia Woolf's novel *Between the Acts* conveys the strain and menace in imaginative terms. In the oppressive atmosphere of a hot day close to rain in June 1939, the owners of a small country house play host to the village pageant. Everywhere there is a feeling of suppressed violence: a snake chokes trying to swallow a toad, animal blood splashes a man's shoe, the newspapers talk of a rape, of Daladier and the falling franc, of the uncertain news from Europe. The pageant is interrupted by a squadron of low flying planes, and its climax, 'The Present Time', is a jangled collage of the past, becoming vicious as the players turn mirrors on the audience – who see nothing. In *Between the Acts* the disintegration is symbolic. Leonard Woolf's *Barbarians at the Gate* analyses the disintegration at a political level. And while German and Russian totalitarianism is the external threat, equally dangerous is the internal weakness of liberal civilization and culture. The Barbarians are at the gate – but more insidious is the collapse of values within.

For the Left the profound shock was not so much Munich (sales of the radical Left Book Club continued to rise) but the Russian-German Non-Aggression Pact of August 1939. The Pact was the complete reversal of the grand battle between Communism and Fascism which Spain had been supposed to be about. Spanish Republican resistance had already ended in March. Some Communists, like Tom Wintringham, George Aitkin and Philip Toynbee, immediately left the Party, while others gritted their teeth and argued

Stalin's case that Munich had proved that the West would do nothing to help Russia and that this was an imperialist war. The shock was greatest to fellow-travellers like Stephen Spender or John Lehmann, who began to think again about the political purges in Russia, and the activities of the commissars in Spain. Connolly was being proved right, and a general retreat began.

The keynote was struck by John Lehmann in the *New Statesman* on the day before war finally broke out. He saw around him 'signs, not merely of a bitter disillusionment about the real power and meaning of democracy in England, but also of a revulsion from all political platforms. Many young writers and artists seem to be feeling now that they put too much trust in parties and catchwords, and that a withdrawal is necessary in self-defence.' Lehmann may have been thinking in particular of Stephen Spender, whose pamphlet *The New Realism, a discussion* had been printed by the Hogarth Press in May 1939. Spender was still left-wing and committed, but now accepted that he was a bourgeois, and that he could only operate by accepting the cultural implications of that fact. Culture became a more important commitment than politics.

Looking back on that time a Communist, Jack Lindsay, commented in an interview that the Russo-German pact caused a falling away of support not only for political reasons. 'There was also an element of fear. It was no longer safe to be in the Communist Party after that.' In France Communists were being arrested, in England some left-wing refugees had already been interned.

The 'Popular Poets' Front' (Richard Crossman's phrase in *Time and Tide*) was broken up. It was ironic that at this point they should realize that they had lost their leaders. In January 1939 W.H. Auden and Christopher Isherwood had sailed for America. Their action only became significant with the declaration of war, and although both were over the age for conscription, their decision to remain in America became a stick with which their enemies could beat both them and their colleagues who had stayed in England.

The Auden/Isherwood case has been much discussed – at the time and since; Connolly called their departure 'the most important literary event since the outbreak of the Spanish War', and a question was asked in Parliament. It is difficult to thread one's way between the unfair accusations and half-hearted justifications which clutter the issue. Louis MacNeice, who was teaching in America when war broke out, put Auden's case:

7

He told me in March 1939 – that it was not his job to be a crusader, that this was a thing everyone must decide for himself, but that, in his opinion, most writers falsified their work and themselves when they took a direct part in politics, and that the political end itself, however good, could not be much assisted by art or artists so falsified. Auden, that is, had repudiated propaganda.

Auden said as much in his essay 'The Public vs. The Late Mr William Butler Yeats' published in the *Partisan Review* in the Spring of 1939. But though friends defended Auden and Isherwood (and indirectly themselves), they also felt betrayed. John Lehmann recalled 'It was all very well to say "We must love one another or die" three thousand miles away when the bombs were dropping here.' These colleagues had not known, for instance, that the pair had gone to America with the intention of emigrating.

In a sense, the departure of Auden and Isherwood *was* the most important literary event since Spain. In itself it was a criticism of European civilization which had nothing to do with immediate political events. It resulted in the further demoralization of the movement which they had helped to form. Both men, through their obvious talent and their less definable moral authority, had become leaders of their generation. Their abdication increased the sense of disorientation and defeat among their followers.

Disorientation and pessimism were general in the closing year of the 1930s. Here is Herbert Read in Geoffrey Grigson's magazine *New Verse*: 'Poetry, at any rate under the present economic dispensation, is dead letters. Poetry is ceasing to be printed; poetry is no longer read. Nothing can bring it back into circulation.' Basil Dean on the state of the Theatre: 'The Theatre was passing through one of its periodic phases of decline. Plays of outstanding merit were even fewer than usual and acting had grown stale and accustomed.' Sir Kenneth Clark, Director of the National Gallery, on support for art: 'For the fine arts there no longer exists in England any of the former patronage. I don't see, however, how the fine arts can exist without it. Instead of patronage we have cliques of little interest to anyone except a very small and usually unimportant group of people.' A leading publisher, Stanley Unwin: 'The literary indifference and the morbid tastes of our public are of danger not merely to our intellectual but to our national life in general. So long as the public will demand books which have nothing to do with literature the publisher can do little to improve matters.'

The decline in national taste was matched by a general loss of confidence among writers. In September 1939 the President of the Publishers' Association, Geoffrey Faber, commented:

For the last year shrewd observers . . . have been noting a progressive decline in the quantity and quality of worthwhile manuscripts. The reason is easy to see. Ever since Munich the atmosphere of Europe has grown more and more unfavourable to creative literary work. . . . 'How can I write with the world in this state?' is a cry I have heard more than once in the past few months.

E.M. Forster was right when he said that 1939 was not a year in which to start a literary career.

To complete the picture, there was an element of nihilism mixed in with the despair and disillusion. Patrick Hamilton's *Hangover Square* (1941) describes an aimless post-Munich world of public houses and wasted time. His schizophrenic hero is in love with a minor film actress, who in turn is the mistress of a Mosleyite:

What if there was a war? Yes – if nothing else turned up, a war might. A filthy idea, but what if a war was what he was waiting for? That might put a stop to it all. They might get him – he might be conscripted away from drinks, and smokes, and Netta. At times he could find it in his heart to hope for a war – bloody business as it all was.

The novel ends in murder and suicide. Further up the social scale in Henry Green's *Party Going* (1939) a rich, idle, irrelevant party of gay young things are caught by fog at a railway terminus on their way to the Continent. They wait (behind locked gates) in the station hotel, flirt and drink, take baths and hurt each other, occasionally looking out on to the huge crowd of ordinary travellers, stranded like them by the fog:

'What targets' one by him remarked, 'what targets for a bomb.'

The war began in London with a speech on the wireless by Neville Chamberlain, a thunderstorm and an air-raid warning, but the immediate holocaust expected by the Londoners who had seen the film of H.G. Wells's *The Shape of Things to Come* failed to materialize. Instead conditions approximated more to Richmal Crompton's *William and A.R.P.* But this time the precautions – and the Black-

Out – were real. The last container of pictures from the National Gallery left for a quarry in Wales on the Saturday afternoon before war began. (The dress rehearsal at Munich had led to the discovery of rolls of dirty canvases that turned out to be forgotten Turners.) The British Museum and the Victoria and Albert Museum sent their treasures to another quarry near Bath. The London Museum and the Tate Gallery found storage in the disused tunnels of the Aldwych Underground. Rodin's 'Burghers of Calais' went to spend the war at Berkhampstead Castle, Eros moved from Piccadilly Circus to Cooper's Hill, Englefield Green. A British Museum official expressed his satisfaction at seeing it as he had always wanted – empty.

All theatres and cinemas were closed, a move which Bernard Shaw was quick to attack as a 'masterstroke of unimaginative stupidity'. (Only the Pier Cinema, Aberystwyth, was open on the night of 3 September.) During the first week of the war 99 % of the theatrical profession was out of work, and looked like being so permanently. The BBC missed a golden opportunity to place anyone they liked on contract before a spate of provincial tours began to make up lost ground. Michel St Denis's London Theatre Studio, one of the best of the few training centres for actors, closed down when its director joined the French Army. The Communist Unity Theatre, which had done very well with a post-Munich pantomime, *Babes in the Wood*, had to abandon a lease they had taken on a West End theatre. A Massine ballet season was cancelled, as were the contracts of the two chief opera companies, Sadler's Wells and the Carl Rosa. The London Philharmonic Orchestra began a desperate battle for survival – at one stage it was reported disbanded. The Promenade concerts were halted and the Royal Opera House, Covent Garden, became a dance hall.

But nothing happened. In the absence of raids the cinemas were open again by 15 September, though as the *New Statesman* commented, 'not with a bang but a whimper'. The cinema industry faced a long-term problem: the government had begun to take over the studios for storage and other work. Elstree became a war factory. In six weeks Alexander Korda managed to throw together *The Lion has Wings*, based on a British air-raid on the Kiel canal, but there was a derisive reception to Merle Oberon's concluding war aims: 'Truth, beauty, and fair play, and – kindliness.'

On the morning after the declaration of war many people returned their library books. Publishers had no idea what was going to happen,

10

and there was a grand slaughter of magazines. Between 1939 and '40 the *Cornhill Magazine, Criterion, Fact, London Mercury, New Stories, New Verse, Purpose, Seven, Twentieth Century Verse, Wales, Welsh Review* and the *Voice of Scotland* all fell silent. The *Writers' Own Magazine*, which had provided useful tips to freelances since 1927, closed down abruptly, and the second half of Stanley Langdale's article 'From the Pen of a Provincial' never was continued.

Writers themselves, although they had known what was coming, felt stunned and unable to work. Dylan Thomas wrote frankly: 'I want to get something out of the war, and put very little in (certainly not my one and only body).' He, like every other professional writer, found that what sources of income there were dried up. 'And all I want is time to write poems,' he protested. 'I'm only just getting going now.' Similarly, George Orwell found that he could no longer live cheaply in the country and subsist by writing reviews – few people wanted reviews any more. Stephen Spender put his heart into a journal linking the collapse of society and the break-up of his marriage. 'I am going to keep a journal because I cannot accept the fact that I feel so shattered that I cannot write at all.' MacNeice's poem *Autumn Journal* also links public and private disaster.

Cyril Connolly, playing on the symbol of high literary culture, no longer wrote in an ivory tower, but in an 'Ivory Shelter', the title of an article for the *New Statesman* in October:

As human beings artists are less free now than they have ever been; it is difficult for them to make money and impossible for them to leave the country. Lock-up is earlier every day, and they are concentrated indefinitely on an island from which the sun is hourly receding. As human beings they are no longer emotionally free, for the infection of war induces mental symptoms which indicate the discomforts and torments to follow.

But Connolly thought he saw some advantages for the writer. At least he was now free of two burdens, 'the burden of anti-Fascist activities, the subtler burden of pro-Communist opinions'. The war was an opportunity, a justification, for the artist to retire and concentrate on his work – to withdraw to his ivory shelter. 'War is a tin-can tied to the tail of civilization, it is also an opportunity for the artist to give us nothing but the best, and to stop his ears.'

It was with this intention that Connolly launched the magazine *Horizon* in January 1940 with backing from a rich patron, Peter Watson, and editorial help from Stephen Spender. Connolly intended to ignore the war and concentrate on publishing good writing: 'Our standards are aesthetic, and our politics are in abeyance.' The deterioration of the military situation forced him to take a less detached view, and throughout the war the mood of Connolly's editorials oscillates between one of faith in the superior claims of Art, and guilt about not being more closely involved in the national effort.

John Lehmann's *New Writing* only just survived the hiatus caused by the start of the war – the Christmas 1939 issue was declared to be its last, but an offer from Allen Lane put new energy into the venture. A sixpenny paperback selection of part new and part previously published material was issued as *Penguin New Writing*. The proportion of new material gradually increased in succeeding numbers, and thanks to a generous allocation of paper, *Penguin New Writing* became a highly successful venture. Meanwhile the Hogarth Press continued to publish hardback anthologies as *Folios of New Writing* (later *New Writing and Daylight*).

There were other signs that literature might just survive. In Oxford the poet John Waller had started *Kingdom Come* in November 1939. Pacifists and anarchists gave their anti-war views a voice with *Now*, 'a forum for controversial writing which could not readily find publication under wartime conditions'. Conservative Christian intellectuals began *The Christian News-Letter* with T.S. Eliot on the editorial board. The Communist *Poetry and the People* was gathering strength, becoming *Our Time* in 1941. *Poetry* (*London*), which had started uncertainly in 1939 under the editorship of the Ceylonese poet J.M. Tambimuttu, was to reappear in November 1940.

Gradually, cultural life of a sort re-emerged. The most striking recovery was in music, which answered an emotional need more easily than plays or books. On 10 October 1939 the pianist Myra Hess began to give lunchtime recitals in the empty National Gallery; they were an immediate success, and were to last throughout the war. Music certainly met a demand; *Time and Tide* reported that by the end of the week in which the National Gallery recitals began there had been twelve concerts in London. 'There would have been audiences for twice as many.' The London Symphony Orchestra and the London Philharmonic managed to weather the initial storm, and while programmes were conservative, there were hopes that the current confusion would eventually end.

The Theatre could be less proud of itself – in the words of a reviewer, 'Many Theatres, but No Theatre'. The Lord Chamberlain now permitted previously censored jokes about Hitler (BBC comedians were allowed the same licence). A strange sign of the times was the revival of Walter Reynolds's *Young England*, a solemnly intended patriotic play whose sentiments were now greeted with gales of laughter. The first serious production of the war was Priestley's *Music at Night*, at the Westminster Theatre, whose management maintained its pre-war reputation with productions of Shaw's *Major Barbara*, Eugene O'Neil's *Desire under the Elms*, and Drinkwater's *Abraham Lincoln*. The Old Vic company mounted *King Lear* with John Gielgud, and *Macbeth*.

With the commercial theatre in unadventurous hands it was left to small theatre clubs to keep serious drama going. The Actors' Company, headed by Alec Guiness, Marius Goring and George Devine, put on Guiness in his own adaptation of *Great Expectations*. The Torch Theatre reopened in December with Clifford Bax's *The Venetian*; wartime difficulties caused the Tavistock Little Theatre to merge with the St Pancras People's Theatre Company. The Threshold, the Gate and the Neighbourhood Theatre (which opened in June 1940) all tried to keep actors in work, and those in the forces in contact with their audience. But prospects were not good. In February 1940 the *Spectator* estimated that of the 18,000 in the theatrical profession (the figure excludes stagehands and musicians) only 3,000 were working, and then at reduced rates.

Mergers and improvizations were also the order of the day in opera and ballet. After successful provincial tours Sadler's Wells Opera and Ballet cautiously re-established themselves in London. Some scratch ballet companies also emerged, the 'Ballet de la Jeunesse Anglaise' and 'Les Ballets Trois Arts'. Harold Rubin took over the Arts Theatre Club and opened it as a dance centre in December 1939. In the following year two of the best dance groups temporarily amalgamated into the London-Rambert Ballet.

The Royal Academy made its contribution to a blighted art world by throwing open its doors in December 1939 to the first ever indiscriminate show of contemporary art. There were 2,219 exhibits, ranging from a Barbara Hepworth sculpture to a portrait in feathers of Princess Elizabeth. The painter and critic John Piper suggested in the *Spectator* that the idea might possibly be to kill contemporary art with kindness. The British Council's selection for the 1940 Venice Biennale – Duncan Grant, Frances Hodgkins, Glyn Philpot, Alfred

Munnings, Edward Wadsworth and Frank Dobson – was shown at Hertford House. The larger commercial galleries remained open, the Lefevre for instance mounting a joint show of contemporary British and French artists, presumably reflecting the current military *entente cordiale*.

Painters were better placed to cope with emergency conditions. World War One had set a precedent for their employment as visual historians, which was some compensation for the closure and evacuation of the art schools, and, as in the First War, artists were employed in camouflage. The War Artists Advisory Committee was established in November, with a government grant of £10,000. All kinds of artists became involved, some on permanent commissions, while others worked on special projects, or sold their work to the Committee. The results were shown at the National Gallery, which was also the location for meetings of the Art and Entertainment Emergency Council, whose members were anxious to prevent cultural activities coming to a complete stop. On the committee were the Gallery's Director, Sir Kenneth Clark, the film directors Anthony Asquith and Paul Rotha, the conductor Sir Thomas Beecham, playwrights James Bridie and Bernard Shaw, A.P. Herbert, Dr J.J. Mallon of the Workers Educational Association, and the designer Milner Gray – in all a representative cross-section of the cultural establishment.

Writers were less fortunate. Lord Esher tried to set up an informal committee, which included Desmond MacCarthy and John Lehmann, to produce a list of writers and painters, etc., who should be exempted from conscription. There were fears that the call-up might be used to silence unorthodox opinions. The plan was to protect no more than fifty people, but the War Office was unwilling to co-operate, since it would be called upon to discriminate between the relative importance of individuals to the state. It also proved difficult to decide which fifty names should be on the committee's list.

One group thoroughly prepared for war were the entertainers. In 1938 the producer Basil Dean, who had organized concerts for troops during the First World War, set up a committee to ensure that, contrary to the bureaucrats' expectations, the theatre would not disappear during wartime. The result was the Entertainments National Service Association. At the outbreak of war ENSA took over the Drury Lane Theatre (where the audiences for Ivor Novello's *The Dancing Years* had been thinning out) as production offices.

After battles with the vested interests of managers, musicians, actors and agents, ENSA was established as the official troop-entertaining organization, and after further battles their services were extended to civilian factories in mid-1940. The first ENSA concert was at Camberley a week after war broke out. For reasons of security the entertainers arrived in Bren Gun carriers; ENSA was to discover that 'security' sometimes made it difficult to find the troops they were supposed to entertain.

The difference in national mood between 1914 and 1939 meant that there was no rush to join the armed forces; conscription would take care of one's future all in good time. True, it was advisable to volunteer if one had a particular regiment or branch of the services in mind, but volunteering was no guarantee of acceptance, and many young and not-so-young men spent frustrating hours in adjutants' offices trying to find a post. The feeling was hardly that of Rupert Brooke's swimmers into cleanness leaping.

The majority of men under thirty settled down to waiting for their call-up papers, and the writers among them did what they could to finish off work in hand, or set themselves programmes of work that circumstances made it unlikely they would fulfil. Not all, of course, were willing to go to war. Conscientious objectors faced local tribunals at which, on the whole, they received a fair hearing. Pacifism had been a minor but influential political theme of the 1930s, and nearly 60,000 people applied for exemption from military or national service during the Second World War. About half of these were registered as Conscientious Objectors on condition that they did some specific form of work. For those whose scruples permitted the wearing of uniform a Non Combatant Corps was formed in the army. In the First World War three out of ten COs had been imprisoned for refusing to contribute to the war effort; in the Second the number was three out of a hundred. But only three and a half thousand pacifists were given unconditional exemption. One or two writers left for America or neutral Eire, among them Roger Roughton, the editor of *Contemporary Prose and Verse*, who gassed himself in Dublin in 1940.

Conscription presented a problem for the artist or writer. It was unavoidable and meant the end of his former activities and associations. An ingenious solution for some was to join Victor Cazalet's Anti-Aircraft Battery. Cazalet, a monied Conservative Member of

Parliament with wide connections in the theatre and the arts, treated the 16th Light AA Battery rather in the manner of the local squires who had raised personal troops during the English Civil War. The Battery was intended to provide congenial and reasonably safe surroundings for writers, actors, dancers, painters and poets who might otherwise be crushed in the military machine. It is clear that this is the 'territorial searchlight battery manned entirely by fashionable aesthetes who were called "the monstrous regiment of gentlemen" ' referred to by Evelyn Waugh in *Men at Arms* (1952). It was claimed that the Battery had a longer waiting list of applicants than the Brigade of Guards.

The Battery lived up to its aesthetic reputation by appointing James Pope-Hennessey its librarian, and displaying a tendency to wear silk pyjamas in barracks. Cut flowers were sent down to the Battery from the Cazalets' greenhouses. Stationed first at Rochester, the Battery then saw action in Portsmouth Docks, before the War Office caught up with this unusual formation and its members were dispersed to ENSA, or less pleasant sites like the Faroe Islands. Dylan Thomas abandoned a half-formed plan to plead conscientious objection and volunteered for the Battery, but was rejected as medically unfit.

For those who had not volunteered and been accepted, sought out Victor Cazalet, or registered as COs, the immediate problem was employment. Two institutions seemed most likely to be able to use writers in wartime, the Ministry of Information and the BBC. The Ministry of Information came into being on the outbreak of war, taking over London University's Senate House in Bloomsbury. From the first the Ministry suffered from a fundamental contradiction; on the one hand it was supposed to propagandize and promote news of Britain's success; on the other it was supposed to censor any information that might be of use to the enemy or damaging to the war effort. The first two years of the Ministry were spent in organization and reorganization, and it proved a graveyard for ministerial reputations. There was perpetual conflict between the professional civil servants and the journalists and writers drafted in to help, a conflict typified by the early confusion between Civil Service and Fleet Street jargon. To a civil servant the letters on a file 'PA' mean Put Away, i.e. to shelve. They are also the initials of the Press Association Wire Service, with the result that a lot of information failed to reach the right destination.

Journalists protested that their expertise was being neglected, and that officials of the English Speaking Union, the British Council, the Conservative Central Office and the Royal Institute of International Affairs were getting the plum jobs. The 'big house in Bloomsbury' was racked by internal conflicts, while the Press mounted a campaign against it from outside. The Ministry's very obvious failings during the early part of the war made it a convenient target for all the general criticism of the inertia and mismanagement of Chamberlain's government. On 30 October 1939 an air-raid warning was sounded accidentally in the Bloomsbury area. When reporters rang the Ministry to find out what was happening they got no reply. The entire staff had gone to the shelters. This sort of story, with malicious embellishments, helped to relieve some of the frustration of dealing with the Ministry. Graham Greene turned his experience of working there in 1940 into a story for *Penguin New Writing*, describing a futile day of memos and meetings; Evelyn Waugh put the absurdities of the Ministry to work to provide the plot for his novel about the 'phoney-war' period, *Put Out More Flags* (1942).

If journalists felt neglected, writers felt ignored altogether. J.B. Priestley recalled, 'There were plenty of writers, innocently anxious to serve their country, working there in Malet Street. Not one of them was given a position of any importance and authority: lawyers, advertising and newspaper men came first.' Writers were certainly eager to serve, inside or outside the Ministry. The popular novelist Sir Hugh Walpole suggested that an advisory committee be established: 'Artists and authors performed great work during the last war, and there is a general feeling among them now that no use at all is being made of their abilities.' The file on this proposal, now in the Public Record Office, is a case history in the attitude of bureaucracy to the arts. The current Minister, a judge, Lord Macmillan, was sympathetic, but had doubts: was Walpole 'the right man to represent the whole of the profession as chairman?' Proposed members of the committee – all very 'establishment' names – were picked over for co-operativeness or faults. Scribbled beside Dorothy L. Sayers's name is 'very loquacious and difficult'.

It is clear from the discussions within the Ministry that the bureaucrats thought that authors were not serious people and could not be trusted. An official of the Ministry of Labour who was consulted replied that a committee would lead to 'continuous bickering and would not be of real help to the Department. After many years experience in working on Committees with authors, I have found them, apart from their special gifts, extraordinarily ignorant and ill-informed people on most topics.' Unfortunately this distrust was not limited to officials. The President of the Publishers' Association, Geoffrey Faber, also advised against writers:

> Authors are, with rare exceptions, egocentric persons. They are not cohesive, they are not good at collectively tackling an impersonal problem. They mostly lack both knowledge and judgment of the means whereby their own books are actually sold; and this lack is the more dangerous because they are apt to assume they know all about it.

On such patronizing advice the idea of an Authors' Committee was abandoned, and instead the responsibility for selecting authors to write suitable material for the Ministry was left to the General Production Department. Coincidentally, the job was earmarked for a former employee of Geoffrey Faber.

The Ministry's handling of the affair was too much for the literary agent A.D. Peters, who had joined the Ministry in order to help organize the supply of literature. Describing himself as 'existing here in the void', he told his superiors, 'authors and publishers are criticizing the whole conduct of literary affairs inside this Ministry with a bitterness which I consider fully justified'. He insisted that his resignation be accepted, and judging from the ensuing correspondence, the civil servants were glad to see him go. Although the Ministry did help literature indirectly, in that it employed writers on its staff and commissioned a certain amount of hack propaganda writing, a chance to use the enthusiasm of writers was missed. Denied responsibility, here was another reason for the writer to feel rejected, and in turn to reject responsibility.

The BBC was almost as unpopular as the Ministry of Information in the early months of the war, largely because its carefully planned dispersal turned out to be not immediately necessary. The small television service stopped abruptly two days before war began, when the emergency operation swung into action. The pattern of regional broadcasting was dropped in favour of a single-channel national programme which had to cater for all tastes, and satisfied few of them. The BBC departments were evacuated to the regions, the Variety and Religious Departments and the BBC Symphony Orchestra to Bristol, Features and Drama to the small town of Evesham in Worcestershire. 'Security' was again a problem, the Director General of the BBC complained that MI5 was too slow in giving clearance to artists, and the Ministry of Information insisted on checking all broadcasters, including musicians, which led to considerable delay and an excess of record programmes and Sandy Macpherson at the BBC Theatre Organ during the early weeks of the war.

The Talks Department was actually run down at the beginning of the war, and had difficulties with security over the choice of speakers, but the Ministry of Information soon realized that morale-boosting talks were going to be an important part of the BBC's war effort, and the department began to expand again. No drama was produced during the first six weeks of the war, the department having been sent to Evesham to share facilities with the BBC's monitoring service. Monitoring of foreign broadcasts was vital to intelligence-gathering, but many of those who carried it out felt their duties more irksome than patriotic. Geoffrey Grigson, former editor of the now defunct *New Verse*, had found a job in the service:

> We hated each other. Ah, that was extraordinary. Even a killing hatred at times, cooped up as we were down the long tables. We hated ourselves, and so hated those whose unpleasantness of any kind, whether by authority or lack of it, by cracking the whip or sidling to the whip-wielder, gathered our irritation upon them.

The horrors of Evesham behind barbed wire and armed sentries are confirmed by another monitoring service employee, Gilbert Harding. He described the arrival of the Drama Department: 'The town was inundated with young persons of either or doubtful sex, carrying Siamese cats and teddy bears.' The Siamese cat belonged to Val Gielgud, the head of the Drama Department, who was very relieved when his team was moved to Manchester at the end of November.

Gradually the BBC, like the rest of the population, settled down. The first excitements of the declaration of war were over, and no fresh excitements appeared. The period of the 'Phoney War', or the 'Sitzkrieg', had begun. Mollie Panter-Downes reported to the *New Yorker* at the end of October: 'There is still an astonishingly general belief, or hope, or perhaps a mixture of both, that something will happen.' For the moment, nothing did.

London, during the 'phoney' war was a dark, unreal place full of shadows and rumour, trying to dispel its fear with a false gaiety. We danced, we travelled to Paris at tree-top height in unarmed planes, we filled up forms and had too much of everything. Young men who tried to enlist were snubbed; women besieged the various relief organizations and, finding that their services were not required, arranged dinner-parties in the black-out.

The atmosphere recalled by Mrs Robert Henrey in 1946. Young (and old) writers and artists found life particularly hard. An article in the *New Statesman*, 'The Liquidation of the Free-Lances (By One of Them)', in April 1940 summed up their predicament and their bitter conclusions: 'No young writer or artist, after this war is over, will ever dare to be without a safe job. . . . When the free-lance is finally liquidated, our art and literature will all be produced by little men in striped trousers, Anthony Eden hats and rolled umbrellas, who are punctual at their offices and incapable of dangerous thoughts.'

Complaints about the general stagnation of cultural life were only to be expected, when it was impossible to find any means of supporting oneself, let alone creating art. George Orwell noted in his diary,

The money situation is becoming completely unbearable. . . . Wrote a long letter to the Income Tax people pointing out that the war had practically put an end to my livelihood while at the same time the government refused to give me any kind of job. The fact which is really relevant to a writer's position, the impossibility of writing books with this nightmare going on, would have no weight officially

The loss of livelihood was widespread. In the spring of 1940 Vera Brittain was interviewing possible adult escorts for children being evacuated to Canada:

Through our office streams a long procession of unemployed actors, couriers, entertainers and cinema managers whose genial peacetime occupation has completely disappeared. Before we had interviewed applicants for a week, we could make a long list of the civilized forms of employment connected with amusement, travel, music, art, journalism and the stage, which have been slaughtered by the grim inexorability of war.

Even if the employment problem could be solved, war conditions continued to bear down in the form of exhausting war work, restrictions, the shortage of transport, the shortage of practically everything else, and an increase in taxation. Already the rigid Black-Out was causing a shift in the nation's use of its leisure.

These shifts were carefully monitored by Mass Observation, a sociological organization set up by the anthropologist Tom Harrisson, the poet Charles Madge, the film maker Humphrey Jennings and others in 1937. Mass Observation was one of the positive outcomes of the social concerns of the Thirties; it did what its name implies, using hundreds of volunteers to note the wide variety of ordinary and extraordinary activities and opinions among the population at large. The intention is summed up in its study of the first four months of war, *War Begins At Home*: 'Sociology can and should reflect and interpret public opinion instead of the "public opinion" which is really the private opinion of newspaper proprietors, BBC directors and the three or four men who control the news-reels.' Sometimes the sociology was a little over-solemn. In an attempt to 'establish a base-line for future reference' Mass Observation analyzed 1,220 pictures on display in West End galleries during October and December 1939 looking for references to the war. Only 2% turned out to have any, and most of these were 'portraits of middle-aged men in uniform'.

Mass Observation concluded what everybody knew, that it was the Black-Out that was having the greatest impact on people's lives. All outside activities, from walking the dog to attending political meetings, had declined, while 'staying-in' and going to bed early had markedly increased. 'The word "Black-Out" has become a synonym and symbol of a shut-down on intellectual life or leisure. The Air War has blacked out civilization.' *War Begins At Home* attacks the complacency of the country's governors who seemed completely out of touch with the needs of the population. The 'war-puritanism' of the government was compounded with a general failure of nerve; 'every institution helped to stagnate itself by suffering a sort of psychological collapse at the outbreak of war. This collapse often went much further than the economic or legislative prescriptions made necessary.' In particular the BBC was attacked for its 'outbreak hysteria'.

Commercial institutions, the pub, the dance-hall and the night-club were quick to adapt to the changed conditions, and the West End saw a boom in business. Other profit-seeking interests altered their methods too:

So sudden it brought him up sharp, the tart, stood back in the doorway, shone a copper beam, from the torch she carried, full on her left breast she held bared with the other hand. She murmured, 'Hulloh love.' Longingly he ogled the dark purple nipple, the moon full globe that was red Indian tinted by her bulb, with the whiff of scent. 'Jesus' he moaned, but it was too near his sub-station.

21

'Staying-in' was at least a stimulus to reading, and by May 1940 Christina Foyle, director of London's biggest bookshop, had detected the first signs of the wartime boom in demand for books, particularly the classics. She added drily, 'We have noticed a general falling-off of sales of political books.' The one political work which did do very well was *Mein Kampf.*

Publishers were becoming aware that their businesses were seriously threatened by war conditions. Compulsory war insurance and the rising cost of paper forced the average price of novels up from 7/6d to 8/3d, while Excess Profits Tax creamed off the compensation of increased demand. But the real problem was paper rationing. Publishers were immediately restricted to 60% of the paper they had used between August 1938 and August 1939, and then found that the ration was progressively reduced as the war went on. The choice of dates establishing the baseline for the allocation was somewhat arbitrary, and publishers were quick to point out that it had been a bad period for books generally, and for their firm in particular. Publisher Stanley Unwin battled against the rationing authorities throughout the war. His firm, Allen and Unwin, had a particular problem in that their basement storeroom had been commandeered as an official air-raid shelter. Shelterers tended to make off with the books.

What looked like the last straw for publishers came in July 1940 when the government proposed including books in the new Purchase Tax. A Committee for the Defence of Books was formed, and Sir Hugh Walpole, Geoffrey Faber, A.P. Herbert and J.B. Priestley joined Stanley Unwin in a vigorous campaign. Unwin wrote later:

> No member of the delegation which pleaded with the late Chancellor of the Exchequer for the exemption of books from purchase tax is ever likely to forget Sir Kingsley Wood's confidence that books were of no importance, or the way in which he brushed the Archbishop of Canterbury and the rest of us aside with the statement that there were plenty of books in the country.

To the publishers' relief, however, the proposal was dropped.

In the face of general criticism, and as part of the huge increase in its responsibilities, the government was forced to do something about the arts. In the words of Ivor Brown in the *New Statesman*, entertainment was given 'the status and dignity of a Problem':

> The Entertainment Problem has been surveyed from various points of view and tentatively fingered by the Treasury, the War Office (not to men-

tion the Admiralty and Air Ministry), the Ministries of Health, Home Security, Labour, and Information, by the Board of Education, by the Charitable Trusts, and by every publicist who knows how to win the war.

Members of unofficial groups like the Art and Entertainment Emergency Council were adamant that the old sources of patronage for the arts were drying up, and that a new patron must be found. Gingerly, the government began to take on the role. This was done in a roundabout way, by persuading the Pilgrim Trust (established by the American millionaire Edward Harkness in 1930) to grant £25,000 towards helping amateur music and drama. As a result the Council for the Encouragement of Music and the Arts came into being on the Pilgrim Trust's money on 19 January 1940. In March the government matched this grant with an additional £25,000, and these twin sources of income continued until 1942, when the Pilgrim Trust dropped out and the government took full responsibility. In these early days professional performers were expected to benefit only indirectly, although a series of guarantees to concerts by the London Symphony and London Philharmonic Orchestras helped them through the worst days of 1940. Gradually, the populist and – in the best sense – amateur enthusiasts lost ground to the supporters of professionalism, a trend which has continued to this day, for the Arts Council is the direct heir of CEMA.

It was left to the *Daily Express*, now vigorously supporting the war it had not wanted, to make the inevitable protest.

The government gives £50,000 to help wartime culture. What madness is this? There is no such thing as culture in wartime.

At first it did not seem that there was much fighting in wartime either. Mass Observation summed up the mood of early 1940:

At present, the war does not satisfy anyone, let alone the bellicose. It is being treated by the Press and the BBC especially, very much as if it were an enormous sporting event, in which one side brings down one of the other's aeroplanes, 15 love, then there is a retaliation, 15 all, and so on, to innumerable deuce games and sets stretching far beyond the horizon.

The horizon, however, was beginning to close in. The first food rationing measures came into force in January. While all was stagnation and over-confidence in the Maginot line, Norway became an active theatre of war at the beginning of April following the German occupation of Denmark. *Hitler, the Beast of Berlin* opened at the

London Pavilion Cinema. A British force was sent to oppose the German invasion of Norway, but had to be evacuated at the end of the month. British morale, which had soared at the news of action, fell again, leaving hostility and suspicion towards the Press and radio for producing misleading reports. A side consequence of the German occupation of Norway and Denmark was that Britain was cut off from supplies of Swedish wood pulp, which had answered 80% of the country's newsprint needs. Newspapers and magazines began to slim.

A direct consequence of the Norway débâcle was the resignation of Chamberlain and the formation of a coalition government under Winston Churchill. But precisely as Churchill was taking over, on 10 May, the Germans began to overrun Holland and Belgium. The Sadler's Wells Ballet, on tour for the British Council in Holland, got out of Arnhem just ahead of the German tanks, but were forced to leave behind the costumes, scenery and music for their productions of *Les Sylphides*, *Façade* and *Dante Sonata*. On 14 May the Local Defence Volunteers, quickly renamed the Home Guard, was formed.

The defeat in Europe meant the opening of a very unpleasant chapter for European exiles in Britain. There were some 70,000 alien refugees, mainly from Germany, Austria and Czechoslovakia, and most of them were hoping to make their way to America. The known Nazi sympathizers and some Communists had been interned at the beginning of the war, while the others had been placed in security categories by special tribunals. The newspapers, notably the *Daily Mail*, *Daily Sketch*, and *Daily Express*, who had been in favour of appeasing Hitler before the war, began an 'intern the lot' campaign. A round-up began on 12 May and by the middle of June most male 'enemy aliens' had been interned. The entry of Italy into the war on 11 June had added her nationals to the list.

The refugees had been making a contribution to English cultural life for some years, particularly the Jewish academics who had been driven out of Germany. The Warburg Institute and Library had moved from Germany *en bloc* in 1933. A Free German League of Culture had been founded in Hampstead in 1938, and the Austrian Club had mounted *The Good Soldier Schweik* and *The Beggar's Opera* after the outbreak of war. Now actors, academics, writers, artists, musicians, many of whom were in England to avoid the concentration camps of Germany, found themselves wakened in the middle of the night and bundled off to imprisonment without being told where

24

they were going or being allowed to say goodbye to their families and friends. It is not surprising there were a number of suicides.

Internees were placed first in temporary camps, of which the worst was a derelict cotton mill at Bury in Lancashire. From there they were moved to the Isle of Man, which was intended as the final collection point before deportation to Canada or Australia. In the Isle of Man the internees began to organize a new cultural life for themselves. (The landlady of a requisitioned boarding-house unknowingly contributed some of her linoleum to the collages of Kurt Schwitters.) The playwright Hans Rehfisch, who had been preparing his play *Well of Promise* for a London production, instead found himself directing *Julius Caesar* in modern dress at the Gaiety Theatre, Douglas. Since there were so many academics an unofficial University of the Isle of Man sprang up, with a distinguished staff unwillingly supplied by Oxford, Cambridge, London University and Dartington Hall.

After the initial outburst of chauvinism had died down, the internment policy was reconsidered. After all, these were useful, and in the case of the scientists, vital men. Liberal opinion protested, assisted by a campaigning Penguin special, *The Internment of Aliens*. Gradually releases for certain categories of work began – but seventeen internees in Hutchinson Camp on the Isle of Man, signing themselves 'artists, painters and sculptors', protested that although the release was being considered of

all sorts of classes – agriculturalists and food producers, dentists and scientists – only the artists have, as is so often the case, been forgotten. Apparently we are not needed.

It would be fair to say that artists were *not* needed in the dying days of May 1940. In the West End *Garrison Theatre* at the Palladium presented a minesweeper shooting down a German bomber, while 'a platoon of tin-hatted poilus march and countermarch through a twenty-foot Arc de Triomphe, the chorus dress (and subsequently undress) as WAAFs' and the programme girls wore ATS uniform. Across the Channel on 25 May the British Expeditionary Force began its retreat to Dunkirk, the last troops getting away on 4 June. A short story by Peter Opie, 'It was a defeat', describes London on the day the first survivors of Dunkirk began to filter into the capital. A group of drunken aimless people are talking in a night-club: 'Did you see London on Saturday? or on Friday? or on Thursday?

Thursday was the first day that London realized that the war which had started six months ago was in progress.'

As the soldiers from Dunkirk went home to their towns and villages, spreading stories of the mismanagement of their war, a great change took place in England. The war had now really started, and it seemed that H.G. Wells's holocaust was after all about to begin. On 22 June came the German armistice with the French. A genuine revolution of feeling was taking place in England, and artists and writers shared in the nation's change of heart. But already there was a touch of bitterness. J.B. Priestley, the man who contributed much towards turning the image of Dunkirk from a defeat into a moral victory, wrote in July:

Most of us imagined a year ago, in our innocence, that if there should be a war, then it must be a war in which public *morale* would be of immense importance, and that therefore much use would be made of the services of authors, who understand something of the public mind and know how to use the various arts of persuasion. We know better now. . . .

CHAPTER TWO

Hell Came to London and other Stories

Officer:	*The war's not going very well, you know.*
Pilot:	*Oh my God.*
Officer:	*We're two down, and the ball's in the enemy court. War's a psychological thing, Perkins.*
Pilot:	*Yes Sir.*
Officer:	*Rather like a game of football.*
Pilot:	*Yessir.*
Officer:	*You know how in a game of football ten men often play better than eleven?*
Pilot:	*Yes Sir?*
Officer:	*Perkins . . . we're asking you to be that one man.*
Pilot:	*Sir.*
Officer:	*I want you to lay down your life, Perkins. We need a futile gesture at this stage. . . . It'll raise the whole tone of the war. . . .*

'The Aftermyth of War', *Beyond the Fringe* (1960)

'There can have been no moment, since the invention of novels, when fewer people wish to read them.' So opens Brian Howard's book review in the *New Statesman* for 7 September 1940. That afternoon at about five o'clock German aircraft appeared over the East End of London, and began to bomb the Docks. By the evening huge fires were burning in the warehouses and timber yards, their light making a mock sunset in the East that glowed until it was joined by the genuine light of the dawn. Nearly 500 civilians were killed, and 1,600 injured. It was the heaviest air attack yet made on a city, and the Blitz had officially begun.

During July and August 1940 German air-raids had crept gradually

27

nearer to London as the Luftwaffe tried to clear the way for a sea-borne invasion, and the British worked frantically to prepare against it. The first bombs to be dropped on the City of London fell, possibly by accident, on 24 August. A reprisal raid on Berlin followed, and the decision was taken by the German High Command to switch from attacks on the RAF's airfields to attacking London itself. The first architectural casualty of the Blitz was St Giles's Church, Cripplegate, struck on 24 August. The photographer Cecil Beaton's entry in his diary stands for all the descriptions of gutted buildings in the following months:

I marvelled at the freaks of air raid damage and the unfathomable laws of blast. Scattered cherub's wings and stone roses were strewn about – whole memorial plaques of carved marble had been blown across the width of the church and lay undamaged. The entire frontage of the deserted business premises opposite was wrecked, and Milton's statue had been flung from its plinth. Yet the lamp-post was standing erect with no pane of its lantern broken.

By November the Ministry of Information's list of non-military targets damaged by bombs included practically every building of historic importance in London.

Gounod's *Faust* was playing at Sadler's Wells on the evening of 7 September. After the performance the audience, fresh from seeing Faust and Mephistopholes descend to Hell, came out to a night sky glowing fiercely from the fires in the Docks. *Faust* was the last performance at Sadler's Wells until June 1945; the building was taken over as a rest centre for people driven from their homes by the bombing. A few days later the Carl Rosa Opera Company lost all its costumes and scenery when the People's Theatre, Whitechapel, was hit. London's limping cultural life was being knocked down for the second time.

In the early days of the Blitz, a period of continuous nightly bombing, people caught in theatres and cinemas were treated to improvized entertainments while the bombs crashed down outside. The composer Norman Demuth remembered the enthusiasm of the audience at the Henry Wood Promenade Concerts:

Night after night everyone was compelled to remain in [the] Queen's Hall till three o'clock in the morning while fun and games held sway on the platform; the most astonishing of all this hilarity was a complete perform-ance of Mendelssohn's Violin Concerto, conducted, and played by soloist and orchestra entirely from memory.

As the bombing continued night entertainment became impossible. (In May 1941 the Queen's Hall itself was burnt down and the London Philharmonic lost many instruments in the fire.) A week after the Blitz began only two theatres were still open at night, and a few days later the revue *In Town Again* at the Criterion was abandoned, leaving a clear field for the comics and nudes at the Windmill Theatre, who struggled on in front of tiny audiences. An early victim of the collapse was the Mask Theatre Company at the Westminster, which had begun to establish a reputation after the theatrical hiatus at the beginning of the war, but could not beat the combination of Black-Out and bombing. A switch to matinée performances was only a partial solution for the theatres, and one by one the viable productions set out on tour.

London's loss was the provinces' gain, but the *New Statesman* reported in December that whereas there would normally have been at least 1,500 members of Equity working in London, there were only twenty-six. Physically, London's theatres got off relatively lightly during the Blitz. There was high drama in May 1941 when a parachute mine went through the roof of the London Palladium, and hung entangled and unexploded in the flies. The Naval officer who successfully defused the mine (since these were sea-mines they were the responsibility of the Navy) was given free tickets to the Palladium for life.

At the National Gallery the lunchtime concerts started by Myra Hess retreated to the Gallery's basement shelter, and continued even while an unexploded bomb was being dug out of the Gallery's Inner Court. The Tate Gallery was hit in September, October and December, and again once a month from January to May 1941, but the only painting damaged was Richard Wilson's *Destruction of the Children of Niobe*, which had been brought to London to be cleaned. The British Museum suffered damage to the Pediment Hall in November, and much more serious damage in May 1941, when 150,000 books in the Library were destroyed. Already 30,000 bound volumes of newspapers had been lost when the Colindale Library had been hit the previous October. About a third of London's art dealers managed to keep going on a thin market, but as Eric Newton, the art critic of the *Sunday Times*, pointed out: 'The West End – let's face it – is no longer a fit place for the accumulation of valuables.'

Night life of a less cultural kind did continue, though there, too, the West End survived rather than made a profit. The sudden change in national mood from boredom and despair to seriousness and urgency after the fall of France had made night-clubbing seem inappropriate, and the police had closed a number of night-clubs down. As a result unlicensed drinking clubs, masquerading as 'bottle-parties', had sprung up, but the bombing put them out of business. The prostitutes who had used them were forced, like the cinemas, to operate only in the afternoon. After a fortnight of bombing, Basil Woon recorded that night-life was 'nearing the crisis':

Among the clubs which refuse to be 'blitzed' are Murray's, the Paradise (which advertises a nightly 'Blitz Reunion Party'), the Havana, the Coconut Grove, the Cosmo and the Cabaret. None of them are coining money. Café de Paris is closed, but hopes to reopen next week with a floor show. . . . You can dance, dine, and sleep at Hatchett's, the Hungaria, the Lansdowne, the Mayfair and Grosvenor House.

The hectic, fatalistic atmosphere produced an epidemic of heavy gambling.

Few people had much time to worry about the fate of bottle-parties, or historic buildings for that matter. The *Daily Herald* reporter Ritchie Calder noted people's reactions to the damage to St Paul's and Westminster Abbey: 'They took it all philosophically, perhaps registering momentary indignation or regret. They regarded it all as wanton and unnecessary, but their concern was rather with things of the present than things of the past.' The things of the present were deciding where to shelter when the air-raid warning sounded, the demands of work in the ARP and emergency services, fire-watching, trying to do one's ordinary job in buildings with the windows blown out, or with no building at all, trying to get to one's job through streets blocked with debris on bomb-damaged public transport, trying to cope with erratic supplies of gas, water and electricity, having to make constant detours because of unexploded bombs which sometimes kept you out of your home for days at a time and, if one had been unlucky, trying to find a new home, preferably in a steel-framed building.

There was an increasing feeling of strain. Harold Nicolson, Parliamentary Under-Secretary for the Ministry of Information, wrote in his diary on 19 September:

Night after night, night after night, the bombardment of London continues. It is like the Conciergerie, since every morning one is pleased to see one's friends appearing again. I am nerveless, and yet I am conscious that when I hear a motor in the empty streets I tauten myself lest it be a bomb screaming towards me. Underneath, the fibres of one's nerve-resistance must be sapped.

Things of the spirit suffered. Vera Brittain noted in her diary 'how excessively boring danger becomes when you are in it perpetually; how completely it destroys concentration upon ideas, books, music, philosophy, and other things far more interesting than the mere preservation of life.'

Although the population of London dropped by a quarter by the end of November, there was a general determination to carry on if possible. Mass Observation noted that there had been a general toughening in public opinion after the initial shock of September, but the Blitz was leaving little time for thought.

One very vital effect of the air raids is this blurring of the future. There is a tendency for people's whole outlook to be foreshortened, so that life exists from day to day. At present there is a marked falling-off in intellectual pursuits, and in many of the uses of organized and private leisure. This is partly due, no doubt, to a simple physical cause as well as to the above psychological one. People are still not getting enough sleep.

In December, Mass Observation commented, 'although people are awake for more hours, they are, in fact, doing *less* with their spare time'.

Cyril Connolly was certain that people were not using their time to read. He wrote in December: 'The reading public panicked with the fall of France, their literary curiosity, which is a luxury emotion, dependent on a background of security and order, vanished overnight.' And literature was physically threatened. A bomb on Mecklenberg Square shattered the offices of Leonard and Virginia Woolf's Hogarth Press; book-cases were blown off the walls and waterpipes burst over the mounds of rubble, books, paper and type. The press was moved to Letchworth. Shortly afterwards a bomb on Tavistock Square destroyed the Woolfs' former home. Leonard Woolf wrote:

It was a curious and ironic sight, for on the vast conical heap of dust and bricks precisely and meticulously perched upright upon the summit was a wicker chair which had been forgotten in one of the upper rooms. Nothing beside remained except a broken mantelpiece against the bare wall of the next-door house and above it intact one of Duncan Grant's decorations.

'Bloomsbury' was literally coming to an end.

The climax of the physical destruction of literature was the great raid of 29 December, an attempt to produce a second Fire of London and burn the heart out of the city. The majority of bombs fell in an area north and west of St Paul's; St Paul's Churchyard and Paternoster Row had been the traditional location of the book trade for three hundred years, and twenty-seven publishing firms had their offices and warehouses in the area. It was a Sunday night, and most of the buildings were locked and unguarded. Five million volumes were destroyed in the fire that followed, and most of the publishers, including Hutchinsons, Blackwoods, Longmans, Collins, Eyre and Spottiswoode, Ward Lock and Sampson Low, had their premises destroyed. The book distributors Simpkin Marshall lost most of their stocks, plus 150 years' worth of records and their catalogue system. The raids also burnt out St Bride's Church in Fleet Street and badly damaged the Guildhall, where 25,000 volumes in the library were destroyed.

The journalist Charles Graves described the City after the raid in his diary:

We walked up Ludgate Hill, stepping over hoses, with the dank, smoky smell unmistakably coming from burnt-out buildings that had been well and truly spurted with water by the Fire Brigade. Numbers of City workers walked about with dazed and stunned looks. They were the people who had arrived the previous morning and found that their place of employment was gutted and were coming back on the following day to stare at the ruins simply because they had nothing better to do and because it was such a habit to go to the office from their suburbs. . . . Firemen were still hard at work; smoke and steam rose in various directions and each of those charming little alleyways, once the haunt of publishers, was full of policemen and firemen in high boots. Even in St Paul's itself there was still that queer, dank, smoky smell.

The publishers were themselves partly to blame for their losses, having failed to leave anyone in charge of their premises. Herbert Mason, the photographer who took the celebrated picture of St Paul's above the flames, said, 'There were so few people. It was pathetic.' Fire-watching became compulsory for all firms in January 1941. The burnt-out publishers managed to find fresh premises within two weeks of the raid, but nothing could replace the total of twenty million unissued new books that were destroyed during the period of the Blitz, or the losses to local and national libraries.

The bombing and burning of London continued into 1941. There was a further fire raid on 11 January, and then something of a lull until the end of February. In March provincial cities and ports were the main targets (the terrible raid on Coventry had been on 14 November), which gave some time for rest and reorganization in London. On 16 April London had its worst raid yet, advertised by the Germans as 'the greatest raid of all time' and known simply to Londoners as 'the Wednesday'. The raid lasted eight hours, and 450 planes dropped 100,000 tons of bombs. This was followed by 'the Saturday'. More than a thousand people were killed in each raid, and 148,000 houses were destroyed or damaged. An even bigger raid on 10 May set fire to the House of Commons and the Deanery of Westminster Abbey, and there were fires right across London. 1,436 people were killed, 1,792 injured, the highest casualties for a single raid. Fire-fighting went on afterwards for eleven days.

Throughout the Blitz the authorities were anxiously monitoring the state of public morale. The slogan was 'London can take it', but during the early days, at least, there were doubts whether the East End of London would. The raids on the Docks smashed the flimsy houses of an impoverished area that was poorly provided with shelters and lacked the efficient social services needed to cope with the shock and homelessness. It has been suggested that had the raids concentrated on the East End the workers there would have risen against the government. Certainly the Royal Family recognized that the daylight raids on Buckingham Palace helped to redress the balance. In the boroughs of West Ham and Stepney there was an almost total collapse of organization and morale, but from it a new leadership emerged, and a determination to see political reform.

Journalists and diarists noticed how quickly the public shelters evolved their own version of the class system. There was 'a spontaneous migration of the like to like. Or, one might say, lice to lice'; the most spontaneous migration of all was to the Underground system. Fearing that once down there the population might never re-emerge, the government had forbidden the use of the Tube stations as shelters, but they were simply taken over. The authorities bowed to a *fait accompli*, and had to improvize means of dealing with the medical and social problems the deep shelters created. Although the majority of Londoners preferred their own homes and their individual Anderson shelters, the Tube shelterers have remained in people's memories as symbols of the Blitz. The *New Statesman* estimated that 200,000 people were sheltering nightly in the Underground in November 1940. The Underground population did not fall below 70,000 a night. The Communist Party was quick to exploit government inactivity during the early days of improvization, and even a pro-British propagandist like the American journalist Negley Farson had to admit that the campaign made some headway with bombed Londoners: 'these people were beginning to lose faith – faith in all degrees of people higher up.'

Gradually order was restored, and with the bunks, portable lavatories and medical attention, came culture. In Bermondsey amateur actors performed Chekov's *The Bear*, the concert party of 106 Pioneer Corps supplied entertainment south of the river, while in middle-class Swiss Cottage the Tube station had its own magazine, *The Swiss Cottager*. Unity Theatre's Outside Show group put on agitprop entertainments in shelters and rest centres. The Council for the Encouragement of Music and the Arts gave a hundred and fifty concerts, and ENSA, now given permission to entertain civilians, followed suit. This led to a clash between popular and high art. A member of CEMA's council complained, 'ENSA came roaring in with its music-hall stars and its barrage of publicity. Next the government decided that this was making the shelters too popular.' Some of the larger shelters had film shows and libraries, while the London County Council laid on evening classes.

The best place to be in a raid – if one could afford it – was one of the large, steel-framed hotels. For the well-off, the Dorchester became the focal point of London after dark. The Turkish baths had been converted into a luxurious air-raid shelter, while dancing and dining went on throughout the Blitz in the downstairs grill-room. American journalist Ralph Ingersoll felt that there was something too self-conscious about the gaiety. 'It was an overdone movie, beautifully costumed but badly directed by a man who had made B movies all his life. There is too much reality in London for make-believe.' As a member of what survived of the fashionable demi-monde, Cecil Beaton made the Dorchester his refuge:

> There the noise outside is drowned with wine, music and company – and what a mixed brew we are! Cabinet ministers and their self-consciously respectable wives; hatchet-jawed, iron grey brigadiers; calf-like airmen off duty; tarts on duty; actresses (also); *declassé* society people, cheap musicians and motor-car agents. It could not be more ugly and vile.

34

In a world severely short of any display of luxury the newspaper gossip columnists seized upon this glamorous image of Londoners taking it:

Descriptions have appeared of revels in an underground playroom-grill, which, apparently, is filled each evening with a gay galaxy of stage and cinema producers, smoking big cigars; actors and actresses trying to catch the producers' eye; and, of course, the usual sprinkling of playboys and playgirls, most of these in uniform. In this gay cavern, states repute, the Blitz is forgotten until closing time, whereupon the roysterers descend still further into the bowels of the hotel to luxury dungeons to sleep or otherwise until the All Clear.

The contrast with the squalor of the shelters in the East End, in the Tilbury foodstore in Whitechapel or the railway arches at Hungerford Bridge, was obvious, and the Communist MP Phil Piratin resolved to do something about it. On 15 September he led about a hundred people to the Savoy, the nearest hotel to the East End, and when the air-raid siren went demanded access to the Savoy's shelter. It was a repetition of the 1938 demonstration, when fifty unemployed men tried to have tea at the Ritz. By law the demonstrators had to be allowed in, but unexpectedly an 'All Clear' sounded fifteen minutes later, and to the relief of the management the demonstrators had no choice but to leave. On the way out they remembered to tip the staff.

Inevitably the *hubris* of night-life London had to be paid for, and on 8 March 1941 retribution came. In early December the restaurateur Martin Poulsen had reopened the Café de Paris, a night-club whose main room was modelled on the ballroom of the *Titanic*. (His partner, an Italian, had been interned.) The Café de Paris was a success partly because Poulsen had cornered the West End's supply of champagne, and partly because it was underground beneath the Rialto cinema. Charles Graves wrote: 'Poor Poulsen had fooled everybody into thinking it had four proper floors above it. It hadn't.' On the night of 8 March two 50-kilo bombs went through the roof and floor of the cinema and down into the night-club. The second bomb broke on the dance-floor instead of exploding, but thirty-four people were killed (including Poulsen) and over a hundred injured. In the confusion that followed looters robbed the dead and wounded. A survivor in hospital found that the girl in the next bed was the mistress of a gangster who specialized in beating the emergency services to shops and offices, in order to grab where the bombs had smashed.

35

The raid of 10 May 1941 was the last major raid on London, but of course no one knew it at the time. It was not until 22 June, when the Germans attacked their ally Russia, that the realization dawned that London had survived, and that the German Air Force was now engaged elsewhere. People did not know that they had come through the worst; indeed there were a great many things they did not know, for it was vital that the Germans should be kept in the dark about the effectiveness, or otherwise, of the bombing. Concessions made to the need for news had sometimes disquieting effects. Mollie Panter-Downes had reported to the *New Yorker* in October 1940:

> In these anxious days, an unnecessary refinement of torture is added by the Ministry of Information department responsible for releasing news of air-raid damage. Some of its references to 'famous squares' and 'well-known London stores' that have suffered sound like crossword-puzzle clues and cruelly agitate the thousands of people who have friends or relations living on squares or working in London stores.

Those who did know what was going on, the firemen, were angered by the official policy. One of them recorded, 'The soothing syrup of Press and BBC, laid on very thick at this period, used to infuriate them. "Slight material damage. Few Casualties. What do they think we are, ——in' mugs?" '

The reason for stressing the lack of information caused jointly by the chaos and official censorship is that while the Blitz was a common and levelling horror, it was a highly individual experience. Just as it was possible to travel from one end of London to the other and see no bomb damage at all, it was equally possible to travel through shattered street after shattered street. Though Chelsea suffered almost as much as Stepney, the social geography of London produced differences between East End and West End, as the evolution of the shelter population shows. (When an attempt was made to rehouse East End homeless in unoccupied mansions in the West End, the people themselves resisted the move.) At the simplest level one's individual experience depended on how close one was to being killed, injured, or merely inconvenienced.

Yet somehow the months from June 1940 to June 1941 have become fused into something called 'the Blitz', something now remembered with nostalgia, something also to be exploited, as the success of a mediocre musical, *Happy as a Sandbag* launched in London in 1975, has shown. The collective image has imposed itself on and even erased individual recollections. Tom Harrisson, the founder of Mass Observation, reported in 1975 on an experiment that had been carried out with Mass Observation's archives at the University of Sussex:

We had people who kept nightly diaries of the blitz as it fell rewrite from memory what they thought they felt and did then. There is usually little or no logical relation between the two sets of accounts, 34 years apart. Memory has glossified and sanctified these 'finest hours'.

What we are dealing with is myth, in this case, as the authors of the revue *Beyond the Fringe* neatly put it, 'the aftermyth of war'. Many writers in London found themselves recording what seemed in retrospect to be the city's last heroic age. That is the myth of the Blitz: part falsehood of glossified and sanctified 'finest hours', part truthful courage and endurance, part nostalgia for a moment of genuine common exaltation.

The first books on the Blitz were written, and some published, before the Blitz was over. The earliest were by visiting American journalists writing propaganda aimed at bringing America out of her neutrality onto the side of Britain. The journalists were also broadcasting direct from London, and their image of London at that time was reflected back on to the city. Louis MacNeice, who was teaching in America at the beginning of the Blitz, recalled that 'the lurid technique of the American radio and press had hidden all Europe in an aura of death'. The reporters soon found themselves living their own fantasy; in September 1940 Alfred Hitchcock's film *Foreign Correspondent* was showing in London, its climax depicting Joel McCrea broadcasting to America from the BBC during an air-raid. Broadcasting House was hit in October and seven people were killed. A parachute mine did further damage in November.

Basil Woon's *Hell Came to London*, describing the first two weeks of the Blitz, has the typical urgent and overcharged feeling of many Blitz accounts. 'A thousand literary masterpieces will germinate eventually from the bloody debris of London,' he predicted. In this he was unfortunately wrong; most writers took the attitude of Auxiliary Fireman Maurice Richardson in *London's Burning*: 'Not much sense saving it up in notebooks for a future war novel. Better get it down quick.' The titles of the books available in January 1941 tell a selective story of the war as the myth of Dunkirk, the Battle of Britain and the Blitz evolves: *Return via Dunkirk, The Epic of Dunkirk, The Road* to *Bordeaux* and *The Nine Days Wonder* (of Dunkirk), the latter by the Poet Laureate John Masefield. Americans contributed *Their Finest Hour, Report on England, The Wounded Don't Cry* and *They'll Never Quit*. Arthur Mee supplied Christian uplift with *1940: Our Finest Hour*.

The Royal Air Force dominates as a subject, and not merely because the Battle of Britain was a heroic event which captured people's imagination. As the newest fighting service it was the most active in shaping its image through an efficient publicity department. The official publications *Bomber Command* and *Battle of Britain* by the peacetime librarian of the House of Commons, Hilary St George Saunders, became best-sellers overnight. Orders for 300,000 copies of *Battle of Britain* were placed on the morning of publication. (Saunders, as 'Francis Beeding', also wrote thrillers such as *Not a Bad Show – a War Thriller*.) The celebrated short-story writer H.E. Bates was given a commission – as 'Flying Officer X' he published his picture of life at a Bomber Station, *The Greatest People in the World*, in 1942. The RAF Public Relations Branch also recognized the usefulness of the poet John Pudney, whose semi-official poetry earned him comparisons (almost certainly unwelcome to the poet) with Rupert Brooke and W.E. Henley. *Readiness at Dawn, Fighter Pilot, Epic Deeds of the RAF*, and *Deeds That Held the Empire by Air* kept the RAF high in the best-seller lists.

The diaries of Charles Graves, themselves published during the war, give a fascinating picture of the process of myth-making. In December 1940 he is in discussions with the Air Ministry about a book to be called *The Thin Blue Line*, 'suitable for the Public School boys of 18', the favoured recruiting material of the RAF. He has lunches in private rooms with Air Commodores, gets fighter pilots to write down their experiences – and Windmill girls, too, who turn out to be prudish. He does not neglect to discuss a £1,000 advance on royalties, the film rights and a possible Air Force order for 10,000 copies of the book. While 'casting' the story he encounters an air-craftsman about to start flying training: 'Looking carefully at him, I observed that he has the long, untidy hair, cleft chin, deep-set eyes, good nose with bone showing that Cuthbert Orde [the illustrator of *The Thin Blue Line*] selects as typical of a successful Fighter pilot.' Written in a month, the books appeared in April 1941, and sold out immediately. Charles Graves then turned to the Navy and the convoys, with *Life Line*.

In the interests of Mass Observation, Tom Harrisson read every single publication of this type that appeared in the first two years of the war. His conclusions, published in *Horizon* in December 1941, were, 'Never have I felt that I owed so little to so many.' The survey shows that there were definite classes of book, just as the war had definite periods. Early in 1940 there were a number of evacuation novels, 'distinctly middle-class and often distinctly unsympathetic to the "masses"'. At about the same time compilations of notebooks and letters began to appear, being easier to produce under war conditions. Dunkirk at least meant that there was something to write about, the ensuing Battle of Britain produced a flood of RAF hero books such as Graves's. The Blitz book marks a change in social attitudes: 'now the working-class are 100% heroes. Extravagant admiration is lavished without regard for modesty, dignity or accuracy.' The scares about parachutists and the 'Fifth Column' produced a rash of spy stories, and at the time he was writing his report, Harrisson noticed that 'peace books' were on the increase, polemics arguing for a better world after the war, or popular novels with no hint of war at all. In all of them he detected a strong right-wing note: 'To judge from most war books, Britain is fighting this war to protect the world against Auden and Picasso, the Jews and any form of collectivism.'

It is unfair to characterize all accounts of London as mythical in the pejorative sense, but one may ask if Negley Farson really did hear this conversation, set on one of the Thames river boats that had temporarily replaced the bombed-out bus service:

'You'd like to get a crack at 'em?' said the skipper.

'Aye!' she [a nurse] replied, her face flushing; '*that* I would!'

The men all grinned. And one of them who looked like a businessman, said, 'Well, we're all in it now, Miss – and you more than some of us. So I shouldn't worry.'

'Oh I'm not!' she said, staring up at a silver balloon. 'But I think our Air Force is fine!'

'What about our AFS boys?' growled the barge-tender.

'Oh, they're fine; they're fine, too – heroes, I call them.'

'So they is: bloody – excuse me, Miss – bloody 'eroes . . . every one of 'em!'

Not all books conceal the strain and depression that was also felt. As a pacifist, Vera Brittain wanted to show that the effort going into the war should have been put into keeping the peace:

Today it is raining, and wounded London looks shabby and sad. Her spirit is unbroken, but her elegance and comfort are gone. Some parts of the city have temporarily lost the ordinary facilities of civilized living; there are rumours of shelter epidemics. . . . Far down the river, a broken sewer pours into the Thames; its putrid odour is blown by the wind as far west as the Strand. . . . Soon, I reflect, London's poorer population, like melancholy troglodytes, will spend its whole life in the Underground.

As for the shelters themselves, here is a fascinating description of the huge Tilbury shelter in the East End – fascinating because it was not written down to be published:

Figures showing faces lit up – rest of bodies in silhouette.
Figures lying against platform with great bales of paper above also making beds.
Perambulators with bundles.
Dramatic, dismal lit, masses of reclining figures fading to perspective point – scribbles and scratches, chaotic foreground. Chains hanging from old crane. Sick woman in bathchair. Bearded jews blanketted sleeping in deck chairs.
Lascars Tunnel (bundles of old clothes that are people).
Bunks with women feeding children.
Dark wet settings (entrance to Tilbury).
Men with shawls to keep off draughts, women wearing handkerchiefs on heads.
Muck & rubbish and chaotic untidiness around.

The author is the sculptor Henry Moore, who turned these notes into his now celebrated shelter drawings [Plate 21]. The artistic transformation had raised the subject out of the squalor of its actuality – but the results were too avant-garde for the ordinary public. *Penguin New Writing* reported that his subjects did not recognize themselves when the drawings were shown: 'Many Londoners confronted with these drawings feel baffled and insulted. Here is a whole new underground world from which they feel themselves excluded, though the elements were so familiar.'

'Everyone is bloody 'eroes' was the more comforting myth, even with the intelligentsia. Maurice Richardson, whose *London's Burning* begins: 'I joined the AFS to dodge the Army', communicates the left-wing middle-class writer's delight – and embarrassment – at close comradeship with the workers. The feeling of communality and solidarity that a few had gone to Spain in search of was now being compulsorily experienced in every training camp in the land, and it was not turning out to be the mystical release some had expected. The Blitz produced one work of humour, George Stonier's 'Shaving Through the Blitz', which takes a sometimes fantastical, sometimes ironic view of events:

'I think the Blitz makes people better somehow, don't you?' she says.
No, I don't. I think it kills a lot of people; I think it makes a few brave and others mad, and the rest more interested, forthcoming and sly. Do I like that? In a way (and this distresses me), I do.

The Blitz also produced propaganda of a kind less welcome to the authorities: political literature campaigning for an end to the mismanagement and class differences the Blitz had underlined. Ritchie Calder led the way with *The Lesson of London* and *Carry on London*, which expose the failure of the emergency services and the breakdown of local authorities at the start of the Blitz: 'We heard a lot about London's citizens being in the "Front Line", but to statesmen it was a glib metaphor.' Calder was arguing for specific social improvements, and so does not conceal the fear and near panic at the start of the bombing, but he too believed in the emergence of a new sense of unity and common purpose rising, literally, from the ashes. For him the myth – part true, part false – is a potential political weapon:

The people who are holding the Front Line are fighting and suffering for a new democracy, which they can understand and to which they themselves are giving the meaning – 'democracy' without the capital. The coin is being reminted, its true worth fresh assayed in the fires of human endurance, and its superscription is that simple remark of the docker 'We are all in it together.' Because, if it is not a 'we-are-all-in-it-together' democracy, there is going to be hell to pay.

Calder and Negley Farson are not so far apart.
The tone for political books had been set by *Guilty Men*, published by Victor Gollancz in July 1940 immediately after Dunkirk. The authors, Michael Foot, Frank Owen and Peter Howard, reviewed the political history of Britain from 1929, in order to show how it led to the defeat of Dunkirk. The Guilty Men were the members of Chamberlain's National Government and the 'old gang' who had appeased Hitler and let the unemployed rot. The message was 'never again'.

Although the leading booksellers W.H. Smith refused to handle it, *Guilty Men* sold in huge numbers, going through nine impressions in the first month of issue alone. On his way to the House of Lords the historian Lord Elton saw it being sold on the pavement in Whitehall as though it were pornography.

More criticism of the past came from C.E.M. Joad's *What is at Stake and Why Not Say So?* Frederick Warburg started a series, Searchlight Books, under the general editorship of George Orwell, to 'criticize and kill what is rotten in Western civilization'; Francis Williams similarly edited a series of pamphlets for Kegan Paul. Orwell, who had joined the Home Guard with ideas that it would become a people's army, considered Hugh Slater's *Home Guard for Victory* 'as much a political pamphlet as a technical manual'. Its author was expelled from the Communist Party for breaking their ban on co-operation with the Home Guard.

The Blitz had a distinct effect on the Communist Party's former mouthpiece in the Left Book Club, John Strachey. The Russo-German Non-Aggression Treaty had been a severe shock, but since he was not a formal member of the Party he could not formally resign. A letter to the *New Statesman* in April 1940 announced his severing of ties. (In 1941 he contributed to Victor Gollancz's attack on the Communists, *The Betrayal of the Left*.) During the Blitz he served as an air-raid warden in Chelsea, and his account *Post D* is straightforward and unheroic, the coolness and detachment empha-sized by his use of the third person. But his *A Faith to Fight For*, the Left Book Club choice for January 1941, is conversely politically passionate. 'The events of 1940 have made me far more certain than ever before that Socialism is a right and true thing.' His socialism is humanitarian, not totalitarian, calling for a just economic system that would be efficient because it was just. Justice was not in the interest of the rich who seek to suppress the truth, and in a passage which looks forward to Orwell's *Nineteen Eighty-four* he argues: 'The lies of the Government and the rich become the only words which break the silence of the subjected peoples. This is total lying.' He has this assessment of the value of historic buildings threatened by high explosive:

The men who in 1940 surrendered Paris in order, they said, to save its buildings were incomparably the greatest vandals who ever lived. For the Pétains showed that they had no conception of what the pictures of the Louvre, or the statues of Chartres, were made *for*.

Strachey served in the RAF, and joined the Labour Party, becoming a junior minister in the 1945 government.

The most influential writer of all, certainly the man who reached the most people, was J.B. Priestley, who began at the time of Dunkirk to broadcast a series of 'Postscripts' after the nine o'clock news on Sundays. Reading them now, these short talks seem almost innocuous, simply pointing out the courage of the common people, that the mistakes of the past must not be repeated, that it was not just a question of fighting, but of having something to fight *for*, and that that meant social change. Priestley, who described himself in an interview as 'an independent man of the Left', has always protested that his impact has been overestimated, and overpraised, though 'I meant what I said in them, of course'.

> I found myself tied, like a man to a gigantic balloon, to one of those bogus reputations that only the mass media know how to inflate. I never asked for it, didn't want it.

Priestley ended the first series of 'Postscripts' at his own request, but a second series on a different day, 'Make it Monday', was given more edge. After questions in Parliament the series was taken off, the BBC telling Priestley it was the decision of the Ministry of Information, the Ministry telling him it was that of the BBC. Priestley had become the most celebrated broadcaster next to Winston Churchill, and there is a strong suspicion that it was Churchill who took him off the air.

When Priestley protests at the reputation of the 'Postscripts', he is protesting against the myth. There is no doubt that he wanted change, as his polemical *Out of the People* (1941) shows. And others seem to have recognized the significance of his message. Harold Nicolson had dinner during the September Blitz with a retired Major General and his wife, who had served in India:

> Priestley gives a broadcast about the abolition of privilege, while I look at their albums of 1903 and the Delhi Durbar and the Viceroy's train. Priestley speaks of the old order which is dead and of the new order which is to arise from its ashes. These two old people listen without flinching. I find their dignity and patriotism deeply moving. I glance at the pictures of the howdahs and panoply of the past and hear the voice of Priestley and the sound of the guns.

A request to do an extra broadcast saved Priestley's life, for he left his room in the Langham Hotel opposite Broadcasting House. When he re-emerged from the underground studios he found a bomb had carried away his wing of the hotel.

By the beginning of 1942, although war books continued to flood the market, critical opinion was turning against them. When the American-produced film *Mrs Miniver* appeared in July 1942 its exploitation of the Blitz myth was attacked by William Whitebait (the pseudonymous George Stonier) in the *New Statesman*:

The most that *Mrs Miniver* achieves is an easy pathos; sentimentality (and class sentimentality at that) takes on a tone of holiness, of smug simplicity, which personally I found it rather difficult to bear. 'This is a people's war,' says the vicar delivering a sermon in his bombed church; but it isn't, it is only (look round at the faces, look back over the story!) the best people's war.

By 1943 boredom with the subject had set in. This is Marie Scott-James in *Time and Tide*:

The new historical novel engendered by the war on the Home Front is on the whole a depressing phenomenon. Contemporary novelists, necessarily preoccupied with current events, are busy enshrining them in fiction long before tranquil recollection can impose form and meaning on the chaos of actuality.... It is too soon for any but a very distinguished writer to improve upon the facts.

Some authors did manage to improve on the facts, although they are few, and took longer to reach publication than the instant documentaries. Graham Greene's *Ministry of Fear* (1943) uses the Blitz as a background to a psychological theme loosely tied to a spy story. The menace of Organization is also the theme of Rex Warner's *The Aerodrome*, published in 1941 and probably at least partly written before war broke out. A harshly written novel, *The Aerodrome* does not portray war, but a battle between individualism and a form of totalitarianism that could be equally fascist or communist, a struggle symbolized by the relationship between a village community and the Air Force which takes it over. His next book *Why was I Killed?* (1943) is a less successful political allegory.

At the outbreak of war the novelist Henry Green (his real name was Henry Yorke) joined the Auxiliary Fire Service, and he used his experiences in training and during the Blitz for a novel, *Caught* (1943). A mannered, elliptical prose style is mixed in with working-class dialogue in a way that no documentary writer would attempt. The Fire Service created a rare opportunity to cut across the class barriers which limit so much English fiction, and there are fine descriptions of fire-fighting in the Blitz, but it provides situation and background rather than subject.

The Blitz enabled one writer to find himself. Before the war William Sansom had worked for the advertising agency J. Walter Thompson, and in his spare time had written 'formula' stories, without any success at all. Having been turned down by the Navy, he too joined the AFS in order, as he said in an interview, 'to do something manual'. Stationed in Hampstead High School for Girls, his team was frequently sent into the Docks. What he saw there made him give up his preconceptions of what a short story should be, and he sat down and wrote for his own benefit a brief scene, 'The Wall'. Quite by chance the business manager of *Horizon* saw it, and passed it on to the editor, Cyril Connolly. To Sansom's surprise it was accepted. 'I decided never to write for an imaginary audience from then on.' Instead a whole series of stories, part descriptive, part allegorical, appeared, being collected as *Fireman Flower* in 1944. During the post-Blitz lull Sansom played the raw recruit in Humphrey Jennings's documentary *Fires Were Started* (Plate 11).

One novel which (at this distance) does seem to convey what must have been the fear, absurdity and chaos is James Hanley's *No Directions* (1943), describing one night of Blitz in a rundown tenement in Pimlico. It is told in a modified stream of consciousness, switching from one character to another so that their jumbled and disjointed thoughts match the upside-down world caused by Black-Out, fire and explosions. Instead of trying to describe directly what is almost indescribable, the physical effects of the Blitz are filtered through the emotional states of the characters, drunk, frightened, ill, old, who only comprehend part of what is going on. But the result is a convincing picture of the surreal horror and muddle that the Blitz must have been. Hanley reuses some of his material in *A Dream Journey* (1976).

At a much simpler level Robert Greenwood's *The Squad Goes Out* (1943) gives a sympathetic and sometimes comic picture of social integration in a volunteer ambulance team in Bermondsey, though with an occasionally cloying touch of sentiment. At the time of their publication neither *The Squad Goes Out* nor *No Directions* made very much impression, possibly because the fashion had turned against

Blitz novels. None, apart from possibly Henry Green's *Caught*, has been heard of since.

Not surprisingly, the Blitz inspired a large number of poems, though few good ones. As in the case of James Hanley's novel the verse in the best of these creates a distancing from the physical effects which bring us closer to the emotional experience. Louis MacNeice achieved this in 'The Trolls' and 'Brother Fire', and C. Day Lewis in 'Word Over All', but the violence and absurdity of the raids was ideally suited to Dylan Thomas, who turns an image of burning London into an act of assertion. The world is reborn in the last stanza of 'Ceremony After a Fire Raid':

> Into the organpipes and steeples
> Of the luminous cathedrals,
> Into the weathercocks' molten mouths
> Rippling in twelve-winded circles,
> Into the dead clock burning the hour
> Over the urns of sabbaths
> Over the whirling ditch of daybreak
> Over the sun's hovel and the slum of fire
> And the golden pavements laid in requiems,
> Into the bread in a wheatfield of flames,
> Into the wine burning like brandy,
> The masses of the sea
> The masses of the sea under
> The masses of the infant-bearing sea
> Erupt, fountain, and enter to utter forever
> Glory glory glory
> The sundering ultimate kingdom of genesis' thunder.

Though the use of verse provides an effective distancing, knowledge of the actual circumstances of the Blitz also illuminates. This is especially true of the second section of T.S. Eliot's 'Little Gidding' in *Four Quartets*. Eliot served as a fire-watcher at the offices of Faber and Faber every Tuesday night, and it was here that he would have accumulated the physical details – the end of an air-raid just before dawn, the sound of retiring aircraft, the burning buildings and the hail of shrapnel from anti-aircraft guns – which go into his encounter with the ghost of W.B. Yeats:

> In the uncertain hour before the morning
> Near the ending of interminable night
> At the recurrent end of the unending

> After the dark dove with the flickering tongue
> Had passed below the horizon of his homing
> While the dead leaves still rattled on like tin
> Over the asphalt where no sound was
> Between three districts whence the smoke arose
> I met one walking, loitering and hurried
> As if blown towards me like the metal leaves
> Before the urban dawn wind unresisting.

This discussion of myth has so far left out an important aspect: the fact that at certain times there is a *need* for myth. The conversion of the defeat of Dunkirk into a moral victory is one example of myth being formed, a myth which overlaid the political significance of the defeat until 1945. There is also a need for heroes, however reluctant:

> Much that is untrue and misleading has been written on the pilot in this war. Within one short year he has become the nation's hero, and the attempt to live up to this false conception bores him.

The anti-heroic author is Richard Hillary, a Spitfire pilot who was shot down during the Battle of Britain and whose hands and face were roasted by the fire in his cockpit. *The Last Enemy*, an account of his experiences in training and later in hospital as his face is painfully reconstructed, has no great literary merit, but it *is* affecting, partly because it is not a war-in-the-air book. Instead Hillary is concerned with moral attitudes. He had entered the RAF as one of the 'long-haired boys' of the Oxford University Air Squadron, and he had the arrogant, non-political but anti-establishment stance of a clever member of the professional class. His encounter during training with the moral seriousness of the Tory Christian landowner Peter Pease was a challenge to his assumptions, and in August 1940 he changed his views to a more 'responsible' attitude. The timing is significant, for it coincides with the invasion crisis and the general change of heart in Britain. His decision would have appealed to the strain of British conservatism which Tom Harrisson noticed.

Recovering from his burns with much suffering, Hillary becomes involved with Peter Pease's fiancée after Pease is killed. His wounds drive him in on himself, he hates himself for being useless, worries about the past, and is angered by blimpish patriotic slogans. His shell is broken by the experience of helping to dig out a woman trapped during the Blitz. The bomb victim's compassion for Hillary's destroyed face decides him that at least he can pass on his experiences:

I could write. Later there would be other things, but now I could write. I had talked about it long enough, I was to be a writer, just like that. I was to be a writer, but in a vacuum. Well, here was my chance. To write I needed two things, a subject and a public. Now I knew well enough my subject. I would write of these men, of Peter and of the others. I would write for them and would write with them. They would be at my side. And to whom would I be speaking when I spoke of these men? And that, too, I knew. To Humanity, for Humanity must be the public of any book. Yes, that despised Humanity which I had so scorned and ridiculed to Peter.

This simple sense of commitment had immense appeal to an intelligentsia alienated by their hesitations about the war, and the government's refusal to give them anything more than a nominal role. *The Last Enemy* was a success both with the critics and a public impressed by Hillary's laconic courage. But there was a price to pay:

Myths grow like crystals . . . as soon as a suitable core is found, they group themselves around it and the crystal is formed, the myth is born. The question, of course, is who makes a suitable core. Obviously it must have some affinity with that vague, diffuse sentiment, that craving for the right type of hero to turn into a myth; obviously he must express something which is the unconscious content of that craving.

The quotation is from Arthur Koestler's essay on Hillary, its title– 'The Birth of a Myth'.

Effectively, the myth took Hillary over. His success depressed him, for he found that people praised *his*, not his dead friends', courage. The book had cleared him of the guilt he felt about surviving death, but he now felt guilty about the book. He suspected that the women who slept with him were aroused by his disfigurement. Having written a book, what could he do to live up to it? The answer also lay in literature, a reading of T.E. Lawrence's then unpublished novel of life in the RAF, *The Mint*, lent to him by the painter Eric Kennington [Plate 26]. The comradeship depicted there pulled him back. 'It was reading *The Mint* that decided me to return.' In spite of his crippled hands he argued his way into training as a night-fighter pilot. He was killed in an accident during a practice flight on 7 January 1943.

Koestler was certain that it was the myth that killed him. 'He had to die in search of his own epitaph.' But, since a myth can only be shaped, and not created by an individual writer, Koestler is uncertain of the lasting form of the myth. His own version is inconclusive:

Hell Came to London, and other Stories

It is the myth of the Lost Generation – sceptic crusaders, knights of
effete veneer, sick with the nostalgia of something to fight for, which as yet
is not. It is the myth of the crusade without a cross, and of desperate
crusaders in search of a cross. What creed they will adopt, Christ's or
Barrabas', remains to be seen.

The writing seems overheated now, but the correspondence that
followed shows that the essay appealed to the emotions of the period.
(For those readers who bothered to vote, Koestler's article was by far
the most popular contribution to *Horizon* in 1943.) But Koestler's
inconclusiveness is ominous. Here, it seemed, literature had risen to
the occasion, and *The Last Enemy* had articulated a common emotion. Yet though Hillary wanted to write 'for Humanity', he had no
certain creed to give it.

Whatever the quality of the results, the myth-makers of the Blitz
were fulfilling a genuine need. So it appeared by 1944, when serious
writers, worn down by the difficulties of war and alienated from the
national effort, were calling for a healing and reintegrating myth, for,
as John Lehmann put it, 'a myth which we in England felt we were
about to recapture for one moment of astonishing intensity in 1940,
when everything seemed to be falling into place'.

The last word goes to Elizabeth Bowen, writing in 1949. Her novel
In the Heat of the Day, set in 1942, shows how quickly the moment of
intensity passed into memory, even before the war was over:

That autumn of 1940 was to appear, by two autumns later, apocryphal,
more far away than peace. No planetary round was to bring again that
particular conjunction of life and death; that particular psychic London
was to be gone forever; more bombs would fall, but not on the same city.
War moved from the horizon to the map. And it was now, when you no
longer saw, heard, smelled war, that a deadening acclimatization to it
began to set in.

When the short-story writer Julian Maclaren-Ross arrived in London
in 1943 a woman accused him of being a 'Soho non-blitzer', a lesser
man because he had missed the Blitz. In self-defence he could only
explain that he had been in the Army. The bombs had fallen equally
towards him in his camp on the Downs, but he had missed the
essential experience.

The intensity of 1940–41 goes beyond the literature of the Blitz. The
image of London the cultural centre is a figure for a wider question –

what happens to a civilization under siege? Do books, paintings and music become more or less important as they become less and less available? And, a more subtle question, do the specific conditions of wartime distort the valuations set on culture? The sight of the dome of St Paul's Cathedral standing out against the smoke of blazing publishers' warehouses grasps the heart, but does that image lead to anything more than a sentimental appreciation of what is lost, when what may be needed is a critical commitment to maintaining the standards of what survives?

There is no doubt that the war was a stimulus to the appreciation of books, paintings and music. Stephen Spender recalls in his autobiography:

there was a revival of interest in the arts. This arose spontaneously and simply, because people felt that music, the ballet, poetry and painting were concerned with a seriousness of living and dying with which they themselves had suddenly been confronted. ... There was something deeply touching about this interest in the arts; it was one of the few things which can still make me regret the war.

Spender might be accused of subscribing to the general myth that during wartime things were somehow better, but his account is confirmed by the words and actions of people at the time. Cyril Connolly reported in June 1940 on the paradox of the artist's position: 'There can be no doubt that the war (crippling though it be to the artist who is affected economically, or by conscription) is yet causing a deepening interest in art and the artist by which they may later profit.'

Virginia Woolf has left a remarkable picture of an artist's response to the imminence of destruction in 'Thoughts on Peace during an Air Raid', describing her feelings while raiders are over her house at Rodmell in Sussex:

The sound of sawing overhead has increased. All the searchlights are erect. They point at a spot exactly above this roof. At any moment a bomb may fall on this very room. One, two, three, four, five, six ... the seconds pass. The bomb did not fall. But during those seconds of suspense all thinking stopped. All feeling save one dull dread, ceased. A nail fixed the whole being to one hard board. The emotion of fear and of hate is therefore sterile, unfertile. Directly that fear passes, the mind reaches out and instinctively revives itself by trying to create.

It was work rather than the horror of war which led to Virginia Woolf's suicide on 28 March 1941, for the effort of writing *Between the Acts* led to a depression which overwhelmed her. The causes of her mental instability lay in the distant past – but the war certainly produced thoughts of suicide, for both she and Leonard Woolf had planned to kill themselves if the Germans successfully invaded.

Literature, though hampered by wartime conditions, was by no means dead, and by April 1941 John Lehmann could even feel optimistic:

it seemed as if the war was going to make all serious literary activity impossible in this country. Since then, it has proved itself tougher and more independent than most people imagined, and even the blitz and the paper-shortage and the rapid spread of the call-up have failed to interrupt it drastically. Writers have gone on producing poems and stories and articles – and also indulging in their squabbles with one another; and, perhaps even more surprising, the reading public has shown an undiminished appetite.

This was of course a partial view. At exactly the same date, George Orwell was reporting to America's *Partisan Review*: 'So far as I know, nothing of consequence is being written, except in fragmentary form, diaries and short sketches, for instance.'

Orwell's is also a partial view, coloured by his own depression. He wrote in July 1940, 'I can't write with this sort of business going on. . . . In any case I feel that literature as we have known it is coming to an end.' By contrast C. Day Lewis, who had been feeling increasing disenchantment with the Communist Party, experienced a definite poetic impulse from his life in the Devon countryside and his service with the Home Guard. The products are his translation of Virgil's *Georgics* and a group of pastoral/military poems. Analysing in his autobiography the feelings which 'it takes a seismic event such as war to reveal to most of us rootless moderns', he describes his quickened love of place and renewed sense of patriotism. 'More and more I was buoyed up by a feeling that England was speaking to me through Virgil, and that the Virgil of the *Georgics* was speaking to me through the English farmers and labourers with whom I consorted.'

A younger generation, hardly formed as men let alone as writers, were undergoing the breaking-down process of military training which precedes reformation. In his book *Auden and After* (1942) the poet Francis Scarfe traces through his poems between 1939 and July 1941 succeeding feelings of horror, disorientation, disillusion, frustra-

51

tion, and eventual acceptance: 'with the entry of Russia into the war [I] wrote my first poem that sympathized with the war.... Or, I should say, not "sympathized with the war" but with the human values which are at stake.' The poet Alun Lewis pondered on the influences of marriage and militarism: 'Thinking back on my own writing, it all seemed to mature of a sudden between the winter of 1939 and the following autumn. Can't make it out. Was it Gweno and the Army? What a combination!!! Beauty and the Beast!' Others, less articulate, must have experienced much the same thing.

In March 1941 John Lehmann felt the literary world poised for some great change:

Everywhere, it is already apparent, a new consciousness is stirring, both among those who have joined the armed forces and those who are still in so-called civilian life; a consciousness that, not merely as a matter of self-preservation for the moment, but also in order to equip ourselves for a far more strenuous future when the results will be far worse if we do not avoid the dismal, sleep-walking mistakes of the past, the old ways of life and the old slogans will have to be scrapped. And in this new consciousness creative writers will have an important part to play. Their part is not to exhort, not to string patriotic jingles together, but to transmit the truth as all the fine instruments of their imagination discover it.

What the fine instruments of rationed, restricted and censored wartime imaginations discovered will be discussed in later chapters. For a more hard-headed assessment turn to Orwell at the same period, to his diary for 22 April 1941:

Sowed while at Wallington 40 or 50lb. of potatoes, which might give 200 to 600lb. according to the season, etc. It would be queer – I hope it won't be so, but it quite well may – if, when this autumn comes, those potatoes seem a more important achievement than all the articles, broadcasts, etc., I shall have done this year.

CHAPTER THREE

Under Siege

'War moved from the horizon to the map.'

Elizabeth Bowen

In May 1941 Mass Observation noted that there was a marked decline in people's interest in the news. That may have been because the news was so bad. Even the events that turned the course of the war – Germany's invasion of Russia and Japan's attack on America – were causes for gloom at the moment of their occurrence. The German invasion of Russia began well, Japan's attack at Pearl Harbour weakened the American Navy, while the British were forced back in Malaya and Burma. Hong Kong was occupied on Christmas Day 1941, and on 15 February 1942 came the miserable surrender of Singapore. British forces were defeated in Greece and Crete, and the victory over the Italians in Libya was quickly reversed when Rommel arrived on the scene. In June 1942 Tobruk fell, and Rommel seemed poised to sweep into Egypt and seize the Suez Canal.

In 1942 Austerity closed its grip. The Battle of the Atlantic had been fought throughout 1941 to maintain the supplies of arms, fuel, raw materials and food from America that Britain needed in order to survive. The winter of 1941–2 was bitterly cold, coal production declined and its distribution became uncertain. Rationing became stricter, and luxuries disappeared (sometimes under the counter or on to the Black Market), while shortages of every kind of commodity were a regular problem of everyday life. The Blitz was over, but there was a constant threat of air-raids, and the shelters and Tubes continued in nightly use.

In June 1942 Joseph Grigg, an American correspondent in Berlin who had been interned when the Americans declared war at the end of 1941, but who had later been exchanged, published this revealing comparison in the *Spectator*:

superficially, there is, in fact, much that Berlin and London have in common. People stumble around in the same black-out. There is no great difference in the basic rations. There are queues, propaganda posters, thin newspapers and uniforms everywhere. You meet some of the same war-time shortages and hear people grumbling about much the same sort of annoyances.

Grigg goes on quickly to say that these are only superficial like-nesses. 'In everything of real importance there is no comparison between the two countries. Food, drink, general living conditions, morale, and, above all, confidence in the outcome of the war – in all these Great Britain is so far ahead.' In view of the needs of wartime propaganda he could hardly say anything else; one wonders if the superficial likenesses were not more important from day to day, but it is true that later in 1942 confidence began to grow. On 4 November came the announcement of the defeat of Rommel at El Alamein, followed by the American and British landings in Morocco and Algeria. More significantly for the final outcome of the war, the German forces in Russia were stuck at Stalingrad, and in January 1943 the balance changed dramatically with the German surrender in the Stalingrad pocket. At the end of 1942 Mollie Panter-Downes noted that the phrase 'after the war' was coming back into circula-tion. On 1 December the government had published Sir William Beveridge's report on a future Britain without Want, Disease, Ignorance, Squalor or Idleness.

For Londoners, civilian or uniformed, 1942 and 1943 became something of a 'middle passage'. The terrors and excitements of the Blitz were over; now came the long preparation for the invasion of Europe, and, with the combined weight of America and Russia, the gradual wearing down of German strength. During the middle passage the emotional demands were different, and the less admirable qualities of people were allowed to show. William Sansom summed it up in his history of Westminster at war:

Perhaps the only real generalizations that can be made are that during blitzes people generally did smile and co-operate without much grumbling; and that afterwards, in the enervating Lull, having all learned in time of danger to live more deeply, the emotions were freed, and expressed more at either of their limits of anger and generosity – where before such emotions were never expressed, masked so that they were perhaps not even felt.

With the withdrawal of war to beyond the horizon even the realities of the Blitz began to stale. George Stonier wrote in the *New Statesman* in April 1942, 'The false exhilaration that set hundreds of diarists going with a sense of history in the making has worked itself out long ago; we have all been bombed, and written about and read about being bombed.' George Woodcock, editor of the anarchist and pacifist magazine *Now*, reported to the New York magazine *View* in April 1943:

This is a freak season, for weather and war alike, and here in London the domestic and the international scene has an air of inconsequential unreality in the mellow light of this extended autumn merging into a premature spring. Still the people of London do not quite believe in the war. In spite of the air raids, the invasion scares, the news from Russia, the unexpected victories in Africa, it has for them no existence as a great cataclysmic fact – as the last war had for the 1914–18 Londoners.

Woodcock (who also forecast that the Labour Party would dwindle 'into a rump') paints a picture of civil discontent and passive resistance that is coloured by his anarchist bias; nonetheless there was an uncomfortable unreality about being in a city under siege – yet still enjoying most of the features of civilized life. The civilian occupation of writing continued to exist, but at one remove. In April 1942 John Lehmann complained of

the steady drain of authors of every sort into the war-machine, either into the Armed Forces, or into jobs which allow them little or no time or opportunity for writing. This difficulty was less apparent in the first two years, though from the very beginning a number of authors found themselves obliged, for one reason or another, to abandon the more ambitious works they had planned. After a time, there was even a certain revival of creative writing, as some of the older authors, recognizing that the fantastic emergency bureaucracy of 1939 had no use for them, found time to think over the problems of their art and their attitude to the world during the long months of the *sitzkrieg*. But now that the call-up has reached – and passed – the overthirties, an increasing proportion of these authors are either being completely silenced, or forced to cut down their independent literary activity.

George Orwell (who by now had solved his economic problems by joining the External Services of the BBC) expressed the problem of writers employed to write: 'To compose a propaganda pamphlet or a radio feature needs just as much work as to write something you believe in, with the difference that the finished product is worthless.'

During the siege of London the number of writers able to carry on their trade was small; their facilities were restricted. Yet these conditions had paradoxical effects. There was a huge increase in demand for whatever writers *could* produce; the writers themselves drew together in self-defence. For those who were in a position to write, the life they led then has become, retrospectively, a golden age. So it appears in John Lehmann's autobiography:

There were not a great number of us; most of those who were destined to spend at least part of the war in uniform had already gone; nearly all who remained knew one another (or very soon got to know one another) personally, and living more or less under siege conditions with very little opportunity of movement far afield, we were continually meeting to discuss together, so that ideas were rapidly absorbed into the general bloodstream and hostile camps and intellectual schisms never lasted long or remained very serious. We were united in a this-has-got-to-be-seen-through attitude towards the war which was taken for granted, and also in a determination to guard the free world of ideas from any misguided military encroachment. We *needed* one another, and for purposes larger than our own security or ambitions.

Lehmann's fellow editor Connolly called this period more acidly a 'five-year sentence in gregarious confinement'.

What John Lehmann is describing is a literary society momentarily stabilized by the physical geography of London. Such brief conjunctions of time, people, and circumstances, producing a mixture of unconventional behaviour and artistic enthusiasm, have become known as 'Bohemia', which is both a state of mind and a place. From 1940 until a few years after the war, London had such a Bohemia. Here is a group of writers, poets, painters, musicians, actors (plus the necessary complement of hangers-on, mistresses, entrepreneurs, patrons and journalists), all of varying talent and achievement, who collectively experience a specific set of emotional and economic conditions. There is only the vaguest awareness that they constitute a group or that they hold any ideas in common, yet they unconsciously reflect a joint experience in the art to which they are committed. The

56

limitations and difficulties shape and stimulate ideas. That is Bohemia
the state of mind. But the group must be fairly small, its members
must meet each other regularly, and in a limited area. That is
Bohemia the place. Look at the place:

'Now we will go to the Black Horse, the Burglar's Rest, The Marquess of
Granby, the Wheatsheaf, then the Beer House and after 10.30 back to the
Highlander which closes later at eleven and after this eat curries in St Giles'
High or steak at the Coffee An'.'

This was Julian Maclaren-Ross's introduction to literary life in
London late in the summer of 1943. The speaker is J.M. Tambimuttu,
the editor of *Poetry* (*London*).

'Only beware of Fitzrovia,' Tambi said . . . 'It's a dangerous place, you
must be careful.'
'Fights with knives?'
'No, a worse danger. You might get Sohoitis you know.'
'No I don't. What is it?'
'If you get Sohoitis,' Tambi said very seriously, 'you will stay there
always day and night and get no work done ever. You have been warned.'

This meeting between an unlikely modern Virgil and an even more
unlikely Dante, and that night's journey through a blacked-out
Inferno, are described in Maclaren-Ross's *Memoirs of the Forties*.

Maclaren-Ross, a short-story writer recently discharged from the
Army, quickly became one of the features of the landscape he
describes. It was a territory bounded on the south side by Piccadilly
Circus and Leicester Square, to the north by Goodge Street, its
approaches to east and west guarded by Broadcasting House and the
Ministry of Information. At the centre the restaurants, pubs, clubs
and brothels of Soho. 'Soho' now stops on the north side at Oxford
Street, but in the Thirties and Forties it was considered to include the
area further north, of which Rathbone Place and Charlotte Street
form the spine. In the Thirties a form of separation had begun, owing
to the popularity in artistic circles of the Fitzroy pub on the corner of
Charlotte Street and Windmill Street. The area has a tradition of
housing artists that goes back beyond the Pre-Raphaelites. It became
known unofficially as Fitzrovia, and during the war if Soho was the
stomach of London, Fitzrovia became its often fuddled brains.

Although still visited by such survivors of the Twenties and
Thirties as Augustus John and Sylvia Gough, the Fitzroy Tavern was
only titular headquarters by the time war broke out. It had acquired a

touristic reputation which drove the genuine figures out, and it later became notorious as a haunt of homosexuals, who lacked the moderate social and legal acceptance they have since won. John Lehmann's novel *In the Purely Pagan Sense* (1976) describes the life of a literary homosexual at this time. The nerve centre of Fitzrovia was the Wheatsheaf, in Rathbone Place. Its major attraction was that it sold Younger's Scotch Ale, a stronger brew than southern English beers. While the Fitzroy has now lost its collection of naval cap badges, First World War recruiting posters and military caps, the Wheatsheaf is still decorated in dark wood and leaded glass, with panels of Scottish tartans, and one may still order Scotch Ale from the corner of the bar where Maclaren-Ross could be found night after night.

Everyone went to the Wheatsheaf. A poet on leave, like Alan Ross, would go straight there, hoping that Tambimuttu had already arrived. As an editorial entrepreneur 'Tambi' had acquired an entourage of males and females who journeyed with him, and the availability of the girls – 'aspiring poetesses' – made Tambi's princely acceptance of hospitality more bearable. His dilatory attitude to publishing *Poetry* (*London*) had to be borne, for he was one of the few editors working at all. Since everyone went to the Wheatsheaf – and there were times when it was inconvenient to encounter those one had offended, or owed money, or both – it was necessary to have somewhere else to go for a quiet chat with a new girl, or to make a business deal. The Bricklayers' Arms, round the corner in Gresse Street, answered this purpose. (It was known colloquially as The Burglar's Rest because it had once been raided by thieves who drank most of their loot on the premises.)

A few yards north of the Wheatsheaf, on the corner of Rathbone Street and Percy Street, lay the Marquess of Granby. In spite of the fact that the landlord was an ex-policeman, the Marquess of Granby had the reputation of being a violent place. Maclaren-Ross describes a man being kicked to death on the pavement outside. Further up Rathbone Street lay the Beer House (now the Nuneham Arms), one of the last pubs in England to have no licence to sell spirits and so to stock only beer. Still further north was the Duke of York, which after the war became one of the first haunts of the Beats.

In Soho proper the Highlander in Dean Street had the advantage of staying open half an hour later than the pubs north of Oxford Street, and from Fitzrovia one could head south, calling in at the Black Horse at the bottom of Rathbone Place before crossing Oxford Street

FITZROVIA

A Finch's The One Tun
B L'Etoile
C Schmidt's
D The Duke of York
E Bertorelli's
F The Fitzroy Tavern
G The Marquis of Granby
H The Beer House
I The White Tower
J The Wheatsheaf
K The Bricklayer's Arms
L The Black Horse

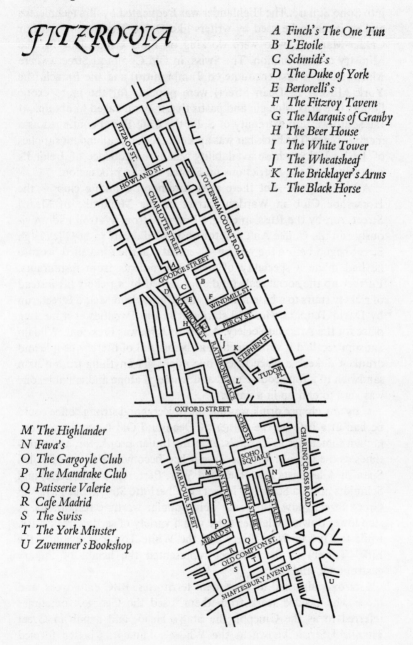

M The Highlander
N Fava's
O The Gargoyle Club
P The Mandrake Club
Q Patisserie Valerie
R Cafe Madrid
S The Swiss
T The York Minster
U Zwemmer's Bookshop

into Soho Square. The Highlander was frequented by film technicians and so came to be used by writers like Dylan Thomas and Arthur Calder-Marshall, who were working on films being made for the Ministry of Information. The Swiss, in Old Compton Street (where Maclaren-Ross first encountered Tambimuttu) and the French (the York Minster in Dean Street) were popular for the more exotic liquors like arak, sloe gin and pastis that they managed to obtain. At the south-western extremity of Soho the Café Royal continued as a meeting place. The back-bar was appreciated for its abundant supplies of Irish whisky, whose availability was a consequence of Ireland's neutrality and the restrictions on Scotch whisky production.

After the pubs shut there were afternoon drinking clubs – the Horseshoe Club in Wardour Street or the Mandrake in Meard Street, run by the Russian emigré Boris Watson. Watson had previously run the Coffee An', a notoriously sordid café in St Giles High Street begun before the war by 'Overcoat Charlie', so-called because he had made a speciality of stealing overcoats from restaurants. Further up the social scale (and approached by a rickety lift instead of rickety stairs to a basement) was the Gargoyle in Meard Street, run by David Tennant who had started it in the Twenties as a meeting place for the Arts and Society. Augustus John was President. William Sansom recalled it with affection as being 'full of literary people and drunken dukes', a place where one might get anything from a ham sandwich to a four-course meal and where, if alone and amiable, one was sure to end up in a party.

If by any chance drink was not the object, good strong coffee could be had at a café on the corner of Dean and Old Compton Streets, known sometimes as Torino's, after the Italian proprietor, and sometimes as the Café Madrid because it had become the haunt of exiled Spanish Anarchists after the Civil War. Bertorelli's (still there) and Schmidts and La Scala (no longer) in Charlotte Street, and Fava's in Greek Street (now also gone) were popular wartime restaurants. A step lower down the ladder there was a variety of seedy Greek cafés, while the Ivy in West Street and the White Tower (previously the Eiffel Tower) in Percy Street represented the height of literary gastronomic ambitions.

Fitzrovia also had its dependent territories. BBC employees, and those who needed work from them, used the George, sometimes referred to as the Gluepot, the Stag's Head, and a pub in Great Titchfield Street known as the Whore's Lament. Chelsea formed

virtually a separate state, threaded through by the Queen's Elm, the
Pier Hotel, the Anglesea, the King's Head, the Australian, the
Crossed Keys, the Red House and the Markham, and especially the
Eight Bells. The Old Swan in Notting Hill Gate was popular on
Sundays (when the pubs shut earlier and the journey to Fitzrovia was
less worthwhile), for it was near the studio shared by the Scottish
painters Robert Colquhoun and Robert MacBryde, notorious
drinkers and fighters. The studio at 77, Bedford Gardens, Campden
Hill, became a regular meeting place for painters: John Minton (who
shared the studio at one time), John Craxton, Michael Ayrton,
Prunella Clough, while in 1943 Jankel Adler, discharged from the
Polish Army, took a studio in the same house. 'The two Roberts'
became close friends with the poet George Barker after his return to
England in 1943. The Old Swan was commemorated by John Heath-
Stubbs when it was demolished after the war to widen the road:

> The gap elicits
> A guarded sentiment. Enough bad poets
> Have romanticized beer and pubs,
> And those for whom the gimcrack enchantments
> Of engraved glass, mahogany, plants in pots,
> Were all laid out to please, are fugitive, doubtless,
> Nightly self-immersed in a fake splendour.

Heath-Stubbs's warning must be borne in mind. Fitzrovia has
become retrospectively romantic, but some nostalgia is legitimate.
The circumstances of war had brought to London the cosmopolitan-
ism of Paris. The streets were full of foreign uniforms – French,
Polish, Dutch, Belgian – emigré officers and civil servants, who lived
well on their wartime salaries and continued their Continental habits
of arguing and entertaining in cafés and restaurants. The Americans
brought money, if not a European style, and maintained the Black
Market economy which grew up around the restaurants, hotels and
night-clubs. Crime is a necessary ingredient for a heady atmosphere;
the prostitutes were busy servicing the services, and deserters without
Identity Cards or Ration Books made their way to Soho and the
underworld. The Continentals moved amongst the indigenous eccen-
trics – the Countess Eileen Duveen, allegedly a genuine countess, a
cured drug addict who lived on benzedrine and cream puffs, Count
Potocki de Montalk, a Polish Monarchist (though it was said he was
Australian) who peddled copies of the *Right Review*, which he

printed on a hand-press (price 1/-), Iron Foot Jack, an immensely strong fairground performer who concealed his long hair by rolling it up into his hat, and the Great Beast himself, the black magician Aleister Crowley, who haunted Dylan Thomas among others until 1944, when he was bombed out and retired to Hastings.

The artists and writers were themselves also eccentric; indeed, those of military age had to be in order to be there at all. Rayner Heppenstall's novel *The Lesser Infortune* (1953) describes his meeting in Fitzrovia no less than three writers who had been discharged from the Army after passing through the Army's psychiatric hospital at Northfield, outside Birmingham, where he had himself spent some time. The characters, 'Dorian Scott-Chrichton' and 'a Welsh and a Canadian poet' are Maclaren-Ross, Keidrych Rhys and Paul Potts, who all became fixtures of the scene in the later part of the war. In the Wheatsheaf:

we struggled through the milling drinkers in the direction of the voice, the dark, waving hair and the pallid hand holding aloft a long, black cigarette holder. Scott-Chrichton wore a jacket of mustard-coloured velvet, chocolate-coloured trousers, with suede shoes to match, and, as Jonathan Hipkiss [Jeremy Clutterbuck] had said, a Sciaparelli tie, upon which was printed a pattern of French newspaper-headings.

Rayner Heppenstall was not discharged from the Army but a posting to the Pay Corps in Reading put him in easy reach of London. Others found their literary talents shifted them to London jobs with the Army Education Corps or Intelligence. These mixed with Conscientious Objectors, the militarily unemployable, prostitutes, con men, gangsters, and students not yet called up (known collectively as 'The Slithy Toves' because of their alleged resemblance to Tenniel's illustrations to *Alice*). The atmosphere was dense with tobacco smoke and alcohol, sometimes exploding into fights, and always noisy with argument. The artist Nina Hamnett might appear rattling her money box – '*My dear*, could you advance me a quid? There's the most beautiful GI passed out stone cold and naked as a duck in my kitchen.'

The pubs were the energetic centre of Bohemia, and most literary figures showed their faces there at one time or another, but there was also a grander level of existence for those who had already made their names. As editors, John Lehmann and Cyril Connolly entertained at lunches and evening parties; the *bon vivant* Connolly in particular

seemed able to obtain rare luxuries. T.S. Eliot gave occasional din-
ners, and from 1942 on the Sitwells, Edith and Osbert, held periodic
literary gatherings, while Edith entertained more informally at the
Sesame Club. On Sundays Viva King held what she called a 'War
Salon' at her house in Thurloe Square, beginning with tea and
moving on to cocktails, where one might encounter Augustus John,
Brian Howard, and Ivy Compton-Burnett with Margaret Jourdain.

On her return from America in 1941 Emerald, Lady Cunard
(mother of the poetess Nancy Cunard) entertained Cabinet Ministers,
generals, and establishment writers at her suite at the Dorchester.
John Lehmann has given an account of these right-wing gatherings in
his autobiography. The prejudices of the guests were 'almost at times
a caricature of the conventional aristocratic class-consciousness,
though sustained with a wit and a vigour of mind that were delightful
to anyone with an ear for dialogue'. A wider selection of guests could
be found at one of Sybil Colefax's 'Ordinaries'. Sybil Colefax loved
the salon life for itself but had relatively little money (she ran an
interior decorating business), and financed her parties by billing her
guests discreetly a few days after the event. Such was an 'Ordinary',
as opposed to a special occasion, but they do not seem to have always
been popular events. Cecil Beaton attended an 'Ordinary' at the
Dorchester in August 1940 when an air-raid prevented the guests
from leaving. 'As the raid was above us and we could not move, the
evening was a success for the hostess.' Harold Nicolson was at a
similar gathering of about thirty people in December 1943. 'Everybody loathes them, and one feels a sort of community of dislike
binding together what would otherwise be a most uncongenial company. Sybil knows in a way that people hate these ghastly functions.'
But there must have been some attraction for the participants,
otherwise they would not have continued to go to them throughout
the war.

Elsewhere in London strange *ménages* flourished privately; one
such was that of the spy Guy Burgess, since described by Goronwy
Rees. Released from the inhibitions of peacetime, men and women
felt the urgency of living for the day, and the pleasures of the day,
when time to enjoy them was so short. Goronwy Rees observed an
'almost tropical flowering of sexuality' in the comings and goings at
Burgess's flat. 'Watching, as if in a theatre, the extraordinary spectacle of life as lived by Guy, I felt rather liked a tired businessman
who had taken an evening off to visit a strip-tease club.'

If one wanted sexual adventure of any sort, it almost certainly began in a pub. In spite of the Black Market, bottles of spirits or wine became harder and harder to buy, there were fewer and fewer parties, and so social life increasingly revolved around the pubs. For those who had learnt their politics in the Thirties they had proletarian and democratic connotations – and the advantage of being fairly cheap. The price of beer (supplies of which could easily run out during the evening's drinking) rose from 6d to over a shilling a pint by 1944. Guinness became the rarest of bottled beers. The official price of whisky, if you could get hold of it, was 25/9d a bottle, or 1/6d a nip. William Sansom recalled that the only wine they could afford was a rough red wine from North Africa, which had to be warmed up with sugar to reduce the acidity, and then allowed to cool. The process, he emphasized, did *not* reduce the alcoholic effect. By 1943 a bottle of claret might cost £3 at a restaurant. Restaurant prices were officially limited to 5/- a meal, but there were ways round the restriction. Charles Graves noted, when a luxury tax on the top restaurants was brought in in 1942: 'The Dorchester charges 12/6d for supper. From June 15th onwards they charge 5/- for supper, 7/6 cover charge, and an extra half crown for dancing.'

Fitzrovia – Soho – call it what you will, had an atmosphere which is difficult to recapture now as one moves from pub to pub, though the names have not changed, and even one or two survivors are still to be encountered there. Atmosphere is a mixture of time and place, and all the circumstances have changed. But for a few years London had a Bohemia as once had Paris and Berlin. The poet John Heath-Stubbs recalled the unspoken rules of the society:

You had to be quite tough – you had to pay your score – drink quite heavily – you had not to resent it if someone borrowed some money and failed to repay you, and you had to accept a harsh rebuff if one transgressed the unwritten code.... One salutary lesson one learnt from life in those pubs was that it was absolutely no good being at enmity with people.

For servicemen on leave the pubs were an exotic outlet for enthusiasms stifled by the military machine. The poet Alan Ross, serving on the Arctic convoys to Russia, snatched what time he could there: 'There was this extraordinary sense of excitement . . . the *only* reality was Soho – the most real place of all.' To civilians working in dull jobs, or even interesting ones at the BBC, the pubs represented an escape into a world that defied the increasing limitations of official wartime controls; the emphasis was on individuality and personality, on the outrageous as opposed to the routine.

The recipe for a Bohemia requires many things that have nothing to do with literature or art, and it is fair to ask how *literary* this London life really was. But then, how often do artists and writers meeting socially actually discuss their work in any formal sense? The conversations of Sainte-Beuve, Flaubert, Gautier, Turgenev and Georges Sand round the dinner table at Magny's Restaurant in Paris in the 1860s, as recorded in the *Goncourt Journals*, are entertaining, witty and bitchy, but not critical in the technical sense. In wartime London the conversation was most likely to be about films or detective stories, and, the perennial subject of authors, the criminal behaviour of editors and publishers. To discuss each other's work face to face could cause trouble. It is unlikely that much writing was done *in* pubs, but they provided the essential stimulus and support of encountering other writers. For those starting out on their careers here the contacts could be made, the commissions received and, if one wanted it, guidance sought. John Heath-Stubbs acknowledges learning from George Barker, Dan Davin from Maclaren-Ross, and many others absorbed unconscious lessons about the business, if not the art, of writing.

The atmosphere of pubs was extraordinary and stimulating, the product of peculiar circumstances – and those circumstances also had their drawbacks. Louis MacNeice's poem 'Alcohol' reveals the nihilism lurking in this 'factitious popular front in booze':

> On golden seas of drink, so the Greek poet said,
> Rich and poor are alike. Looking around in war
> We watch the many who have returned to the dead
> Ordering time-and-again the same-as-before:

It concludes:

> Take away your slogans; give us something to swallow,
> Give us beer or brandy or schnapps or gin;
> This is the only road for the self-betrayed to follow –
> The last way out that leads not out but in.

Again, William Sansom has summed up the conflicting stresses of living through the middle passage:

There is felt always the impotence of not attacking, but being attacked. With this also the strange and sometimes absurd sensation of continuing in

65

many cases without a uniform or any visible reassurance of duty, the phantom of a peacetime job in the grey-painted skeleton of a peacetime environment. There are compensations. In war certain responsibilities are shrugged off or postponed. Others are assumed, but of a different, a more vivid, a shorter-lived nature. There are sensations of new virility, of paradoxical freedom, and of a rather bawdy 'live-for-today' philosophy.

Fitzrovia took its toll after the war, but to judge from Louis MacNeice's poem the debts began to pile up from the start. Many who found themselves together during those years were lonely and rootless people, many died early through drink, or killed themselves in despair. Worse, many failed to live up to their promise. The poet Paul Potts has tried to make a virtue out of failure in his auto-biography *Dante Called You Beatrice*: 'It wasn't until during the war while I was in the 12th Commando [as a batman before being inva-lided out] that I realized that I was going to fail in life, fail to be a real poet and fail to win the woman I loved.'

The violence of the pubs was partly a reflection of the violent times being lived through, but there is something self-destructive about Dylan Thomas's habit of picking fights with soldiers, or the aggres-sion of the painters Colquhoun and MacBryde. Dan Davin's first encounter with the loud affected voice and rude manner of Julian Maclaren-Ross nearly ended in a fight. 'I began to consider how, when the flashpoint came, I must upset the table against his thighs and get my blow in before he recovered his balance.'

Maclaren-Ross, whose *Memoirs of the Forties* first suggested this book, is finally a tragic figure. In Heppenstall's *The Lesser Infortune* the narrator (Heppenstall) steals a look at 'Scott-Chrichton's' note-books. 'Work was planned for ten years ahead. Here and there were lists of books to be written and published over that period, publisher and price included. *You've Had It* by D. Scott-Chrichton. Gollancz (1947), 8s 3d. *The Salesman and the Dairymaid*. By Dorian Scott-Chrichton. Faber and Faber (1954), 10s 6d. I gazed at these mani-festations of sinful pride and marvelled at the purity of the man's ambition and resolve.' Things did not turn out like that. His post-war output was small. In the early Sixties, alcoholic and in debt, the only way he could be persuaded by his publisher to write the memoirs which have done so much to fix the myth of this period was to be paid chapter by chapter. On the final occasion when they met he arrived drunk and late, having misdirected the taxi-driver. Broke or not, he always travelled by taxi. The chapter was delivered, the money handed over, and he disappeared for the last time. He died of a heart attack two days later. It was the autumn of 1964 and the *Memoirs* remain uncompleted.

The moods of anxiety and depression, the overcharged gaiety, the occasional violence, 'Sohoitis', these are the outward signs of a conflict in the minds of writers. The conflict was a debate as to what they should be doing, what their role really was. The self-questioning had gone on throughout the Thirties (and the debate remains unsolved), but the war made the problem especially perplexing. The ivory tower was an impossible location in wartime, the facilities for peaceful contemplation did not exist, for the conflict penetrated ivory walls. But it seemed at times that there was nowhere else for the writer to go. In one of the earliest contributions to the debate, Julian Symons's 'Notes on the Poet and the War' in *Now* No. 2, July 1940, the inhabitants of Bloomsbury and Soho are fully excused from responsibility, but on Marxist grounds, that they are incapable of shouldering it:

> It must be obvious, it must surely be obvious by now, that no organized action can be expected from the artist, that petty bourgeois spectre who spends his evenings gliding between the Fitzroy and the Wheatsheaf, and his weekends in country houses. It is obvious, I hope, that poets today are erratic individualists with a *taste* for Catholicism, Communism, or conscientious objection: that to consider the poet as a social unit is irrelevant and that to condemn him is a waste of time.

Writers in the services had little choice in the matter; they might fight the military system, or they might accept the experiences warfare had to offer, but either way their primary responsibilities were military. In London, at the centre of the literary industry, the situation was different. There might be very good reasons for not being in the services – age, work of a different kind of importance – but there was a high proportion of people who had been filtered out of the military machine, or whose pacifism had kept them out of it, and their non-combatance set them apart from ordinary people.

In London, if other work permitted, one might be in a position to write, but was writing a suitable activity at a time of national crisis? A pseudonymous article in *Horizon* in March 1942 by 'Neuro' described 'guilt, boredom and pathological anxiety about the future' as the competing factors for the prime neurosis of the age, War Guilt. And that was felt most acutely by intellectuals. Guilt had diminished during the Blitz (when London was in the front line), but was on the increase again. The intellectual felt driven into National Service or the Army, but in doing so denied himself his own fulfilment. 'Neuro' recommended that his real work was to continue to be his intellectual self. 'The duty of a man with brains is substantially unaffected by war. It is now as always to try to find an outlet for his powers either in the interests of humanity or if he be a professional artist in the direction of creative achievement.'

The trouble is that this is easier said than done. The interests of humanity in wartime are the immediately physical needs to be answered (like winning the war), rather than lofty speculation or personal creative satisfaction. It is true that not all writers felt a conflict between their work and the war effort, notably J.B. Priestley. When asked if he thought that literature 'had risen to the occasion', he replied, 'I don't think it could', pointing out that most people had other work to do. He did not resent the time he spent on propaganda. 'It was necessary war work.' Priestley's chairmanship of the reforming 1941 Committee and his speeches in the campaign to open a Second Front in Europe show him working directly at a political level, trying to prepare the way for a new Britain after the war, and urging greater military efforts in support of Russia. 'I supported Russia because the Red Army was winning the war and we were not.' Priestley was also able to express his faith in future social justice in plays like *They Came to a City* (1943), and the novel *Daylight on Saturday* (1943) set entirely in an aircraft factory shows that Priestley understood the feelings of ordinary people and felt no distance from them or the conditions of their work.

Priestley, however, is an exception. Constantine Fitzgibbon, in the American Army but working in London, observed that his literary friends, particularly Dylan Thomas, constituted an 'inner emigration':

a curious paradox had arisen. These men, whose political views so far as they had any had led them to identify themselves with the masses emotionally and alienate them from their own class, now found that those same views had alienated them from the overwhelming majority of their compatriots. It is probably true that in most cases their pre-war identification had been largely subjective and illusory, but their wartime alienation was real. And in many cases this was the root cause of much unhappiness and failure.

Unable to find a proper role in wartime society, writers turned in on themselves, but by doing so only emphasized the isolation in which society had placed them.

Resentment of the war was particularly strong among the younger writers who had grown up in the Thirties, and now found themselves paying for the mistakes of politicians since 1918. In a letter to *Horizon* in May 1942, 'On Interpreting the War', Alex Comfort, a pacifist poet and novelist studying medicine in London, defended the younger generation of writers who had been attacked by Spender, among others, for their 'defeatism':

There has been a very marked change of attitude among the 'new' writers since 1937 or so, with which Spender is not in sympathy, and possibly not even in touch – there is an attitude of passivity, which does not see the war as a struggle in the way that Spain was a struggle . . . the writers of the last few years, rightly or wrongly, see this war as a degenerative, not a conflict process.

Pacifists were bound to feel this most strongly, but Comfort goes on to make an important point, not only about the relation of the artist to society, but about the relation of any individual:

They [young writers] have lost the psychological ability to identify themselves with the professed aims of their fellow-men because they realize consciously what those fellow-men realize unconsciously, that we are no longer an integrated body held together by a purpose. We have reached individually that condition of ego-sufficiency which psychiatrists recognize as a cause of clinical neurosis. The state has somehow become, for the majority of Englishmen, 'They', and no longer 'We'.

The only purge for this neurosis, Comfort concludes, would be military defeat. He does not say that as a consequence the problem of literature of any kind would be purely academic.

In left-wing theory the alienated writer could solve the problem of his isolation by reintegrating himself with the working-class. But only Communists – now re-legitimized by the alliance with Russia – still thought in these terms. Most writers had lost faith in political action. The problem was expressed in John Spink's article 'The Strategic Retreat of the Left' in *Horizon* for January 1943. Spink notes the 'backward shift which has taken place recently in discussions on political and moral topics. . . . Translated into strategic terms, the shift appears as a retreat of the Left on a wide front to positions on which the Fascist onslaught, which imposed it, can best be resisted.

It has implied the temporary abandonment of the Marxist, and a return to the humanitarian idealist, criticism of society.'

Spink talks in terms of a retreat, George Orwell in terms of a defeat. In his first 'London Letter' to the *Partisan Review* in January 1941 he revealed that he had recently been in severe trouble 'for saying in print that those who were the most "anti-Fascist" during the period 1935–9 were most defeatist now'. To continue the military metaphor, Orwell sees the intelligentsia as not only in retreat but swept aside and disarmed:

During the Spanish Civil War the left-wing intellectuals felt that this was 'their' war and that they were influencing events in it to some extent. In so far as they expected the war against Germany to happen they imagined that it would be a sort of enlarged version of the war in Spain, a left-wing war in which poets and novelists would be important figures. Of course, it is nothing of the kind. It is an all-in modern war fought mainly by technical experts (airmen etc.) and people who are patriotic according to their lights, but entirely reactionary in outlook. At present there is no function in it for intellectuals.

No function, that is, for people such as Orwell himself. His own position, expressed in his essay 'My Country Right or Left' (1940) and *The Lion and the Unicorn* (1941) was that of a patriot who wanted to turn English nationalist energies towards social revolution. At the beginning of the war, in that intense moment of national regeneration and determination after Dunkirk, Orwell believed that anything was possible: 'Within two years, maybe a year, if only we can hang on, we shall see changes that will surprise the idiots who have no foresight. I dare say the London gutters will have to run with blood. All right, let them, if it is necessary.'

The debate about the true function of the writer in wartime seems most agonizing in the writings of Stephen Spender. Spender was a left-wing intellectual for whom Spain had been a struggle, and for whom Spain had been a defeat. The political crisis of 1938 and 1939 had coincided with the breakdown of his first marriage, and as a poet whose drive came far more from his emotions than did that of the intellectual Auden or MacNeice, Spender suffered the conflict of roles very much in his own person. It was natural that he should turn to the problem of 'Creative Imagination in the World Today'. (The essay appears in the same Autumn 1940 volume of *Folios of New Writing* as Orwell's 'My Country Right or Left' that has just been quoted.) Spender's essay shows the strategic withdrawal of the Left in progress. There is no rejection of political issues as such, but now politics must be the business of politicians, and the business of poets, poetry. The poet has a cultural, as opposed to a doctrinally political duty, to guard the language and the values it expresses against its abuse by propaganda of any sort. This is arguably still a commitment, but of a different kind, and one which drives the poet back on himself, since only within his own imaginative work can he safeguard the values he believes in.

The debate continues at length in Spender's contribution to the Searchlight Book series, *Life and the Poet* (1942). It is not a satisfying book, for the goal which Spender is seeking somehow eludes him. Its firmest note is Spender's farewell to the political commitment of the Thirties:

We were in a false position. Hypnotized by the sense of the necessity of saving civilization from fascism, we were entangled in a net of theoretical ways and means which evaded our grasp. This is the most charitable and, I think, the truest explanation of what happened to the 'Pink Decade' of the 'thirties. These writers, artists, scientists, supported the politics which seemed to offer the one chance of saving their disinterested and civilizing activities. But the intellectual, having given politics his support, became an Orestes pursued by Furies of Ends and Means, Propaganda and Necessity.

Spender specifically denies that he is recanting, but he regrets that in the Thirties intellectuals had been making statements '*when we should have been asking questions*'. He offers an 'organic' instead of a political view of life: 'Society is not a machine of mutually destructive means, but an organic growth around a central philosophy of life and a wide understanding of the needs of satisfactory living. What decides the nature of political institutions is ultimately values deriving from religion, philosophy, scientific methods and art.' This is a clear break with Marxism, but it is difficult to say what Spender puts in its place. He does not say what these cultural values are, nor how the values from which political institutions derive are expected to relate to political institutions as they exist, day to day.

John Lehmann, whose comment on the need for poets to withdraw in self-defence is quoted in Chapter One (p. 7), follows Spender in seeing the role of the writer as more humanitarian than political:

writers [of the pre-war Left] have felt that one of their most urgent tasks has been to keep alive an understanding of the human aspect of the war, beside the tirades and the cold-blooded statistics which may be necessary but which are certainly destructive if they are ever allowed to become too strong. To see the sufferings as they are, to register the full impact of tragedy in the individual's fate: that is the power that must be exercised in full.

The political commitments of the Thirties are replaced during the course of the war by a call for a return to 'personal values'. Writing is, of course, by individuals about individual experiences, the 'impact of tragedy in the individual's fate', as Lehmann puts it; the problem is how these values can be defined. The danger is that the shift of emphasis becomes not a return, but a retreat. As the war dragged on the prevailing mood became one of introversion and despair, the great changes anticipated failed to materialize.

It was left to Cyril Connolly to take a maverick view of the Artist-in-Wartime discussion. He was possibly thinking of Spender's *Life and the Poet* when he wrote in May 1942, 'it is time to realize that every essay, every broadcast, every conversation about the artist and this or that is so much wasted time, and springs out of a sense of guilt and sterility. Are plumbers the unacknowledged legislators of mankind?' In Connolly's view the Art-War antithesis was a fallacy, the artist became caught up with defending art, not making it, or retreated into art-administration, which produces nothing. He had a radical solution to the problem. 'I would therefore declare a moratorium on Art till the war is over. All writers who feel that they are in the war and responsible for winning it should be excused literary activity, and even forbidden it. This alone would remove their guilt, and put an end to the paper-covered books in which they express it.'

The problem was compounded by the reaction against the left-wing intelligentsia noticed by Tom Harrisson. The *Times Literary Supplement* expressed a particular hatred for 'the metropolitan intellectual'. An editorial in April 1940, when Russia was Germany's, not Britain's ally, sought to explain the attraction of Communism for English intellectuals. 'It was rather the impulse to emphasize their distinction from the common herd, or else the longing to escape from their own annihilating isolation and merge themselves in the herd, that painted Bloomsbury red.' This does not make sense, since one reason contradicts the other, but either explanation emphasizes the intellectual's lack of a proper role. The anti-intellectual mood continued in a *Times* fourth leader in March 1941, titled 'Eclipse of the

Highbrow'. The fourth leader is traditionally the place for *The Times* to express the nearest thing it knows to a satirical view, but the intellectuals were sufficiently stung to take the matter very seriously indeed. Stephen Spender told *The Times* it sounded like the Nazis' *Völkischer Beobachter*.

Taking its tone from the recently published *Note-Book in Wartime* of the historian Lord Elton, which contained a number of anti-intellectual comments, 'Eclipse of the Highbrow' is not a very well made argument; its main line of attack is a philistine criticism of the unintelligibility of modern art, mentioning only one artist by name, the recently dead Paul Klee. In the Twenties and Thirties the arts 'were brought down to the level of parlour games', but the days of such trivialities and perversities are now over, for soldiers and civilians are united in war. *The Times* concludes: 'What changes of taste this war, and the reactions following it, may produce, no one can foresee. But at least it can hardly give rise to arts unintelligible outside a Bloomsbury drawing-room, and completely at variance with those stoic virtues which the whole nation is now called upon to practise.'

The Times attack is more interesting as a symptom than for its argument, but there were those on the Left who also felt that the intellectuals were failing in their duty. Orwell told the *Partisan Review* that he had done himself a great deal of harm –

by attacking the successive literary cliques which have infested this country, not because they were intellectuals but precisely because they were *not* what I mean by true intellectuals. . . . My case against all of them is that they write mentally dishonest propaganda and degrade literary criticism to mutual arse-licking. . . . It is just because I do take the function of the intelligentsia seriously that I don't like the sneers, libels, parrot phrases and financially profitable back-scratching which flourish in our English literary world.

As Jenni Calder has pointed out in her study of Orwell, much of his feeling of isolation came from the fact that he, as a true intellectual, had no recognized role. Isolation served to increase his personal bitterness and moral contempt, while attacks on his contemporaries only deepened the divide.

The intellectual's loss of role is the theme of Arthur Koestler's essay 'The Intelligentsia' in *Horizon* for March 1944. As a Hungarian exile Koestler saw the problem from the point of view of the less alienated European intellectual. Tracing the word 'intelligentsia' back to the late nineteenth-century Russian revolutionaries who had caused it to be coined, Koestler argued that the problem was that by the 1930s the working-class had developed its own leadership, and its own bureaucracy – 'men with iron wills and wooden heads', so that the middle-class intellectuals who had once fueled the revolution were excluded.

They were not wanted, had to remain fellow-travellers, the fifth wheel to the cart. The intelligentsia of the Pink Decade was irresponsible, because it was deprived of the privilege of responsibility. Left in the cold, suspended in a vacuum, they became decadents of the revolution just as their predecessors had become decadents of the bourgeoisie.

Koestler still had faith in the intelligentsia, and believed in its value as a critic of society – provided that society would listen. 'To sneer at the intelligentsia and, while depriving it of the responsibility of action, shove on to it the responsibility of failure, is either thoughtless stupidity or a manoeuvre with obvious motives. Nazism knew what it was doing when it exterminated the intelligentsia of the European Continent.'

Others, too, believed in the value of what they were doing. Rex Warner's 'On Subsidizing Literature' in *Folios of New Writing* for Autumn 1941 argues that Churchill's 'Survival' was not the whole answer to the question of what was being fought for, and that the fast-disappearing professional writer had a part to play in defining the shape of the post-war world. At the same moment *Horizon* was asking 'Why Not War Writers?', a manifesto signed by Arthur Calder-Marshall, Cyril Connolly, Bonamy Dobrée, Tom Harrisson, Arthur Koestler, Alun Lewis, George Orwell and Stephen Spender arguing that writers should be given the same protection and facilities as journalists, and by implication, War Artists:

At the beginning of the war, it was assumed that the function of the creative writer was to write a good book about the war . . . after the war. Experience of two years of war has shown to writers that their function is to write a good book about the war *now*.

The authors admitted that there had been hiatus and confusion at the outbreak of war, but 'with the invasion of Russia, feeling has crystallized. It is no longer possible for anyone to stand back and call the war an imperialist war. For every writer, the war is a war for survival. Without victory our art is doomed.'

74

The facilities were not forthcoming, nor were the good books. The 'inner emigration' continued. In February 1943 Connolly called the manifesto '*Horizon*'s most lost of lost causes'.

These are the issues that underlay the casual and unstructured conversations in the Wheatsheaf or the Fitzroy, that were the cause of the noisy arguments, even possibly the fights. Yet for a brief moment artists and writers in London felt a sense of communal identity, if only negatively by withdrawing from the conflict around them. And however nihilistic the mood may have been, one can still feel regret for a period when writers and artists did at least meet and talk with a sense of identity and purpose, however insecure the identity and uncertain the purpose. Alan Ross has supplied Fitzrovia with its epitaph:

It was a time of search and of little money, when the price of a drink and a humanly welcoming bed was the most anyone could wish for. It seems to me now to have been enormously exciting and savagely happy, to have possessed a gaiety that seems never to have been repeated. Was any of it really as one imagined it, a sustaining hunting ground which writers and painters as young as one was then are today recreating in their own image? If they are, neither I nor anyone I know have any idea where it is.

CHAPTER FOUR

New Writing

'*Books are, in fact,
weapons of war.*'

Lord Elton

One of the bitterest paradoxes for writers during the war was that at a time when there was an unprecedented increase in the demand for books, there was a severe reduction in the means to supply them. There is no doubt that there was an enormous boom in reading during the war, a phenomenon well established by the end of 1941. Yet the figures for the production of new editions (new titles and reprints) show a marked decline: in 1937 17,137 books were published, in 1939 14,094, and by 1945 the figure had slowly shrunk to 6,747. Between 1939 and 1945 expenditure on books rose from £9 million to £23 million. Such an increase cannot be explained by the fact that the price of individual volumes rose slightly between those years. The truth is that new books were snapped up as soon as they appeared, so that they could go out of print in a matter of days, while at the same time publishers' stocks of pre-war books were being run down. These statistics relate only to the production and *sale* of books; there was an overall increase in reading simply as an activity. Librarians reported a much greater demand, but it is impossible to calculate how often a book might be read, or by how many people. There are other smaller signs of the times: in April 1941 an Oxford Street second-hand bookstall was offering to buy old books at half the published prices. In the same month a bookseller went to prison for a year for buying books pilfered by a publisher's employees.

It was particularly galling, then, that publishers' supplies of paper should have been measured on the baseline of their consumption between August 1938 and August 1939, when in comparison with the peak year of 1937 few people seemed to be buying, writing, or publishing books. A publisher's quota of paper was issued under a licence from the Ministry of Supply in four-month blocks. At first the ration was 60% of pre-war consumption, but by December 1941 this had been reduced to $37\frac{1}{2}$%. In October of that year the Publishers' Association had generated sufficient concern about paper supplies for there to be a debate in the House of Lords. The arguments for an increase in the supply of paper to publishers were rehearsed: there was a huge demand for books, particularly technical books, and a huge shortage, twenty million volumes had been lost through air attack. Books were a valuable export; about 30% of production went abroad. Lord Elton and the Archbishop of Canterbury weighed in with the moral value of books, and Lord Snell, replying for the Government, admitted that 'books are the daily bread of the spirit, and my own indebtedness to them is beyond all computation'. But there was to be no increase in the paper ration. The arguments for an increase, and the government's reluctance to grant it, remained constant throughout the war.

Publishers felt that the government was being particularly unreasonable because all they used was *1·5*% of the total consumption of paper. An increase of 1% would have solved all their problems. Some statistics of 1944 are interesting. Newspapers used 250,000 tons of paper, Her Majesty's Stationery Office 100,000, periodicals 50,000 and books 22,000 tons. The War Office alone used up 25,000 tons of paper, more than the entire production of books. (Besides the needs of bureaucracy, paper and cardboard were of course essential for munitions.) Publishers faced other difficulties as well. The trade lost skilled men to the armed forces, and there were severe bottle-necks in the actual binding of books, where twenty of the seventy pre-war firms had gone out of business, and the rest were working with only half their staff. The government would not sanction the import of new machinery for binding or paper-making. In terms of machinery, writers also suffered – new typewriters became extremely scarce, could only be bought with a special permit, and were a favourite target for thieves.

Naturally the Ministry of Information was concerned about the situation, but could do little to persuade the Ministry of Supply. However, in mid-1941 it began to help the publication of books of which it approved by contributing paper from its own allocation. Nearly all the foreign-language magazines published in London, for instance *La France Libre*, existed thanks to paper from the Ministry of Information. The Ministry also kept a discreet eye on the content of books. George Orwell traced his difficulty in finding a publisher for his anti-Stalinist allegory *Animal Farm* to the Ministry. (At least three publishers turned him down before Secker and Warburg accepted it in 1944.) 'Publishers take manuscripts to the MOI and the MOI "suggests" that this or that is undesirable, or premature, or "would serve no good purpose". And though there is no definite prohibition, no clear statement that this or that must not be printed, official policy is never flouted.' The most overt case of censorship by the Ministry was the temporary withdrawal of its subsidy to magazine wholesalers exporting *Picture Post* to the Middle East when the magazine became critical of the Desert Army's weaponry.

In March 1942 the Paper Control of the Ministry of Supply did make one concession to the publishers by releasing an extra 250 tons of paper for books 'of national importance', the supply to be allocated by a committee of four publishers. As is so often the case, the publishers could not agree among themselves. They objected to having to disclose business information, and distrusted the impartiality of the proposed allocators, but the scheme finally fell down on the difficulty of deciding what constituted a book of national importance. An internal memorandum of the Ministry of Information revealed a similar difficulty when it considered using discrimination in the paper ration to steer publication and the press. The memo asked in what categories of suitability would fall *Mickey Mouse Weekly*, *The Rainbow*, *Miniature Camera Magazine* and *Thomson's Weekly News*.

The publishers did manage some co-operation. When the stocks and records of the book distributors Simpkin Marshall were almost completely destroyed in the fire raid of 29 December 1940 the Publishers' Association took the firm over and ran it as a co-operative venture. More important was the Book Production War Economy Agreement of January 1942, a voluntary undertaking to restrict standards of production. There was a powerful incentive to join the scheme in that those who did not were given an even smaller ration of paper – only 25%. It was calculated that those who did join managed to get about 60% of their pre-war production of books out of $37\frac{1}{2}$% of their pre-war paper consumption. A further co-operative venture, Guild Books, by which publishers would produce cheap editions of individual books and market them through a joint organization, was less successful, mainly because of the lack of a special paper ration.

The quality of paper itself severely declined. In Orwell's words, 'Writing paper gets more and more like toilet paper while toilet paper resembles sheet tin'. Paper for books was made from home-produced straw, and by 1943 had become rough, yellow and thin from being pulped and repulped so often. The Ministry of Supply therefore launched a salvage drive to collect pre-war books whose pulp would improve the quality. Fifty-six million volumes were collected, of which five million were sent to the Forces, a million to replace damaged library stocks, and the rest to pulp. There was a drawback to this, for book experts complained that when they discovered valuable volumes in the salvage they were not allowed to rescue them. To cope with this problem the Inter-Allied Book Centre was opened in October 1944 to help replenish libraries in England and Europe.

Although the publishers had successfully fought off the threat of Purchase Tax, they could not avoid the Excess Profits Tax introduced to prevent war profiteering. The demand for books meant that publishers were selling much of their pre-war stocks, but were completely unable to replace them. Since the 'backlist' represents part of a publisher's capital, he was being forced to sell this off and pay a heavy tax on it. It is interesting that in 1942 and 1943 publishers began to offer large prizes for new manuscripts, presumably to use up money that would otherwise have gone in Excess Profits Tax.

Faced with these difficulties, it is not surprising that publishers were forced to allow a large number of books to go out of print. By 1942 580 out of the 970 titles in the 'Everyman' series were unobtainable, and a total of 37,000 books available in 1939 were out of print. Specialist publishers who had produced no major editions in 1938 or '39 found that they had virtually no paper ration now that their works – particularly medical books – were desperately needed. One of the few levers an author has against a publisher is that if a book is allowed to go out of print the copyright of the book reverts to the author and he may take it elsewhere. Some literary agents used this to press for reprints, but the publishers had a 'gentlemen's agreement' not to poach in this way.

In desperation authors who could not get published or reprinted turned to the 'mushroom' firms that sprang up. While it was illegal after 25 May 1940 to start a new magazine, it was perfectly legal to start a new publishing firm. All that was needed was a stock of paper, usually pre-war material found in some provincial printer's warehouse. Some two hundred new publishing houses started up in 1940; in October 1943 Sir Stanley Unwin protested in *The Times* that while established publishers were being hampered, 'new firms are starting every week'. The mushroom firms do not seem to have made much contribution to literature, however, preferring mildly pornographic novels or trashy children's books.

The physical restrictions on publication had their effects on the contents. Books became shorter. In the Thirties pressure from the lending libraries meant that a novel *had* to be at least 70,000 words, but now publishers were prepared to consider shorter works, if only because they used less paper. Rupert Hart-Davis, then an editor at Jonathan Cape, wrote a witty review in *The Spectator* in March 1940 suggesting that a combined Censor and Rationing Officer should see to it that all detective stories were restricted to 40,000 words. The biggest change was the sudden popularity of collections of short stories by one author, or, better still, anthologies. Before the war these had not been popular with publishers or public, but that quickly changed. This was not just the result of circumstances of production, for writing and reading habits also changed during the war.

A particular reason for the increase in anthologies was that many of them were camouflaged magazines. It was illegal to start a new magazine, but an anthology of verse and prose was quite legitimate. This was brought home sharply to Miron Grindea, who, oblivious of the regulations, launched *Adam* in September 1941, a magazine he had originally run in Budapest. He was told by an official at the Ministry of Information that *Adam* as a magazine was forbidden, but that it was permissible to bring it out under a different name each time – *Eve*, *Cain*, *Moses*, *Jeremiah*, etc. Grindea refused, although a second *Adam* celebrating H.G. Wells's birthday did come out without a volume number. In 1944 the new radical-liberal political party Common Wealth could not start its own magazine, so bought an old one, *Town and Country Planning*, and ran that as a party publication until it won its argument for an allocation to start *Common Wealth*.

Because of the confusion between magazine and anthology, their irregular production and the rarity of some issues, it is impossible to say exactly how many little magazines there were. Even Denys Val

Baker, who specialized in the subject with *Little Reviews* (1943) and *Little Reviews Anthology*, did not know: 'for every review registered at the British Museum there must be two or three semi-private ones that never reach the bookstalls.' The Cambridge *Bibliography* lists just over a hundred new titles between 1939 and '45. The magazines varied in size and circulation between *Poetry Folios*, printed on a hand press by Peter Wells in his spare time as a farm labourer, to *Penguin New Writing*, which used five tons of paper for each number, enough for roughly 75,000 copies. Five tons was the entire allocation of the Hogarth Press for 1941.

Even *Penguin New Writing* had its difficulties. John Lehmann gave this account of his editorial duties in Number 8, July 1941:

First of all, the authors have to write their contributions; they promise them by a certain day, but in the meantime Fanfarlo's typewriter may have been put out of action by Mrs Greenbaum's landmine, and Robert Pagan's beautiful hand-written manuscript may have met with Nazi fires on its way through the post, and arrive charred and soggy a week late. Next, the contributions have to be set up in type and proofs corrected, enemy action may cause more delays here, and an Editor may have to turn out with the Home Guard and be late with his own blue-pencillings. And when all the proofs are at last returned to the printer, our watchful solicitor may decide that one author has shown too great a levity towards a distinguished public figure or worthy organ of government; cuts have to be made, but when the printer is hurriedly rung up the Exchange suavely replies: ten hours' delay. Suppose, however, that all is ready to time, the great machines ready to revolve: the boat with the paper from overseas may have been delayed, and while the machines are idle, the call-up may claim some of the printer's key workers. Even when the thousands of sheets are safely printed, folded, collated and neatly pressed into their bright new covers, there are still plenty of obstacles lurking: the vans may not get their petrol ration at once, the packers at the warehouse may have decided the week before they would rather fly a Spitfire or man a corvette; and when the parcels have finally been sped from the packing table to bookshops and bookstalls all over the country, a blitz on the way or sudden war priorities in transport may mean another few days of irritation and disgruntlement to a regular reader.

The range in size and influence of the literary magazines was very broad. *Penguin New Writing* and *Horizon* dominated, although the individual movements, Anarchist, Communist, Neo-Romantic, managed to sustain more than one magazine each. (Of course the surviving established periodicals like the *New Statesman* and the *Listener* continued their literary pages, as did the newspapers, within the severe limits on space imposed by paper rationing.) The anthology/magazine tended to be a very mixed bag – a reviewer in *Time and Tide* described the editor of a typical anthology as acting as though he was 'alternately running a co-educational school magazine and conducting a dance band'. More to the point for the professional writer, there was a real demand for his work. Julian Maclaren-Ross recalled: 'There were, in that peak year of 1942, excluding *Horizon* and *Penguin New Writing*, where I was also published, no less than sixteen markets for a short-story writer to choose from ... and stories of mine came out in all these periodicals and magazines including *Lilliput*.'

The revival of interest in books was of course not restricted to live authors, the circumstances of war were also favourable to the dead. The English author who probably benefited most from the war was Anthony Trollope, whose elaborate pictures of Victorian life offered an escape into a retrospectively secure past. Henry James enjoyed a similar vogue. On the other hand the popularity of D.H. Lawrence fell away almost completely. Everyone seems to have at least started to read *War and Peace*, and its popularity led to both radio and stage versions. (The stage production of 1943 lasted three and a half hours.) Russia's entry into the war on the side of the Allies in 1941 widened readers' interest to Pushkin, Blok and Gorki, and ensured that Tolstoy stayed a best-seller. V.S. Pritchett's weekly literary articles for the *New Statesman* helped to sustain the idea of a literary tradition, for the scarcity of good new books had led to an editorial decision to give two thousand words each week to a reconsideration of the classics.

In this general revival of reading, the biggest demand still appears to have been for *new* books. The book designer and poet Seán Jennett noted in January 1945, 'many books that do not date, and that would have been sold out within a few days if they had appeared now, remain on stock with the publisher only, it seems, because they were published before the war'. The reasons for the demand are not hard to find: there was a shortage of the luxuries and entertainments that compete with the price of a book; there was no television; and the radio, if anything, helped. The discussion programme 'The Brains Trust' could cause a book to go out of print simply by mentioning it. During the long Lull a great deal of time was spent, literally, waiting.

Waiting at ARP posts, at gun sites, while fire-watching. The Black-Out made going out in the evening difficult, and there was frequently nowhere to go anyway. Rail journeys were long and slow. A book occupied the time and offered an escape, not necessarily because of escapist subject matter but because a book was an alternative to the immediate and often boring circumstances of ordinary life. A book also, by the very fact that it constituted an organized view of the world, might supply a pattern or a sense of harmony missing from uncertain wartime existence.

From the point of view of the publisher the paradox was bitter indeed. On the one hand these were ideal conditions, as Stanley Unwin has recalled:

> The most expensive item in the running of a book-publishing business . . . is publishing fallibility. That item, for the time being, almost entirely disappeared. The paper rationing reduced the number of new books any publisher could issue, and there was the curious situation of publishers weighing in the balance the return any particular book would yield for the paper expended. There was no need for a publisher to take risks if he did not want to.

On the other hand the restrictions were such that there was no way a publisher could fully exploit the market. Pity then the author, whose manuscript was being weighed in the balance of the paper ration. Since we can only judge by the manuscripts that were set in type, not those that were rejected, it is difficult to tell how cautious publishers became in promoting new authors, but publishers' reluctance to risk paper is certainly another of the distorting wartime factors. The actual number of fiction titles published fell from 4,222 in 1939 to 1,246 in 1945, which, taking into account the total decline in book production, means a fall from about a third to a fifth of the total of all volumes published annually – but this says nothing about the contents or quality of the work that was accepted, or refused.

Whatever their eventual decisions, publishers had fewer manuscripts to consider, good or bad. (The exception was poetry, which blossomed partly as a result of the withering of other means of expression.) Any kind of sustained creative effort became increasingly difficult, not just for novelists, but for all types of serious writer. Scholars were cut off from Europe and found it difficult to get access to material at home. There was the added disincentive that scholarly work once done had little chance of being published until the war was over. Assuming, of course, that there was time to do any. Many scholars were drafted into the temporary Civil Service – or the Political Warfare Executive and the Secret Service, where linguists, political scientists, philosophers and mathematicians found themselves inventing cyphers, breaking codes, and carrying out the complex analyses of information gathered from monitoring reports and intelligence agents. All of it intellectually strenuous work that required full concentration and left no spare energy for scholarship or contemplation.

Arthur Koestler saw serious dangers for the future intellectual resilience of the country in the diversion of so many minds into war work. In March 1944 he wrote:

during the last two years the intelligentsia has to a large extent been absorbed as temporary civil servants in the Ministry of Information, as Public Relations Officers, in the BBC, etc. For the time being 'job' and 'private production' are still kept in separate compartments (with the result that the latter is becoming more and more atrophied); but it is imaginable that a situation may arise in which the two merge; when instead of regarding the former as a kind of patriotic hacking and the latter as the real thing, the energies become suddenly canalized into one stream. ... The danger of this happening is all the greater as conformity is often a betrayal which can be carried out with a perfectly clear conscience.

The situation might have been easier for writers if only the work they were called upon to do had some relevance to what they saw as their true skills. In 1943 Stephen Spender, then serving as a member of the National Fire Service, complained in the *Times Literary Supplement*:

The other day I was rung up by a representative of one of the Ministries and told that if I liked to write a propaganda piece, of a kind which has no value and for which I have no talent, I could be released from all other duties. ... Many poets employed in the services, or exalted to the precarious Paradiso of the Ministries, or the BBC, must feel as I do. Artists are commissioned to paint pictures; but writers are commissioned only to write films, scripts, pamphlets, anything, so long as it is certain that it will not be of the slightest value or interest in five years' time.

Poets were not alone in feeling that their talents were being trivialized. In 1944 the composer William Walton calculated that between 1940 and the music commissioned for the film of *Henry V* his various 'incidental' contributions, to BBC plays, or films, added up to five and a half hours' performance, the length of eleven average symphonies. Would one now rather have the incidental music or the symphonies?

In November 1943 George Orwell took the step of resigning his post with the Indian section of the BBC after what he called privately 'two wasted years'. He immediately became literary editor of the left-wing weekly *Tribune*, but at least he gained a little spare time, and he began to work on what was to become *Animal Farm*. Reflecting on those who had not left the wartime bureaucracy he wrote in October 1944:

I could give a whole list of writers of promise or performance who are now being squeezed dry like oranges in some official job or other. It is true that in most cases it is voluntary. They want the war to be won, and they know that everyone must sacrifice something. But still the result is the same. They will come out of the war with nothing to show for their labours and with not even the stored-up experience that the soldier gets in return for his physical suffering.

Being in the services, however, imposed a new set of restrictions and difficulties. Service life destroys privacy and permanence, two requisites for sustained mental effort. The physical stress of training, (let alone fighting), the endless, repetitious duties of the private soldier or officer, leave little time to sit down, chew one's pen, and think. But the services also had a more insidious influence:

All the time, working inside the mass of an army, all references and relations are to the things also inside; nothing outside – countries, people, new qualities and new values – is noticeable except as the army comes to them, and you gradually stop looking at anything outside.

The experience of Tom Burns, a medical orderly captured in Greece in 1941, was not unique. William Chappell's 'Words from a Stranger', also in *Penguin New Writing* No. 19, for January 1943, is devoted to precisely this theme. 'I think that the majority of people in the Services have this feeling of unreality to a greater or lesser degree although they do not realize it as a definite malaise, and are, perhaps, only aware of a certain spiritual discomfort, that they cannot completely understand.'

Writing, of course, did not cease altogether in the Services, though it continued only with difficulty. The poet and short-story writer Alun Lewis, who was killed accidentally in Burma in 1944, described his life in India as a rhythm of 'periods of spiritual death, periods of neutrality, periods of a sickening normality and insane indifference to the real implications of the present, and then for a brief wonderful space, maybe every six weeks, a nervous and powerful ability moves upward in me'. These may be the typical emotions of a young poet under any circumstances, but one can be sure that they were heightened by the alternating tensions and frustrations of service life. At the other end of the scale, in terms of views, age and reputation, Evelyn Waugh had to use his connections with Brendan Bracken, Minister of Information, in order to extract three months leave in 1944 to write *Brideshead Revisited*, and even then this privilege was only granted because of Waugh's fundamental unsuitability as an Army officer. (The earlier comedy *Put Out More Flags* (1942) was written on a troopship travelling to and from the abortive attack on Dakar.)

One of the best descriptions of the writer's condition in the Services is a short story by John Sommerfield, 'Worm's Eye View', published in *Penguin New Writing* No. 17. Sommerfield had published a novel before the war, and fought in the International Brigade in Spain. A Communist, he joined the RAF and became a fitter, spending most of the war in India and Burma. 'Worm's Eye View' describes a would-be poet's feelings as he tries to revive an idea for a poem, first in a barrack hut in a bleak camp in Cumberland, and then in the heat of India. The story's theme is the isolation of the serviceman from civilian life, a division which falsifies all his images of home, and the isolation of individual men one from another. For John Sommerfield at least the barriers between man and man were broken down in the extreme conditions of a forward airfield in Burma, and his later stories, like 'The Survivors', 'Dog's Life', and 'The Night of the Fire' are written in the first person plural, not the first person singular. This shift from 'I' to 'We' was unconscious. Cut off from all other outlets the writer became once more someone appreciated as an entertainer – and as someone who gave shape to the life of the community.

But that life remained self-enclosed and isolated. The editors of both *New Writing* and *Horizon* noticed the gradual change in the material sent in by servicemen. Connolly saw a widening gulf between soldier and civilian writer that harmed both: 'At the beginning of the war our relations with the armed forces were very close, gradually they have drifted. For as their new careers take hold we have received fewer and fewer contributions from them which are up

1 Fitzrovia 1942: Osbert Lancaster's version for *Horizon*

2 Literature under fire: Holland House Library 1941

3 Cyril Connolly

4 John Lehmann

5 Stephen Spender

**Editors
Poets
Novelists**

6 Louis MacNeice

7 C. Day Lewis

8 Elizabeth Bowen

9 J. B. Priestley

10 Tambimuttu

11 William Sansom

The Younger Generation

12 John Heath-Stubbs

13 Alan Ross

14 Dylan Thomas

15 Sidney Keyes

16 Keith Douglas

17 Roy Fuller

Service Poets

18 Alun Lewis

19 Cityscape 1941: St Paul's Cathedral and fireman artist

to standard, while in consequence we have ourselves become some-thing of a backwater.' This was written in mid-1944; earlier in the same year John Lehmann had detected in the service writers the alienation from self and society that can be seen in the drinkers of Fitzrovia:

> One had been changed by the war – like the man who found he was an insect one morning in Kafka's horrible and prophetic story – into some-thing completely alien to one's old self ... in this new way of life the writers had become aware of gulfs around them they had not imagined existed, or could ignore, in their earlier life. This sense of division and loneliness, which the poem and the story can most powerfully reveal, and which are in themselves with extreme sharpness divided from the pep-reports and grin-records of so much reading matter supplied by the popular press, emerges more and more, as the war goes on, as one of the most acute symptoms of the sickness of our time.

Self-alienation reaches a symbolic extreme in R.D. Marshall's story 'A Wrist Watch and Some Ants', published in *Penguin New Writing* No. 21. A soldier cuts off his own arm after being wounded, and then lies looking at it abstractedly, a part of his own body no longer part of him. Marshall had, in fact, lost an arm in the fighting in the Western Desert.

Soldiers felt divided from civilians, civilians felt divided from soldiers. Guilt about not being in the Army is a theme in Nigel Balchin's novels *Darkness Falls from the Air* (1942) and *The Small Back Room* (1943). Balchin worked as a temporary civil servant, and both books describe the intrigue and pettiness of life in the Ministries. In *The Small Back Room* the protagonist is a crippled scientist whose work in dismantling a German booby-trap bomb gives him a kind of entry into warfare – but even then his crippled leg lets him down.

The fact that this was wartime was in itself isolating. There was an inhibiting awareness that this was a 'period' with a beginning and expected end, cut off from past and future alike. Pre-war experience is no longer valid material for the writer, it is difficult to conceive what post-war life will be like, and meanwhile the present is too close, and too unpleasant. For both soldier and civilian the violence of modern warfare seemed beyond the limits of communication. The fireman William Sansom noted in his journal: 'The experience is too violent for the arts to transcribe; there will never be an adequate reportage to convey to posterity a living idea of the truth of such experience. . . . The results of violence and its reflections may be written down – but never the core of the violent act itself. In the first place, language fails.' But even if one did not wish to confront the violence of the times directly, the times themselves were too immediate to be seen in perspective. Elizabeth Bowen, who published no novel during the war, described the problems of many writers besides herself in 1942:

There is at present evident, in the reflective writer, not so much inhibition or dulling of his own feeling as an inability to obtain the focus necessary for art. One cannot reflect, or reflect on, what is not wholly in view. These years rebuff the imagination as much by being fragmentary as by being violent. It is by dislocations, by recurrent checks to his desire for meaning, that the writer is most thrown out. The imagination cannot simply endure events; for it the passive role is impossible. Where it cannot dominate, it is put out of action.

Like Elizabeth Bowen, the critic Raymond Mortimer could only hope for a future imaginative integration of the emotions of wartime. 'We have come to take war and its claims for granted – it is peace and the pursuit of happiness that now appear abnormal. That young men should have to use the furthest resources of courage in tearing other young men to pieces, in setting fire to women and children, no longer appals or even disconcerts us. . . . Not until the tranquillity comes in which to recollect such emotions will they be material for the novelist.'

In the event, the chief note of the best of the later novels about the war has been what might be called the serious-absurd, the comic characters in Waugh's trilogy, *Sword of Honour*, the insane logic of Joseph Heller's *Catch-22*, the science fiction of Kurt Vonnegut's *Slaughterhouse Five*. Or, for that matter, the fantastical figure of little Oscar in Gunter Grass's *The Tin Drum*. It seems that black humour was the only possible response after the horrors of the concentration camps and the atom bomb had made even the ordinary violence of warfare insignificant.

The art of prose literature neither flourished nor died during the Second World War. Viewed in the wider perspective of historical development, continuity was not interrupted, only disturbed. The question here is what are the signs of disturbance?

The difficulty of writing a novel at all must be clear by now; as the next best thing many writers put what time they had into the short story. H.E. Bates's *The Modern Short Story*, published in 1941, lists a generation of writers, all born between 1900 and 1910, who continued to form 'the backbone' of the craft: 'V.S. Pritchett, L.A.G. Strong, Malachi Whitaker, H.A. Manhood, Leslie Halward, Arthur Calder-Marshall, Pauline Smith, James Hanley, Elizabeth Bowen, G.F. Green, Geraint Goodwin, Rhys Davies, T.O. Beachcroft, Dorothy Edwards.' By the end of the war Julian Maclaren-Ross, Fred Urquart, Glyn Jones, William Sansom, John Sommerfield, Alun Lewis and Dylan Thomas could be added to the list.

Besides these more familiar names, many people had one or two stories published during the war, but few of these are anything more than average accounts of a personal experience. (One or two which do transcend their immediate circumstances, or convey them particularly sharply, have already been quoted.) The pre-war *New Writing* had set the style for a form of documentary story that simply required the author to choose a situation, and describe it. For preference the situation was social rather than emotional, to do with work or class. The documentary film movement of the Thirties had had the same propaganda intention of showing the lives of ordinary people, in order both to give those lives some dignity – and argue for change. The war provided any amount of material for reportage (see *New Writing*'s regular feature 'Report on Today'), but in general propaganda gave way to more personal emotions. John Lehmann commented in *Penguin New Writing* No. 14 in September 1942, 'the centre of balance has shifted from a rather extrovert, documentary type of realism to something more introvert, with a great deal more reflection and feeling in it'. William Sansom's symbolist stories in the manner of Kafka, which he nonetheless mixed with straightforward accounts of fire-fighting, represent the extreme of the reaction.

With everyone living, as it were, inside a newsreel, and with propaganda now the State art, it was inevitable that the centre of balance should shift. The political problems of the Thirties had for the moment been shelved, instead the need was to understand what was happening to oneself as an individual, rather than as part of a movement or class. Documentary had also lost its novelty. In January 1944 Connolly complained about the quality of contributions submitted: '*Horizon* will always publish stories of pure realism, but we take the line that experiences connected with the blitz, the shopping queues, the home front, deserted wives, deceived husbands, broken homes, dull jobs, bad schools, group squabbles, are so much a picture of our ordinary lives that unless the workmanship is outstanding we are prejudiced against them.'

The limitations of the short story applied to the wartime novel as well, though here there were some achievements. Significantly, the best books written in wartime are not directly about the war. A few Army novels did create some interest: Gerald Kersh's account of training as a Guardsman, *They Die With Their Boots Clean* (1941), Arthur Gwynn-Browne's narrative of the first six months of 1940 in France, *F.S.P.* (1942), Eric Knight's story of a runaway soldier, *This Above All* (1941), and C.S. Forester's *The Ship* (1943) all got some attention. In general, however, John Hampson's comment in the *Spectator* in 1943 sums the war-novel up:

> About a third of the novels coming the way of the average reviewer in these times, deal with the war in one or more of its numerous aspects. Few of them stir the emotions deeply. . . . One reads them conscious of some lack somewhere; conscious, too, of the fact that one will never feel any genuine wish to re-read them in the future.

An exception is Julian Maclaren-Ross's collection of short stories *The Stuff to Give the Troops* (1944), which is still worth reading as a picture of the underside of Army life.

Instead of confronting the present, many writers turned to the related themes of autobiography and childhood. Henry Green published *Pack My Bag* in 1940, Herbert Read *Annals of Innocence and Experience*; in 1941 there were autobiographies from John Masefield, Eric Linklater and Philip Lindsay. Elizabeth Bowen published a family history *Bowen's Court* in 1942 and a reminiscence of childhood *Seven Winters* in 1943. Forest Reid, who published a literary memoir *Private Road* in 1940, completed his trilogy of childhood, *Uncle Stephen* and *The Retreat*, with *Young Tom* in 1944. Joyce Cary published two 'adult' pictures of youth *Charley is My Darling* in 1940 and *A House of Children* in 1941. Childhood may suggest the evocation of a happier age of innocence, but Stephen Spender's *The Backward Son* (1940), L.P. Hartley's *The Shrimp and the Anemone* (1944) and Denton Welch's *Maiden Voyage* and *In Youth is Pleasure* of 1943 and 1945 reveal a post-Freud world of conflicting wills and paradise lost – or never found.

There is a reason for this outpouring of memory, and it is not simply that writers found it difficult to deal with the immediate present. The probing back into the past was in search of some explanation for the crisis of the times. Both fictional and auto-biographical childhood took writers back to just before the First World War, and it was in the Edwardian period, seen part-nostalgically, part-critically, that causes were sought. It is not accidental that Henry James should have been popular with readers, or that E.M. Forster, who had not published a novel since 1924, began to acquire a wide following for the first time.

Two writers, Elizabeth Bowen and Rosamond Lehmann, exemplify this search. Elizabeth Bowen's collections of short stories, *Look at all those Roses* (1941) and *The Demon Lover* (1945) convey an atmosphere of retreat and decay in the genteel middle-classes, out of place since Edwardian times. In several stories the present and past are juxtaposed to make a bitter contrast. In 'The Happy Autumn Fields' a woman in a bombed house recalls a family walk in the country as a child. 'We only know inconvenience now, not sorrow. Everything pulverizes so easily because it is rot-dry; one can only wonder that it makes so much noise. The source, the sap must have dried up, or the pulse must have stopped, before you or I were conceived.'

The idea of a vital spring of psychic energy now run dry is central to Rosamond Lehmann's novel *The Ballad and the Source* (1944). It is set, very consciously, in the period that leads into the First World War, and it is told through the experience of a child. The story is reported to her, as in a Greek tragedy, of the career of a woman who has the life-force that the child feels others have lost:

> It was this, this last that had left our house, and perhaps similar houses at that period. There were no words for it, of course, and the sense of it came only intermittently. Looking back now, one might express it by saying that there had been disillusionments lurking, unformulated doubts about overcoming difficulties; a defeat somewhere, a failure of the vital impulse.

The tragedy of the story is that the possessor of this vital impulse uses it for destruction rather than good. On a smaller scale, Ivy Compton-Burnett's series of domestic dramas, of which *Parents and Children* and *Elders and Betters* were published during the war, use the late Victorian and Edwardian world as a setting for the working out of evil within a privileged but undermined class.

Joyce Cary's trilogy *Herself Surprised*, *To Be A Pilgrim*, and *The*

Horse's Mouth (1941, '42 and '44), was a conscious attempt to survey English society from the 1880s to the Second World War. The story stops before war breaks out, although at one time Cary considered taking it on into the Blitz. The 'vital impulse' is hardly lacking in either of his characters Sarah Monday or Gulley Jimson, but the conclusion, with Sarah murdered by Jimson, Jimson dying, and his masterpiece demolished, shows that the destructive element of fate and injustice is also hard at work. (The trilogy established Cary's reputation as a novelist. Apart from a trip to West Africa for the Ministry of Information, he spent the war in Oxford and avoided literary London.)

If Joyce Cary's trilogy is an examination of the liberal-Protestant English tradition, Evelyn Waugh's *Brideshead Revisited* (1945) represents the conservative-Catholic. The comparison is not as neat as that, but is made in order to stress that there is more than self-indulgent nostalgia in what reviewers recognized as Waugh's first 'serious' book. Waugh had already made a gesture in 1942 by publishing two chapters of an abandoned novel as *Work Suspended*, with the following preface:

> This is the book on which I was at work in September, 1939. It is now clear to me that even if I were again to have the leisure and will to finish it, the work would be in vain, for the world in which and for which it was designed, has ceased to exist.

Waugh's friend and biographer Christopher Sykes believes this to be nonsense, but in the context of 1942 and the historical casting-back that has been discussed the gesture is not ridiculous.

Brideshead Revisited is touched with the same regret for 'the splendours of the recent past', Waugh's phrase in his introduction to the revised edition of 1960 in which he apologized for the gluttony and rhetoric with which the book is infused. 'It was a bleak period of present privation and threatening disaster – the period of soya beans and Basic English.' Its subject is the working of divine grace in the life of an aristocratic Catholic family, but the background is the decay of a noble house, literally so, since Brideshead comes to be taken over by the Army during the War. The prologue and epilogue are set in that contemporary 'age of Hooper', the narrator's phrase for the bleak present created for the likes of his grammar-school-ignorant young subaltern. Waugh hated that present and regretted the past which in 1944 he thought had gone for ever. But looking at it again in 1960, he saw how much *Brideshead Revisited* was itself a document of that period: 'It is offered to a younger generation of readers as a souvenir of the Second War rather than of the 'twenties or of the 'thirties, with which it ostensibly deals.'

There are parallels between *Brideshead Revisited* and Cyril Connolly's wartime document *The Unquiet Grave* (1944), not least their 'obsession with pleasure at a time when nearly all pleasures were forbidden'. *The Unquiet Grave* is not a novel; in a sense it is the baroque extreme of the diaries and journals that substituted for much writing during the war. The narrator is Palinurus, helmsman to Odysseus who fell overboard and whose soul had to wander until it found a grave, and originally Connolly concealed his authorship, although the secret was not kept for very long. The book is the record of a spiritual journey which Palinurus/Connolly made in the course of recovery from depression. It is a journey through memories of happier days, and the journey sometimes becomes travel writing as he conjures up inaccessible Paris and the South of France. The travel writer also tours a selection of European literature, a theme interlocking with his desire to be a real writer, not a literary journalist.

We are back with the enemies of promise, and the victim is Connolly himself:

Approaching forty, sense of total failure: not a writer but a ham actor whose performance is clotted with egotism; dust and ashes; 'brilliant', – that is, not worth doing. Never will I make that extra effort to live according to reality which alone makes good writing possible: hence the manic-depressiveness of my style, – which is either bright, cruel and superficial; or pessimistic; moth-eaten with self-pity.

Connolly has the courage to be frank; there were many other writers in London 'affected by the dirt and weariness, the gradual draining away under war conditions of light and colour from the former capital of the world', who also felt depression and self-pity. By the middle of the war there is a prevailing mood of dejection amongst the older writers who had fought the battles of the 1930s, dejection because those battles had proved defeats, dejection because they did not feel sufficiently part of the battle in which the whole of Britain was engaged. A contemporary critic summed up:

Any impartial examination of the literary scene in 1943 reveals an utter disintegration. Novelists, critics, biographers and dramatists seem to be so infinitely separated, so alone and so lonely that there is an almost universal note of artistic despair.

The earlier part of this chapter tried to show the physical constraints that the war placed on prose writing; the latter tries to explain the psychological limitations. A novel is an organized view of society, even when that society is in flux, and wartime conditions were such that writers found it difficult to establish a point of perspective from which to view what was happening around them. Further, an author needs to hold at least some values in common with the society in which his work is done. To many it seemed as though that link had been broken, and the best novels written during the war are by those writers who go over the ground in search of the breaking point. Others, for practical as well as psychological reasons, did not make the attempt, and the books simply were not written.

Literature, however – the desire to write, to give expression to one's individual feelings – persisted. Despair, isolation, loneliness, these are valid subjects for the writer; the question is what form can give them best expression.

CHAPTER FIVE

Poetry (London)

*'Poets arguing about wartime
poetry; jackals snarling over
a dried up well.'*

Cyril Connolly

Given the habit of newspaper editors of reaching for the file to see
what they did last time, it is not surprising that in the early weeks of
the Second World War the popular press should raise the cry 'Where
are the war poets?' Even the *Times Literary Supplement* could not
resist ending 1939 with some advice 'To the Poets of 1940'. If they
were to

fall into resignation or despair . . . the Dark Age is assured. And that is true
too if they try to make harmonies from hatreds or seek the salvation of man
in political formulas labelled Left or Right.

Having thus dismissed a theme that had inspired some of the best
poetry of the 1930s, the *Times Literary Supplement* produced its own
prescription:

The beauty of the new poetry will be in its integrity; it will be brave,
positive and stark, because it is forced to look intently at the worst, but it
will relate the immediate, agonizing facts in universal terms.

But then poets rarely do take the advice of the *Times Literary
Supplement*.

One answer to the question, Where are the war poets?, was that the
poets of the First World War were still very much there, in the minds
of those who now found themselves confronted by the Second. Trying

95

to convey the menace of Libya's desert landscape, Keith Douglas admitted: 'Rosenberg I only repeat what you were saying.' There was also that element of 'war poetry' which they wished to avoid at all costs. John Heath-Stubbs has said in a radio interview: 'If there was one poet my generation really hated – really spat when his name was mentioned – it was Rupert Brooke. He stood for all the attitudes to war which we detested.' Yet all attitudes to war, poetic or other, positive or negative, were conditioned by 1914–18. Roy Fuller reflected:

> Pity, repulsion, love and anger,
> The vivid allegorical
> Reality of gun and hangar,
> Sense of the planet's imminent fall:
>
> Our fathers felt these things before
> In another half-forgotten war.
>
> And our emotions are caught part
> From them;

First-war poets were there in the flesh as well as in memory. Keith Douglas's tutor at Oxford was Edmund Blunden. Herbert Read's 'Ode Without Rhetoric, Written during the Battle of Dunkirk, May, 1940' recalls his First World War experiences against the background of gunfire faintly heard across the Channel from France. His memories of the narrow spaces of the trenches give point to the estranging, distanced violence of the Second World War, a theme that was taken up by many others besides Read.

> Unreal war! No single friend
> links me with its immediacy.
> It is a voice out of a cabinet
> a printed sheet, and these faint reverberations
> selected in the silence
> by my attentive ear.

Read, as a director of the publishers George Routledge and Sons, was to be a key figure for a new generation of poets after 1939. The reputation of Robert Graves, though he was known as the author of *Goodbye To All That*, did not really begin to grow until after the Second World War had ended. His wanderings were brought to an end by the declaration of war, and after being turned down for military service, he spent much of his time in semi-retreat at Galmpton-Brixton in Devon. He wrote historical novels for a living, but made an occasional critical foray. 'The Persian Version' is a wry comment on the use of propaganda:

> Truth-loving Persians do not dwell upon
> The trivial skirmish fought near Marathon.

Cyril Connolly knew where the war poets were: ' "under your nose". For war poets are not a new kind of being, they are only peace poets who have assimilated the material of war. As the war lasts, the poetry which is written becomes war poetry, just as inevitably the lungs of Londoners grow black with soot.' The transition from peace to war in September 1939 was not the wrench it had been in August 1914. For some the war had been going on since 1933, for others it did not really begin until the crisis of June 1940. In August 1941 George Stonier pointed out the difficulty of being a Rupert Brooke about conscription, Munich, or the Maginot Line. 'The reaction, in literature as in everything else, to war was defensive.' The Blitz, though heightening emotions, did not change the defensive mood of poets. Neither the patriotism of Rupert Brooke nor the pity of Wilfred Owen was appropriate to a new war, being fought on new terms.

In the stress and excitement of the times many people found that writing poetry was a release for their emotions, whatever the quality of the results. In June 1940 Connolly complained that *Horizon* was being inundated with poems 'in many cases by people who have never written a poem before, and yet find it comes to them as naturally as blowing out a paper bag'. The boom in writing was matched by a boom in publication. While the number of fiction titles published steadily declined, poetry publication fell far less sharply in the first three years (from 310 in 1940 to 249 in 1942), and actually increased to 329 in 1943, followed by 328 in 1944. Of course, not all these titles came from the *avant garde*. A retired university lecturer, Minnie Haskins, became a sudden celebrity when King George V quoted her poem 'I said to the Man who stood at the Gate of the Year' in his Christmas 1939 radio broadcast. The publishers Jonathan Cape had something of a coup in 1944 when they persuaded Field Marshal Viscount Wavell to put together *Other Men's Flowers*, an anthology of his favourite poetry. And if we are looking beyond the customary definitions, Lord Vansittart's anti-Nazi hate poems in the *Sunday Times* must qualify as 'war poetry'. In 1945 the *Sunday Times* privately printed a selection of its school of war poets, which gives an idea of traditional poets' responses to the war.

One reason for the boom in verse publication was that poetry was the simplest way to satisfy the demand for new material, without using up too much paper. Technical developments in publishing had made it possible to produce a decently made volume of verse that retailed at 2/6d – for instance Faber and Faber's 'Sesame' series. Faber and Faber, Routledge, and to a more limited extent The Hogarth Press, gave important help to contemporary poetry by producing cheap but well-designed group and individual collections. The fact that two poets with differing tastes were in charge of the poetry lists of two major verse-publishing houses – T.S. Eliot at Faber's and Herbert Read at Routledge – had an influence on the pattern of publication. Where Faber's preferred poets continuing on the lines of Auden, Routledge gave encouragement to the new school of Romantics. The two senior poets co-operated closely. When Sidney Keyes, a 'romantic', offered Eliot a collection of Oxford poetry, Eliot sent him on to Read. Keyes wrote to a friend, 'Eliot and Read work together on all new poetry, they share it out'. The result was Routledge's *Eight Oxford Poets*, of whom three were to be killed, three were to stop writing, one was to become a translator, and one, John Heath-Stubbs, survives as a poet and critic.

Book publication could come only after a moderate amount of work had been published in the little magazines. In an introduction to his selection of war poetry *I Burn for England* (1966), Charles Hamblett says:

> Facilities for having verse printed in the surviving literary magazines were mostly in the hands of a small clique of delicate maiden gentlemen, most of whom were too busily engaged in coy little love sublimations with each other to apply their lavender minds to the rough, uneven poetry that was being composed by the rude, licentious soldiery.

But the acknowledgments in Keidrych Rhys's anthology *More Poems from the Forces* (1943) show how wide, even if one was in the services, the opportunities for publication really were: *Augury, Bolero, Bugle Blast, The Citadel* (Egypt), *Caseg Broadsheets, The Cherwell, Eight Oxford Poets, Horizon, John O'London's Weekly, Kingdom Come, Life and Letters Today, The Listener, New English Weekly, New*

Statesman and Nation, New Writing and Daylight, News Chronicle, Now, Orientations (Cairo), *Oxford Press Anthology, Our Time, Penguin New Writing, Parade* (Cairo), *Partisan Review, Periscope, Poems of this War, Poetry* (*Chicago*), *Poetry Folios, Poetry* (*London*), *Poetry Quarterly, Poetry Review, Programme, Resurgam Younger Poets, Salvo for the USSR, Selected Writing, The Spectator, Some Poems in Wartime, Time and Tide, Tribune, Times Literary Supplement Wales,* plus credits to sixteen individual volumes of poetry.

Dylan Thomas once said, 'Poetry editors are mostly vicious climbers, with their fingers in many pies, their ears at many keyholes, and their tongues at many bottoms.' Two poetry editors in particular emerged during the war; one has been encountered already, Tambimuttu (to whom Thomas made his comment), the other was Wrey Gardiner. Both were in similar positions from which to influence the development of poetry: Tambimuttu had started *Poetry* (*London*) in February 1939 – the suffix was in order to distinguish the magazine from *Poetry* (*Chicago*) – and was also poetry editor for the publishers Nicholson and Watson. Julian Maclaren-Ross gives a colourful account of Tambimuttu's relations with the firm, which eventually went bankrupt, in *Memoirs of the Forties.* Wrey Gardiner had taken over the tiny, almost amateur *Poetry Quarterly* in the spring of 1940, and was also owner of the Grey Walls Press. Publication in the magazine could lead in both cases to publication in book form. Tambimuttu had additional influence as poetry editor of Reginald Moore's magazine *Selected Writing.*

The rise of both *Poetry* (*London*) and *Poetry Quarterly* to the important positions they held was almost entirely accidental. A gap had been left by the collapse of Geoffrey Grigson's *New Verse* and Julian Symons's *Twentieth Century Verse*; the demand for poetry caused circulation to expand. Neither magazine achieved the critical status of its predecessors. Both Tambimuttu and Gardiner preferred catholicity to critical dogmatism, for which they have been criticized by the doctrinaire, though they may have done more for poetry by giving it space in which to develop rather than forcing it down fixed channels. The doctrinaire had plenty of opportunity to press their views in more selective publications.

Of the two editors Tambimuttu undoubtedly had more flair, and a number of poets, Keith Douglas particularly, benefited from his interest. On the other hand Wrey Gardiner was distinctly more efficient. *Poetry Quarterly* appeared regularly, whereas *Poetry* (*London*), which was supposed to come out six times a year, appeared only ten times between 1939 and 1945. Number Ten, a large hardback edition, was known colloquially as 'Chums' because Tambimuttu had tried to include everyone to whom he had made hitherto unfulfilled promises of publication. Tambimuttu's permanent presence in Fitzrovia brought him plenty of opportunities for talent-spotting (he was said to be able to smell the quality of a poet's work without reading it), but the consequent Sohoitis meant that once spotted, the talent might have to wait a long time for wider recognition. Keith Douglas's collected poems are a notorious example.

Reviewing the state of poetry in September 1942, Naomi Ryde Smith exactly illustrates the problem of discussing poetry written in wartime:

The hour has thus given to the work of each of these emphatic people the importance we must always attach to what may be the last utterance of any man: it has also encouraged an enormous amount of discussion about and classification of their output. The result is an epidemic of anthologies which overlap one another and a slightly ring-side attitude in the appreciation of their work by the exponents of opposing theories. The hubbub is intensified because the poet-prophets have found so many poet-critics to expound and acclaim them.

The fact that there was a hubbub about poetry in the middle of a fierce world-wide struggle is a healthy sign; the problem for the individual poet was that the accidental circumstances of war could decide his reputation for him. Robert Graves gave this indirect answer to the question 'Where are the war poets?' in his introduction to Alun Lewis's *Ha! Ha! Among the Trumpets*:

It is only when death releases the true poet from the embarrassing condition of being at once immortal and alive in the flesh that the people are prepared to honour him. . . . This explains the heavy black headlines in the Press of March 1944: ALUN LEWIS THE POET IS DEAD. Search the back-files and you will find no preparatory announcement: ALUN LEWIS WRITES GREAT POETRY.

Looked at as 'literary history' the period 1939 to '45 has a definite pattern, both in terms of schools and generations. The established poets of the Thirties continued to work along the themes they had chosen before the war, though they developed further and further away from the original matrix of Marxist and Freudian theory; on the other hand a new generation of poets reacted away from the outwardly directed and 'classical' viewpoint of pre-war poetry of the Auden School towards a romantic and inwardly-directed extreme.

The poets of the 1930s were gradually moving into the position of a literary establishment – but Stephen Spender's assessment in 1942 is a reminder that his generation too was in revolt:

> The war has caused a sharp division of writers into three generations: the generation of those who were consistently blind to events from 1918 to 1939 and who now find themselves in the strongly entrenched positions in literature, the arts, and home affairs which fall to the superannuated in times of war; the 'New Writing' generation of those who were acutely aware of the approaching war, ever since 1933, and who therefore regard it almost with relief, as a fulfillment of their prophecies; the generation of those who are the war's victims, too young to have been in any way responsible for it, and in some ways filled with bitterness against the preceding generations.

Yet though there is distinct difference in terms of style between the generations, the curious fact is that poets reacted remarkably similarly to the new conditions produced by the war.

Writing later what might be called the 'official history' of wartime poetry for the British Council, Stephen Spender in his short account *Poetry since 1939* shows how the shocks of 1938 and 1939 had changed the committed political attitudes of the Thirties writers, particularly his own:

> the war has been a period of reorientation for them in which their whole energies have not gone into the writing of poetry. This can be explained partly by circumstances which have denied almost everyone in Britain the time in which to pursue creative tasks. However, it is partly also to be explained by the doubts of these poets whether the war, which was certainly against Fascism, was for a purified cause. . . . There is a tendency for the poetry of Day Lewis, MacNeice, and Spender to turn inwards towards a personal subject-matter and avoid the world of outer events.

Yet the signal for such a change of direction had been given, symbolically at least, by a poem very much related to outward events, Auden's '1st September 1939'. It is an honest expression of defeat and retreat:

> I sit in one of the dives
> On Fifty-Second Street
> Uncertain and afraid
> As the clever hopes expire
> Of a low dishonest decade:

It is also a defence of the role of the poet as observer rather than actor; it is an assertion of his right to search out truth and preserve it in poetry, not politics:

> All I have is a voice
> To undo the folded lie,
> The romantic lie in the brain
> Of the sensual man-in-the-street
> And the lie of Authority

Auden's political resignation had taken place in January 1939 when he left for America; by 1941, when he published his *New Year Letter*, his attitude had shifted to one of disdain for poets who misled themselves with hopes of political progress:

> Art is not life, and cannot be
> A midwife to society,

Auden's only recommendation in '1st September 1939' was that 'We must love one another or die'. It was unfortunate that this sentiment should be published in England on 20 June 1940, when Dunkirk had set more minds on death than on love. Even his loyal friends came to complain of the 'regrettable transatlantic developments of W.H. Auden'.

Auden had physically removed himself from the scene; those who remained behind conducted a similar political retreat. C. Day Lewis, formerly the most politically active of the group, gave their reasons in his 'Dedicatory Stanzas' (to Stephen Spender) at the start of his translation of Virgil's *Georgics* (1940):

> Where are the war poets? The fools inquire.
> We were the prophets of a changeable morning
> Who hoped for much but saw the clouds forewarning:
> We were at war, while they still played with fire
> And rigged the market for the ruin of man:
> Spain was a death to us, Munich a mourning.
> No wonder then if, like the pelican,
> We have turned inward for our iron ration,
> Tapping the vein and sole reserve of passion,
> Drawing from poetry's capital what we can.

For Day Lewis poetry's capital proved to be the perennial themes of Love, Death and the Imagination (and better verse than the lines just quoted). But poems like 'Lidice' and 'Will it be so again?'

and those celebrating his service with the Home Guard in 1940 show that he did not simply become self-absorbed. Rather, as in the case of Auden, it was the perception of his role as a poet that had changed:

> Today, I can but record
> In truth and patience
> This high delirium of nations
> And hold it to the reflecting, fragile word.

This may be said to describe his position as a poet; in 1941 Day Lewis became an editor for the Ministry of Information, where the word was considered less fragile. After *Word Over All* in 1943 he did not publish another collection until 1948.

Stephen Spender had announced his change of direction in the introduction to his 1939 volume *The Still Centre*: 'I have deliberately turned back to a kind of writing which is more personal, and I have included within my subjects weakness and fantasy and illusion.' The poems of *Ruins and Visions* (1942) chart the progress of his emotions from the break-up of his first marriage to his meeting with the pianist Natasha Litvin, whom he married in April 1941. There are poems inspired by air-raids and the death of friends, but, to quote George Barker's description of Spender, 'this poet with his soul upon his shoulder' somehow fails to communicate his emotions. Reorientation was still in progress, and his critical work at this period is much more interesting, expressing more directly the change of heart. His position as a poetry reviewer and his connections with *Horizon* and *New Writing* also made his critical work more important for other people. Spender was called up into the National Fire Service in 1941, becoming involved in the Service's education schemes.

Louis MacNeice was in America at the start of the war, teaching at Cornell University, and might have stayed there were it not for the crisis of 1940. 'I had no wish to return to a Chamberlain's England, where my fellow-writers were sitting around not writing. From June [1940] on I wished to return, not because I thought I could be more *useful* in England than in America, but because I wanted to see things for myself.' He returned to England during the Blitz and joined the BBC as a scriptwriter in May 1941.

The turn to inward-probing affected MacNeice – in 1941 he wrote the draft of an autobiography, later published as *The Strings Are False*, another example of the wave of reminiscence that swept English writers at the beginning of the war – but MacNeice had always stood a little apart from those with whom he had been grouped, and though in retreat, MacNeice did not abandon the role of commentator. His poems are written as it were from a defensive position, directed at others, noticeably the series of portraits in *Springboard* (1944). A long poem, 'The Kingdom', begins with a celebration of the individual against the wartime pressures of the mass:

> Under the surface of flux and of fear there is an underground movement,
> Under the crust of bureaucracy, quiet behind the posters,
> Unconscious but palpably there – the Kingdom of individuals.

The outward-direction of MacNeice's poetry keeps it hard where Spender's goes soft; his observations are sardonic, sometimes brutal. These judgments are also reflections on his own conduct. His powerful description of the aftermath of an air-raid 'Brother Fire' is an admission of the destructive urge in himself and others which runs completely contrary to any Ministry of Information version of a firestorm:

> O delicate walker, babbler, dialectician Fire,
> O enemy and image of ourselves,
> Did we not on those mornings after the All Clear,
> When you were looting shops in elemental joy
> And singing as you swarmed up city block and spire,
> Echo your thought in ours? 'Destroy! Destroy!'

Like Auden, Spender and Day Lewis, MacNeice recognized that the moment of their poetic propaganda had passed, that each must turn to individual concerns and allow his poetry to develop in accordance with its own needs. But it was the vein of satire in MacNeice which gave the group its bitterest memorial, his 'Epitaph for Liberal Poets', 'who walked in our sleep and died on our Quest':

> The Individual has died before; Catullus
> Went down young, gave place to those who were born old
> And more adaptable and were not even jealous
> Of his wild life and lyrics. Though our songs
> Were not so warm as his, our fate is no less cold.

By turning away from social commentary towards personal contemplation, these poets were choosing the direction already taken by T.S. Eliot. Only Auden went as far in search of a religious answer, and a parallel, not a connection is suggested between Eliot's concern and that of the younger generation – though the parallel is there. Eliot must be excluded from Spender's list of those who were 'consistently blind to events from 1914 to 1939' but his response was conservative, a despairing of change through political action. The 'act of personal contrition, of humility, repentance and amendment' which he felt the Munich crisis called for implied a search for salvation through moral rather than political discipline, a salvation found in the completion of *Four Quartets*.

The *Four Quartets* are not about war, though war contributed some of its imagery. War also helped Eliot to complete the scheme he had begun with 'Burnt Norton' in 1936. He told an interviewer that he was prevented from writing another play, and he welcomed the fact:

> The form of the *Quartets* fitted in very nicely to the conditions under which I was writing, or could write at all. I could write them in sections and I didn't have to have quite the same continuity; it didn't matter if a day or two elapsed when I did not write, as they frequently did, while I did war jobs.

'East Coker' was completed in 1940, 'The Dry Salvages' in 1941, and 'Little Gidding' in 1942. The sequence appeared as a whole in 1944.

The argument of the *Quartets* cannot be summarized here; what is important is that the philosophical meditation on time, moment, perception and expression does lead to some kind of affirmation. That affirmation is, as it should be, in the poetry itself; Eliot achieves an imaginative integration of his themes which is matched by the actual integration of his symbolism in the closing lines:

> All shall be well and
> All manner of thing shall be well
> When the tongues of flame are in-folded
> Into the crowned knot of fire
> And the fire and the rose are one.

Though boredom and banality were common afflictions in London during these years there were also moments of high intensity, when the emotions were exposed and there was a sense of spiritual need beyond the immediate concerns of day to day. The intensity of the *Quartets* matches these moments of high emotion, their poetic affirmation responds to that need; the result is one of the major literary achievements of the war.

The poets who had begun to write in the 1930s lacked T.S. Eliot's conservative Christian certainties. In fact they lacked certainties of all kinds, and it showed in their poetry. In November 1941 Cyril Connolly concluded that the poetic impulse of the previous decade was exhausted, and to make his point he invented a writer, John Weaver, one of the dozens of minor poets inundating *Horizon* with unpublishable poetry. John Weaver's background is typical of the intellectual of *entre deux guerres*: professional parents, educated at a minor public school and a major university, Marxist sympathies, 'at present trying to reconcile communism with religion, pacifism with war, property with revolution and homosexuality with marriage'. Though Connolly is careful to distinguish Weaver from his mentors these confusions could also be found in them:

though years younger than Auden and MacNeice, he is completely dominated by them. He imitates their scientific journalism, their Brains Trust vulgarity without the creative energy of the one or the scholarship of the other, just as he assimilates the piety of Spender and the decorum of Day Lewis into his correct, flat, effortless, passionless verses. And it is Weaver, now at an OCTU or in the Air Force Intelligence, who is responsible for some of the badness of war poetry, who used to write *Comrades we have come to a watershed*, and who now talks about *Love's tracer bullets*.

The satire is aimed at what Connolly calls the school of 'Puritan verse', and since Auden, Spender, MacNeice and Day Lewis are its founders, Connolly is indirectly attacking them. Having cleared the air of Georgian poetic whimsy, the poetry of the Twenties and Thirties must in turn give way to a mood more in tune with the new decade: 'Poetry was taken down a cul de sac to get away from the Georgians, and now it has to find its way back. The academic socialism of the thirties was not strong enough to revive it, we are waiting for a new romanticism to bring it back to life.'

In fact the 'new romanticism' Connolly anticipated had already arrived – the inside cover of that November 1941 *Horizon* carries an advertisement for the first anthology of the movement, *The New Apocalypse*. An alternative to the Puritan school of verse had been in existence well before the war began, though as a tendency rather than a school. Indeed, one reason for the concentration of historical accounts on 'the Auden generation' is that it is more easily defined than the looser group of poets who had absorbed varying amounts of European symbolism, Celtic romanticism, and latterly Surrealism, and for whom the respected names were Yeats, James Joyce and

Ezra Pound. The magazine *New Verse* had found room for others, such as George Barker, Dylan Thomas and David Gascoyne, besides Auden, and the poetry of one of its assistant editors, Kenneth Allott, does not fit neatly into the either/or categories of classic/romantic, Puritan/Surrealist. Allott's two volumes, *Poems* (1938) and *The Ventriloquist's Doll* (1943), represent an almost equal mixture of both tendencies, social comment on the one hand, a freedom of imagery on the other. Allott's virtual silence after 1943 is also significant. It is as though the poetic tide of the Thirties had receded, leaving him high and dry.

A member of an older generation, Edith Sitwell, experienced completely opposite feelings. Here was a figure from the Twenties, who had published no poetry since *Gold Coast Customs* in 1929, suddenly finding her voice again under the pressure of events:

> Still falls the Rain –
> Dark as the world of man, black as our loss –
> Blind as the nineteen hundred and forty nails
> Upon the Cross.

The result of this personal renaissance, *Street Songs* (1942), tries to universalize the experience of war through a mixture of exotic imagery and Christian symbolism. The effect now seems overwrought, but the recurrent references to cold, starvation, and the figure of Death had an emotional appeal for a public familiar with suffering more prosaically expressed. Her reputation is now very low, but – as is the case with far worse poetry of the time – the war gave her genuine and widespread popularity.

Edith Sitwell is an isolated figure; so, too, is David Gascoyne. If Edith Sitwell's roots lay in Rimbaud and the French Symbolists, Gascoyne's were in the Continental Surrealists; he had published the first English study of Surrealism in 1935. Yet although Gascoyne's inspiration and direction were very different from Auden's or Spender's, he too felt that the change from peace to war called for a change in his poetry:

I feel that poetry of the 'magical' category, – product of sheer imagination, unrestricted by pure design and untempered by the wisdom of disillusionment, – may be more stimulating, more immediately satisfying to write; but in the long run it is probably less rewarding, less consoling, than that resulting from conflict between the instinctive poetic impulse and the impersonal discipline, the unadorned sobriety of realistic 'sense'.

The division between 'magical' and 'realistic' which Gascoyne makes here in an introduction to his section of the Hogarth anthology *Poets of Tomorrow, Third Selection* (1942) was carried through into his *Poems 1937–42*. The opening sections, which he describes as religious and metaphysical, are in the Surrealist manner:

> The socket-free lone visionary eye,
> Soaring reflectively
> Through regions sealed from macrocosmic light
> By inner sky's impenetrable shell,
> Often is able to descry:

But later poems in the volume, describing encounters and events in what amounts to an autobiography of the crisis years, are written in a much more direct voice:

> Draw now with prickling hand the curtains back;
> Unpin the blackout-cloth; let in
> Grim crack-of-dawn's first glimmer through the glass.

The same shift towards a simpler means of expression can be seen in the work of George Barker. Like Gascoyne the emphasis of his poetry before the war had been on the surreal and the visionary, but in *Eros in Dogma* (1944) the long and complex poems reminiscent of Ezra Pound are replaced by sonnet sequences and elegies. Barker was teaching in Japan at the beginning of the war, then lived in America until the end of 1943, and the poems are tinged with the mood of exile. His address is more direct, structurally there is an underlying narrative of the poet's journey to Japan and America, of the war and his emotional life. The final poem, 'To Any Member of My Generation', makes it clear that Barker thought of himself as a poet made by the Thirties, and that he shared his contemporaries' desperation:

> Whenever we kissed we cocked the future's rifles
> And from our wild-oat words, like dragon's teeth,
> Death underfoot now arises: when we were gay
> Dancing together in what we hoped was life,
> Who was it in our arms but the whores of death
> Whom we have found in our beds today, today?

The reason for emphasizing the pre-war existence of a romantic or visionary tendency in poetry, and the fact that at least some of its followers moderated their position after the war began, is that the reputations of Edith Sitwell, George Barker, David Gascoyne and others benefited from the failing impulse of the Auden tradition. The extreme case is that of Dylan Thomas. His *18 Poems* (1934) and *25 Poems* (1936) contained all the elements of the 'new romanticism' that Connolly was waiting for: violent natural imagery, sexual and Christian symbolism, emotional subject matter expressed in a singing rhythmical verse which the careless might confuse with the automatic writing of the Surrealists:

> I see the boys of summer in their ruin
> Lay the gold tithings barren,
> Setting no store by harvest, freeze the soils;
> There in their heat the winter floods
> Of frozen loves they fetch their girls,
> And drown the cargoed apples in their tides.

The effect of this poetry was to liberate others from 'the strict and adult pen' demanded by W.H. Auden, but it is noticeable that Thomas, too, wrote more directly in the 1940s. During the central part of the war, between the summer of 1941 and the spring of 1944, Thomas actually wrote little, if anything, although he continued to be published in magazines, and his reputation grew. The poems of *Deaths and Entrances* (1946) are more controlled and less obscure than the pre-war volumes. It is no surprise that poets change as they grow older and more confident of their craft, but the war seems to have made Thomas feel the need to make a more public statement. That, at least, is the tone of 'A Refusal to Mourn the Death, by Fire, of a Child in London':

> Deep with the first dead lies London's daughter,
> Robed in the long friends,
> The grains beyond age, the dark veins of her mother,
> Secret by the unmourning water
> Of the riding Thames.
> After the first death, there is no other.

Dylan Thomas has been described by Stephen Spender as 'perhaps the only one capable of exercising a literary influence as great as that of Auden', and during the war it did appear that he had, unwillingly, founded a school. To examine the rise of that school we must turn from literary criticism to literary politics.

Whatever doubts writers may have had about their role in the wider national struggle, they never ceased to battle among themselves. Wrey Gardiner commented in the Spring 1941 number of

Poetry Quarterly: 'What was once the free expression of the soul of a great nation has become a dirty trade practised by obscure people in vague corners employing the same technique as the exploiters of patent medicine, and with less justification.' The 'dirty trade' was poetry, the battle was for control of the outlets for publication and criticism.

There is no doubt that the survivors of the Thirties, principally Connolly, John Lehmann and Stephen Spender, had wide influence through *Horizon* and *New Writing*, and their established positions gave them access to the BBC and the review pages of periodicals and newspapers. Jealousy was inevitable. Reviewing the Hogarth Press *Poets of Tomorrow, Third Selection* (edited by John Lehmann), George Woodcock claimed in *Poetry (London)* that there was a conspiracy on the part of the 'mandarins' of the Thirties movement to keep it going with a group of neo-1930s writers, in this case Laurence Little, David Gascoyne, Laurie Lee and Arthur Harvey, who were 'flotsam from the pre-war past . . . poets of yesterday, rather than of tomorrow'. Keidrych Rhys, editor of *Wales* and *Poems from the Forces*, protested at 'the tame journalistic-values that still govern the unflourishing, unchanging state of letters in liberal England', of which *Horizon* was typical. Charles Hamblett's views have already been quoted (p. 129).

The image of a group conspiring to establish a 'movement' in the 1930s has been disputed. C. Day Lewis has pointed out that it was not until 1947 that he, Auden and Spender met together in the same room. But the image existed nonetheless. In an important article published, somewhat surprisingly considering its contents, in *New Writing and Daylight* in June 1943, Henry Reed blamed the Auden/ Spender group for the conflict between the generations: 'this group seems steadily and always, to have misinterpreted itself as a group of *rebels*. This conception seems to have been prompted by nothing more substantial than the transient ebullience of political enthusiasm.' The collapse of that enthusiasm had ended the artificial coherence of the group – and produced some 'extraordinarily disappointing' verse from Auden and Spender, but the damage had been done.

The myth that the Auden-group were rebels had been sedulously fostered by the Auden-group themselves: it was therefore necessary that the newcomers should be rebels also, this time (it was almost a dialectic process) against the politically-conscious, over-intellectualized writers of the early 'thirties.

Looking at the lists, of contributors to the three main anthologies representing the 'newcomers', *The New Apocalypse* (1940), *The White Horseman* (1941), and *The Crown and the Sickle* (1944), it is clear they were no more cohesive a group than their predecessors, and that the only common factors were indeed hostility to Auden – and hostility to London, for many of the contributors were from Scotland and Wales, or Northern Ireland. The best known of the movement were Henry Treece (by origin Welsh), J.F. Hendry (Scots), G.S. Fraser (Scots), Norman MacCaig (Scots), and Nicholas Moore (English). The editors of a related anthology *Lyra* (1942), Alex Comfort and Robert Greacen, were English and Northern Irish respectively.

The Celtic atmosphere was reinforced by the group's admiration for Dylan Thomas, though it is clear that Thomas did not admire them. In 1938 Henry Treece had been preparing a book on Dylan Thomas (eventually published in 1949 as *Dog Among the Fairies*), and he tried to get Thomas to sign what he was already calling an Apocalyptic Manifesto. Thomas refused: 'I agree with and like much of it, and some of it, I think, is manifestly absurd.' Treece's essay 'How I see Apocalypse' may explain why:

In my definition, the writer who senses the chaos, the turbulence, the laughter and the tears, the order and the peace of the world in its entirety, is an Apocalyptic writer. His utterance will be prophetic, for he is observing things which less sensitive men have not yet come to notice; and as his words are prophetic, they will tend to be incantatory, and so musical. At times, even, that music may take control, and lead the writer from recording his vision almost to creating another vision. So, momentarily, he will kiss the edge of God's robe.

G.S. Fraser gave a more sober account in *The White Horseman*. Apocalypticism, he explained, was a 'dialectical development' of Surrealism which accepted the Surrealists' psychological discoveries, but still tried to control its material, even though: 'From the writer's highly technical point of view, it might be said that Freud's main discovery is that it is impossible really to talk nonsense.' The poet must *fuse* with his material, conveying description and feeling in a series of images. (Fraser refers to Pound's Imagist experiments, and beyond that one can detect traces of French symbolist theory.) But the most important claim that Fraser makes for the Apocalyptics is his assertion of the psychological significance of the movement: 'If the poetry of the Auden generation had a certain immediate political

111

and social value, the poetry of the Apocalyptics is likely to have a certain permanent clinical value for the human race.'

It must be made clear that it is the theory that is interesting – not, unfortunately, the practice. The Apocalyptic movement produced a great many bad poems. The chief subject matter is Death, a figure stalking a *grand guignol* landscape of purple and black mountains, dotted with gibbets, broken byres, ravaged fields and winter woods, and littered with skulls, swords, mystic missals, lanterns and chalices. The gothick flora and fauna are principally thorns, thistles, snakes and ravens. The note of nightmare deliberately evokes the unconscious mind, for all is symbolic of psychological conditions, mainly depression, terror and pain. But there is little control over the imagery; it evokes, or fails to evoke, and mostly fails. To quote Henry Treece against himself:

> A consonant brings birth or death;
> From womb to tomb is a letter's length

and frequently not just letters but words, phrases and whole chunks of verse seem interchangeable. Here are the first two stanzas of Hendry's 'Apocalypse':

> Who are the speaking wound
> And world thrust stride over death,
> Star burred with symbols and
> The blind ghost shaping fountain's
> Horror strewn with mind
> Through the talking fiend?
>
> A cloud-skull strangling sun
> A spine-haired cannibal sky
> Stabs the blown heart green. Man
> Polared east of sex and west
> Of death crowns iron
> Orbits with a bone.

Yet in spite of the poverty of so much of their work, the Apocalyptics do seem to have been in tune with the times. Death, pain and depression were familiar features of everyday life; at least the Apocalyptics presented them with some flair. Certainly they carried out a remarkable *putsch* against the literary establishment. *New Writing* held out, *Horizon* stopped short at Dylan Thomas, George Barker, W.S. Graham and Norman Nicholson (these were Connolly's chosen 'new romantics', not Apocalyptics), but *Poetry (London)*, *Kingdom Come, Now, Adelphi* and *Life and Letters Today* all fell under the neo-romantic spell. Wrey Gardiner announced the surrender of *Poetry Quarterly* in Autumn 1942:

> Neo-Romanticism and the Apocalyptics have tinged the literary scene with colour and richness and hope. They are not afraid to show that they have feelings. They stand in absolute and irreconcilable contrast to the desiccated despair, [dis]honest niggling and brazen rather bawdy cynicism of the prewar decade.

Besides these going concerns, the new movement had powerful allies in Herbert Read at Routledge, and Tambimuttu at Nicholson and Watson. As well as the Apocalyptic anthologies, *Transformation*, *New Road* and *Opus* were started as further outlets, and the Celtic Fringe saw the revival of *Poetry Scotland* and *Poetry Wales*. Ivor Jacobs commented in *Horizon* in October 1943, 'it seems that the Auden Aftermath mean business and their hold on English publishing presents them with golden opportunities, that is, golden opportunities for smart Alecs on the make'. The jealousy does not seem to have been always one way.

The Apocalyptics were the extremists in a wave of romanticism that surged through English culture during the war years, affecting painting and music as well as poetry. This was not entirely as Henry Reed put it, a dialectical response to the political preoccupations of the 1930s. There was a need for some kind of emotional satisfaction which a return to the self-concerns of romanticism seemed able to provide. At a time of regimentation the argument that 'any rigorous ruling, in poetry as in life, is the antithesis of happiness' had special appeal. In this 'return-to-self' the pre-war generation were not so far from the newcomers, but it was the newcomers who reacted most violently to the conditions in which they found themselves. G.S. Fraser considered those conditions a justification for the Apocalyptic's excess:

> With the war, we are all forced in a sense to become stoics – to depend on ourselves and the universe, the intermediate social worlds having been largely destroyed. We depend more and more on our own uncorroborated imaginings. ... The obscurity of our poetry, its air of something desperately snatched from dream or woven round a chime of words, are the results of a disintegration, not in ourselves, but in society.

Fraser's claim may seem exaggerated, but there were many who believed that a disintegration was taking place in society, and that art was bound to reflect it. Herbert Read argued:

it is not war in the ordinary sense which we are enduring, but a world revolution in which all conventions, whether of thought or action, break down and are replaced – not by new conventions, for conventions are of slow growth – but by provisional formulas which are immediately tested under fire. This process, obvious enough in military strategy and social organization, cannot be excluded from the cultural sphere. Painting and poetry, drama and the film – are involved in this insurrectionary test.

The collapse was felt most strongly among those most likely to be victims of it, the generation liable for conscription between 1939 and '45. Alex Comfort, one of the more considerable poets associated with the movement, stated: 'I belong to a generation brought up in the certainty that it would be killed in action on behalf of an unreality against an insanity', and signified his refusal by becoming a pacifist. The younger poets, he argued, were only reflecting the malaise of society:

For most of the poets here [the anthology *Lyra*], the war is a cosmic calamity, like the rain or the big winds – even in the Army they are on the surface of it, not in it. It may be true that ego-isolation of this kind pre-disposes to neurosis. It is certainly true that it is not confined to poets, but reflects the secret feeling of very many ordinary people.

The answer to the alienation and introversion of wartime existence was, according to the Neo-Romantics, a return to the spiritual and cultural values that had been crushed by the mass-mobilization of society. Again it was a pacifist, D.S. Savage, who argued the case most strongly:

In Shakespeare's time, we may say, the individual was in a real sense the centre of society: the social framework could be said to radiate from a centre in personal life. With the progress of civilization the centre has been shifted until the exterior structure of society no longer relates directly to the individual person. It has become externally centred upon itself, and the individual integrated into its structure, not as a person, but as an object. Personal creativeness is thus isolated from the social structure, thrust outside and refused social forms and sanctions: the isolated position of the modern artist is symbolic of the isolation of the personal principle itself.

Savage's case, put here in *The Personal Principle* (1944), was that Britain's self-defence against totalitarianism had only led to totali-

114

tarianism being introduced voluntarily. The problem of the poet was only an extreme version of the problem of every individual, the lack of self-creating control over his life and environment. Creativity could only be restored when society had become once more a series of small, self-governing units, a society that was organic rather than organized, in fact, a responsible anarchy.

In the middle of a world war, when the individual was indeed mobilized, propagandized and directed by an all-powerful state machine, such arguments for 'personalism' had great appeal, and were taken up by the magazines that came under Neo-Romantic influence. The attitude seems unreal and irresponsible, but it shows how despairing and isolated the poets felt. Their rejection of the society on which they blamed their predicament was so total that they could find virtue in society's incomprehension of their poetry. They attempted to transcend immediate material problems by writing verse that was intended to be magical and incantatory, and for a time a considerable number of people were persuaded that extreme subjectivity was the only possible poetic response to the conditions which faced them. Neo-Romanticism answered the psychological needs created by wartime living, with the disappearance of those pressures (or rather their mutation into the pressures of the Cold War), the Neo-Romantic movement evaporated, the vacuum being filled by a counter-reaction as fierce as theirs had been against the poets of the 1930s.

Finally, it must be stressed that the Neo-Romantics were by no means alone in feeling alienated from a disintegrating society, the general despair and withdrawal has, after all, been the major theme of this book. The most violent opponents of the Neo-Romantics felt the same need for a renewal of the spirit that would lead to the regeneration of literature. John Lehmann called the newcomers 'a sickly fungoid growth on decaying jam', but in the same breath talked of the 'tragic sense' that would emerge as a result of the war:

I find in the work of nearly all poets under forty signs of a very profound revaluation of values and a search for some outlook that is more in tune with the lessons of ten years of intensive history, some more satisfying faith than they were aware of the need for a few years ago.

It seems then that the advice of the *Times Literary Supplement* was largely ignored. Though the majority of poets abandoned their hopes of salvation in political formulas many, it appears, fell into resignation and despair. 'Brave, positive and stark' hardly describes the poetry discussed in this chapter. But there were those who, however, unwillingly, were forced to look intently at the worst. These are the subject of the following chapter.

CHAPTER SIX

Poems from the Forces

'The integration is the action, I
Can only scribble on the margin:'

Roy Fuller

The question remains, Where are the war poets? So far the subject has been not so much war poetry as poetry in wartime; the universal character of the war, the equal involvement of soldier and civilian, meant that the distinction between the two kinds of poetry was necessarily blurred. Nonetheless, though it has many of the characteristics of the poetry already discussed, there is a separate category of 'service poetry', if only because poets of a certain age found themselves in uniform, and reflecting on the fact, – 'the OCTU generation' as one of them, Sidney Keyes, called it. There is also the bald truth that more than forty published poets were killed on active service during the Second World War. These are war poets, whatever their achievement.

Certainly there was no shortage of would-be poets of all ranks, the urge to write poetry that Connolly had noticed was felt just as strongly in uniform as out of it. At Christmas 1942 the *Crusader*, the weekly newspaper of the Eighth Army (then facing the Afrika Korps in the Western Desert), announced a poetry competition: 403 poems were received from 280 competitors; a selection was published as *Poems from the Desert* in 1944. As the Eighth Army fought its way up Italy the Education Corps followed up with *Poems from Italy*, selected from 596 entries. There are thirty-three contributors to *Air Force Poetry*, fifty-five to *Poems from India*. This tells us nothing about the standard of what was produced – as Siegfried Sassoon tactfully put it in his introduction to *Poems from Italy*: 'It will be observed that the poets are both ancient and modern in their technique.' It is a reminder, however, that where other forms of self-expression suffered, it was still possible to write poetry. Alan Ross has said: 'The Navy – at least when one was at sea – was ideal for writing, once you got used to the noise and complete lack of privacy.' The time spent in training, in troopships, in transit camps and depots, all the waiting for the brief periods of violent action, could provide space for poetry without the continuity (as Eliot observed) necessary for prose.

As members of the OCTU generation, service poets were of an age to feel rebellious towards the poets that had preceded them, that 'dialectic' of generations that Henry Reed described. Keidrych Rhys, drafted from the editorship of *Wales* into an anti-aircraft battery, launched his attack in the introduction to the early anthology *Poems from the Forces* in 1941:

The poet in uniform in particular finds himself in a thankless position, born into the wrong times, accepting conscription with grace, with a bunch of tame versifiers on one side and an older generation whose views he does not wholly support on the other. The intellectuals of the depression have betrayed him. The culture side has been left to people so limited in their grasp as to, consciously or unconsciously, oppose the war. The culture of the country has been left to two magazines, neither of which poets respect or feel it is any honour to be in.

There is nothing exclusively 'service' in this attack on *Horizon* and *New Writing*; the fact of being in uniform only heightened the tension felt by the poet between his personal needs and the society in which he lived. Alan Rook, who rose to the rank of Major, wrote:

I do not ask you to dramatize the soldier-poet. For every profession is full of enmity against the individual, and alive with hate for those who oppose their solitude against the many little annoyances of a daily routine. This is the inescapable lot of the artist, and is not created, only emphasized by the peculiar conditions of war.

The 'peculiar conditions of war' underlined the poet's isolation. Reviewing a batch of younger poets in 1943, Clifford Dyment used the revealing phrase, 'these poets are less critics [of war] than prisoners of war'.

In giving expression to this complex *malaise* of modern man, the younger poets strike me as being at once true to their day and untrue. They are true in that they are aware of what is deep and unrealized; untrue in that they miss almost completely what is *not* deep and *is* realized. Collective urgency thinks only of action; poets, however, are always wondering about causes. For this reason poets must – however seriously they persuade themselves to the contrary – be at a disadvantage in times like the present. Thus, during the Blitz, the people of England, concerned only with the immediate task of endurance, made merry: the poets, however, wrote elegies on lost man.

Poets were prisoners of war within the military machine, the mechanized expression of the total mobilization of life. The Army was the mass organization of mass organizations, deliberately breaking down the individual's personality as part of his training, turning him into an efficient component with a number rather than a name. As an Apocalyptic, G.S. Fraser took his reaction to an extreme. The Army, he found, was:

a machine made up of human beings, not of abstract concepts, and a machine which works: the only defence against it which an organic human personality has, probably, is to sham dead. And it is possible that it is this, quite against my conscious will and my conscious moral political beliefs, that my personality has been doing.

And Fraser was a volunteer, not a conscript.

'Shamming dead' in the hope of avoiding further pain is not a psychological condition that helps the writing of poetry. Death is, of course, a constant subject of war poetry; what is remarkable is how many poets in the Forces felt as though they were dead already. Laurence Little's 'Tram Ride', for instance:

> I shall wake
> Up, when this ride is over,
> And find that I am dead, and this thin
> Room a coffin, for I am cold inside
> And death is drifting upon me
> With each man's breath.

Alan Ross concludes his poem 'Messdeck':

> The light is watery, like the light of the sea-bed;
> Marooned in it, stealthy as fishes, we may even be dead.

Norman Hampson's 'Assault Convoy' conveys the suspension of belief in the future necessitated by the imminence of possible death:

> Our future is unreal, a thing to read of
> Later; a chapter in a history book.

And later:

> We are dead, numbed, atrophied, sunk in the swamps of war.

Training in the RAF, Timothy Corsellis (killed in 1941) felt the stiffening atrophy as his squad practised drill:

> Forward and backward to the desperate drum
> Of the increasing madness
> The wheel whirl roll unfurl,
> Encroaches in the dead mind in a dying body,
> Eats further into the interior.

The ultimate life-in-death was of the prisoner of war. In a POW camp in Italy a captured South African war correspondent Uys Krige wrote:

> This is a dead world, a lost world and these are lost men, lost each in
> his own separate limbo, banished from his own memories, exiled even
> from himself. Here
> even dreams are dead.

The means of death itself seemed distant, the bomb aimed at a whole town, the gun fired at an unseen target. Alan Ross's 'Radar' concludes:

> Control is remote; feelings, like hands,
> Gloved by space. Responsibility is shared, too.
> And destroying the enemy by radar
> We never see what we do.

The intimacy of the static lines of trenches across the Western Front during the First War was supplanted by an abstraction. Barry Amiel calculated:

> Death is a matter of mathematics.
> It screeches down at you from dirtywhite nothingness
> And your life is a question of velocity and altitude,
> With allowances for wind and the quick, relentless pull
> Of gravity.

The results were no less destructive:

> Ten out of ten means you are dead.

On the positive side, the geographic character of the war meant that there was no repetition of the claustrophobic atmosphere of the trenches – though that has remained the characteristic image of war in the twentieth century. Instead, poets found themselves obliged to travel and to absorb fresh material, the theme, for instance, of Bernard Gutteridge's *Traveller's Eye* (1947). India had a particular impact, where the soldier was confronted not only by a strange scenery and climate, but an unfamiliar and politically hostile culture as well. But though travel produced fine poems such as Norman Cameron's 'Green, Green is El Aghir', there was also a tendency to see the sensuous reality of foreign places in terms of the abstraction of a map, a recurrent image rooted in the practical demands of warfare. Robert Medley's 'Egypt':

> Show me the palm of your hand,
> Consider, my friend, your fate drawn like a map.

Equally, travel inspired home thoughts from abroad. This is Trooper N.T. Morris's response to Mount Aetna:

> Coke mountain,
> Belched from the earth's bowels,
> Your steaming steeps
> Remind me of Wednesbury, Wigan,
> And slag
> On the South Yorkshire heaps.

Military circumstance created a chance culture in Egypt that is a near microcosm of literary life in London, complete with its mixture of soldiers and civilians, factions and decadence. The membership of this Bohemia was completely accidental. Terence Tiller, Bernard Spencer, John Spiers and Romilly Fedden were academics at Cairo University; others, Olivia Manning, Robert Liddell, Lawrence Durrell, had been working for the British Council in Greece and the Balkans and had been driven south by the German invasion. The exiled Greek government established itself at Alexandria; the poets George Seferis and Elie Papadimitrou linked up with the British exiles. The chances of war brought others from London – Hamish Henderson, G.S. Fraser, John Waller, Dorian Cooke, Keith Douglas. The nominal neutrality of Egypt created a sense of unreality that parallels the unreality of London; London's 'inner emigration' had its mirror image in the enforced exile of Cairo and Alexandria, encapsulated in the title given by Bernard Spencer and Lawrence Durrell to their magazine *Personal Landscape*. The cultural soil was sufficiently rich to support other magazines besides – *Salamander*, and Army-based publications like *Citadel* and *Parade*, though G.S. Fraser described his attempts to run *Orientations* as a monthly forum for soldiers as a complete failure, greeted with jeers from the civilian poets.

The accidental culture of Egypt involved a small number of people, a group of exiles thrown together by little more than the fact of their exile, and inevitably self-referring; Olivia Manning defended them against *Horizon*'s accusations of having lost touch:

> Whether willingly or not, they have become cosmopolitan; they have met and been influenced by refugee writers of other countries; they have learnt foreign languages not commonly learnt by English people and so absorbed new literatures. The character of poetry written out here may suffer from being outbred as that written in England during the same period may suffer from being inbred.

Lawrence Durrell's post-war sequence of novels, the 'Alexandria Quartet', is one product of the cross-currents of Egypt in wartime.

Under pressure from external events and the awareness that World War One had left a 'tradition', service poets restricted their gestures and shrugged off the responsibility that oppressed them. Jocelyn Brooke begins 'Embarkation Leave':

> Let me be honest, at least: I cannot evoke
> The appropriate and elegaic mood
> To suit the occasion;

and remarks 'The currency of emotion is inflated.' Roy Fuller rejects the role that tradition seemed to have forced on him:

> My photograph already looks historic.
> The promising youthful face, the matelot's collar,
> Say 'This one is remembered for a lyric.
> His place and period – nothing could be duller.'

Gavin Ewart's 'When a Beau Goes In' plays on the euphemisms for death and destruction in service slang, implying in laconic tones a mood of self-protection:

> When a Beau goes in,
> Into the drink,

It makes you think,
Because, you see, they always sink
But nobody says 'Poor lad'
Or goes about looking sad
Because, you see, it's war,
It's the unalterable law.

The service poet felt (like the majority of his unliterary comrades) anti-heroic and anti-lyrical. Wilfred Owen had said that all a poet could do was warn, but Donald Bain's Second World War poet was even more restricted:

We only watch, and indicate and make our scribbled pencil notes.
We do not wish to moralize, only to ease our dusty throats.

Such an attitude seems entirely justified. The refusal of excess, the concentration on saying accurately whatever it was felt *could* be said, the experience of action and the confrontation with the self that the presence of death provoked, constituted a discipline which gave the service poets an edge that others lacked. Keith Douglas expressed it very simply:

I don't know if you have come across the word Bullshit – it is an army word and signifies humbug and unnecessary detail. It symbolizes what I think must be got rid of – the mass of irrelevancies, of 'attitudes', 'approaches', propaganda, ivory towers, etc., that stand between us and our problems and what we have to do about them. To write on the themes which have been concerning me lately in lyric or abstract forms would be immense bullshitting.

Four service poets in particular exemplify the themes not just of war poetry but of poetry in wartime: Sidney Keyes, Alun Lewis, Keith Douglas and Roy Fuller. There is nothing original in the choice of these four; their reputations have long been established; the standard of their work (and the fact that there is sufficient from which to form a judgment) justifies their position. However, each individually illustrates the problem of being a poet in wartime in a distinctive way. Two at least sought through their military conduct a resolution to what they saw as poetic problems.

To begin with, the first of these, and the first to be killed, Sidney Keyes, was not a poet of war, simply someone killed while in the services. Of the four he is the clearest exponent of the romantic reaction to the 1930s, a position that might have changed if he had been given more time and more experience. Born in 1922, he was still at school when war broke out, going up to Oxford in the autumn of 1940. Though they constitute his major themes, the death and pain in Keyes's work are psychological, not literal.

Keyes's talent as a poet was recognized while he was still an undergraduate. Oxford in wartime was a contradictory city; the town was taken over by ministries evacuated from London; the nearby motor factories and aerodromes were very much at war; but the University did its best to concentrate on what it regarded as its proper work. Wartime students were in a difficult position; they knew that they could be there for but a short time, and it was hard to concentrate with the certainty that call-up papers would suddenly plunge them into the middle of the war. Until that day came the only thing to do was to contrive to ignore the war.

The result was that for students Oxford was an unreal place, 'stifling as a cocoon, and noisy with trivialities', as a friend of Keyes put it. In this unreal city Keyes did as he would have done in peacetime: worked, punted on the river, fell in love unhappily, put on plays, edited the student magazine *Cherwell*. Beyond that, he continued to develop as a poet.

The first result was *Eight Oxford Poets*, for whom Keyes acted as spokesman. (The others were Heath-Stubbs, Drummond Allison, Keith Douglas, J.A. Shaw, Gordon Swaine, Roy Porter and Keyes's co-editor Michael Meyer.) Keyes wrote: 'We are all, with the possible exception of Shaw, *Romantic* writers, though by that I mean little more than that our greatest fault is a tendency to floridity; and that we have, on the whole, little sympathy with the Audenian school of poets.' Keyes is speaking principally for Heath-Stubbs and Allison – Douglas had left Oxford by the time Keyes arrived. Drummond Allison was killed in 1943, and only a posthumous volume, *The Yellow Night* (1944), remains as evidence of his potential. John Heath-Stubbs's poor eyesight kept him out of the Forces; *Wounded Thammuz* (1942) shows that collectively they were evolving a metaphysical poetry that explored man's psychological states through myth and symbol – though stopping short at what Keyes called 'the present trend towards a new and overwrought Romanticism' of the Apocalyptics.

The poetic interests, however, are similar: Blake, Wordsworth, Keats, Yeats, Schiller, Hölderlin, Rilke, Romanticism amplified by the psychological symbolism of Surrealism. Heath-Stubbs has said in an interview: 'We didn't mind a poem being obscure provided it worked on the emotional level.' Rilke had special appeal, for the Rilkean theme that each man carries his own death within himself seemed particularly appropriate to Keyes's condition – as to many others:

The Romantics raised a spectre they could not lay; it was, broadly speaking, death as a part of life, conceived in terms of sensual imagery . . . it has resulted in a clearly apparent *Death Wish*, as the only solution to the problem – since the solution must come in sensual terms. It was left to necrophilious Germany, to Rilke in fact, to provide the best solution short of actually dying.

Sensuality and death, a Keatsian 'half in love with easeful death', are the themes of Keyes's 'Remember Your Lovers':

> Young men walking the open streets
> Of death's republic, remember your lovers.
>
> When you foresaw with vision prescient
> The planet pain rising across your sky
> We fused your sight in our soft burning beauty:
> We laid you down in meadows drunk with cowslips
> And led you in the ways of our bright city.
> Young men who wander death's vague meadows,
> Remember your lovers who gave you more than flowers.

It was not that Keyes, or any other member of his generation wanted to die, but that they felt condemned: 'We are all beating our heads against a wall, without purpose or result.'

Keyes's first individual collection of poems *The Iron Laurel* was ready for the printer in January 1942, but, possibly because he knew that his call-up was near, Keyes held back until he had completed a long, speculative poem 'The Foreign Gate', which tries to set the fact of death in war in perspective. The gate in question is the entrance to the metaphorical cemetery of the after-life, where the dead of present and past wars become, like lovers or the natural elements, part of the myth of a perpetual duality of life and death, their condition resolved by the continuity of the pattern. The war was forcing itself on Keyes's attention, and it was just before his papers finally came that he formally acknowledged, with unease, the role that he was expected to play:

War Poet

I am the man who looked for peace and found
My own eyes barbed.
I am the man who groped for words and found
An arrow in my hand.

In the Army Keyes found himself having to fight off the numbness that military training induced. He wrote of the Army

reducing everyone to an artificial object; and I am sometimes frightened by the fact that it achieves this object so easily. I am not yet myself reduced to the (literally) dead level, and hope not to be. But already, I find it necessary to think continually, 'I am not a man but a voice. My only justification is my power of speaking clearly. Therefore it doesn't matter in the least what happens to my body; in fact, the body exists to be given, not to be owned. The gift is equally valid, whether to a gun or a lover.'

His argument shows Keyes transforming the present as it were into a symbol for some higher reality. The poems of his second collection, *The Cruel Solstice* (1944), reflect some of the impact of Army life, poems inspired by places encountered during training, imagery of barbed wire and gun, but his method was still to turn immediate conditions into myth. Thus the routine of guard duty becomes the ritual of religion, 'Two Offices of a Sentry'. Death remained an archetype rather than an actuality, for it was not until March 1943 that he was sent on active service.

The manuscript of *The Cruel Solstice* was with his publishers before his battalion embarked for Algeria to take part in the last stages of the battle for North Africa. Death caught up with Keyes quickly enough. Just over two weeks after he entered the front line for the first time, he was killed in unexplained circumstances during the battle for Hill 133 on the Medjez Road. The poems he was working on disappeared.

Alun Lewis was allowed more time, both as a man and a poet, for he was able to develop and change his attitude to war in a way that Keyes was not. Born in 1915, a Welshman, the son of a schoolmaster, he had studied at University College, Aberystwyth, and Manchester University, and experimented with journalism before himself becoming a teacher. His first poems had been published in the *Observer* and *Time and Tide* in 1937, so that he was altogether more experienced than Keyes, though still very uncertain of his attitude to the war. In

126

1937 he had felt that he was a pacifist, and in 1939 considered registering as a Conscientious Objector before finally volunteering as a non-combatant clerk with the Royal Engineers. Hardly an appropriate start for the man whom Herbert Read was to call 'the Rupert Brooke of this war'.

Though several poems written during the early part of his training register the boredom and discomfort of Army life, and its deadening effect – 'The Sentry' begins: 'I have begun to die' – Lewis felt a growing commitment, intensified by his having to care for survivors from Dunkirk. 'After Dunkirk' records that he has found his voice again, and a renewed purpose, but it is the Army's purpose, and therein is contained the paradox of self-sacrifice. He adjusts to and accepts the circumstances, however,

> as the crystal slowly forms,
> A growing self-detachment making man
> Less home-sick, fearful, proud,
> But less a man.

Having unsuccessfully applied for a transfer to the Education Corps, Lewis decided early in 1941 to apply for training as an infantry officer. At the same time publication in *Horizon* of a poem written early in his Army career 'All Day it has rained' attracted attention from those who were looking for evidence that war poetry *was* being written, and Allen and Unwin offered to publish a collection. The direct observation of soldiers 'sprawled in our bell-tents, moody and dull as boors', the poet's nostalgia and regret and the exactly placed final reference to the First World War poet Edward Thomas seemed to set the tone for the unheroic – yet none the less mortal – poets of the Second. In March 1942 Allen and Unwin published *Raiders' Dawn* with the claim 'The War Poet has arrived at last!'

In fact 'war poems' form only a part of *Raiders' Dawn*, there are romantic and metaphysical poems on themes from literature, and love poems for his wife Gweno, but the drier tones of those describing Army life are the most distinctive:

> We are the little men grown huge with death.
> Stolid in squads or grumbling on fatigues,
> We held the honour of the regiment
> And stifled our antipathies.

His second collection *Ha! Ha! Among the Trumpets* (1945) covers the period of his preparation to go to India with his regiment at the end

127

of 1942, the journey by troopship, and finally India itself. The tone is more consistent, a withdrawn and contemplative lyric as he leaves his wife for exile overseas. But though becoming an officer did not make him any less critical of the prejudice and inefficiency in the Officers' Mess (see his story 'Almost a Gentleman' on his officer training), Lewis felt that the war was something that required a commitment, or at least an act of acceptance. He recorded in his journal that he had told his wife just before embarkation:

> I say we must lose ourselves in the war and go each into the unknown and neither of us must cling to a past memory or a future hope but we must give to the world and suffer the world and become its accidents, and so grow rich.

It is difficult to tell whether by suffering the world Lewis meant a positive sacrifice or a negative surrender – he later wrote 'Acceptance seems so spiritless, protest so vain. In between the two I live' – but his journal and his actions in India confirm what he had forecast, 'the restless writer in me will probably impel me to abandon neutrality and seek in India as in England the true story and the proper ending'. The reward was the poems written in India. Soldiering plays only a minor part; the country itself is the theme, a colourful wasteland, seductive and appalling at the same time:

> The dwarf barefooted, chanting
> Behind the oxen by the lake,
> Stepping lightly and lazily among the thorntrees
> Dusky and dazed by sunlight, half awake;
>
> The women breaking stones upon the highway,
> Walking erect with burdens on their heads,
> One body growing in another body,
> Creation touching verminous straw beds.
>
> Across the scorched hills and trampled crops
> The soldiers straggle by.
> History staggers in their wake.
> The peasants watch them die.

But to observe India and record it was not enough, it is as though Lewis wished to close the implied gap between the country and the soldiers sent to trail across it. Given the chance of a safe job as an instructor, Lewis preferred to remain a combat officer. He told

Robert Graves, who was advising him on his work: 'I wanted something more: I wanted to fuse finite and infinite, in action.' A letter to
another friend shows that he wanted the experience of action to give
him, in his own word, 'authority':

> I want to run the gamut; and it's quite a mature wish, too; it isn't for
> the thrill of it nor the horror of it, though both these attract. It's for two
> reasons – to have authority in the long fight for peace and to share the
> comradeship of war, and of death.

While waiting for his regiment to be sent into action in Burma,
Lewis wrote 'The Jungle', a poem which synthesized several of his
themes, and which, only because of the accident of war, becomes a
kind of conclusion. The jungle, exotic and menacing, is the setting for
a meditation on the national and personal motives that have caused a
group of soldiers (though they are never described as such) to have
arrived to rest beside a jungle pool. In comparison with the political
and economic realities of the West, the jungle seems temporarily
paradisical.

> we who dream beside this jungle pool
> Prefer the instinctive rightness of the poised
> Pied kingfisher deep darting for a fish
> To all the banal rectitudes of states,

Yet in spite of the ease induced by sleep there is still an inner threat,
the menace of corruption within each individual heart:

> And though the state has enemies we know
> The greater enmity within ourselves.

Lewis turns to the power of love, the ever-present danger of the
failure of love, and finally to death. The service poets' theme of
death-in-life, 'We are the ghosts . . .', modulates into a contemplation
of death as action (ambiguously, the death of others or ourselves),
death as release, death almost, it seems, as an act of love:

> And if the mute pads on the sand should lift
> Annihilating paws and strike us down
> Then would some unimportant death resound
> With the imprisoned music of the soul?
> And we become the world we could not change?
> Or does the will's long struggle end
> With the last kindness of a foe or friend?

'The Jungle' is not, of course, a true conclusion; it marks the stage Lewis has reached in his search for a fusion of finite and infinite when, after only a few days in the forward area, he died in a pistol accident.

Keith Douglas saw action, and survived long enough to be able to write about it in both prose and verse which manifests the change he knew that action would bring about. 'I enlisted in September 1939, and during the two years or so of hanging about I never lost the certainty that the experience of battle was something I must have. Whatever changes in the nature of warfare, the battlefield is the simple, central stage of the war: it is there that the interesting things happen.' Douglas had shown promise as a poet – and as a draughts-man – while still at school. *New Verse* published one of his poems, written when he was sixteen. In 1938 he went up to Merton College, Oxford. The mixture of aesthetic and athletic interests in his character (he joined the University Officer Training Corps for the riding) reminds one of his contemporary Richard Hillary; so too does his self-confident and questioning attitude to authority.

Douglas's early poems are lyrical and romantic, but his drive was to follow the principle of poetry he had laid down in *Augury: An Oxford Miscellany of Verse and Prose* (1940): 'In its nature poetry is sincere and simple.' 'Invaders', written in 1939, which begins,

> Intelligences like black birds
> come on their dire wings from Europe,

looks into a bleak future, and suggests that he is preparing to give up a romantic attitude:

> I shall never write a word to escape,
> our life will take on a hard shape;

He already wonders if he will survive, and 'Canoe', written in 1940, hints that he will not. He begins:

> Well, I am thinking that this may be my last
> summer,

The conclusion justly mixes lyrical sadness and precise description:

> Whistle and I will hear
> and come another evening, when this boat
>
> travels with you alone towards Iffley:
> as you lie looking up for thunder again,

130

        this cool touch does not betoken rain;
        it is my spirit that kisses your mouth lightly.

Keyes's 'Remember your lovers' has the same particularly Oxford note of sensual nostalgia.

Douglas did not begin his military training until July 1940, joining a mechanized regiment as a Second Lieutenant in February 1941. In June he sailed for the Middle East. Just before he left England he wrote a poem which, though there is no direct reference to being a writer, may be considered as his variation on the 'war poet' theme:

        Remember me when I am dead
        and simplify me when I'm dead.

Douglas accepts the distancing that time will give to judgments on him, and invites the reader to make his decision on those terms: 'see if I seem/substance or nothing'. The verdict is left to the reader, but he still asks to be remembered – and he is certain that he will die.

Though now in the Middle East, and in a position to describe 'a new world/the vegetation is of iron/dead tanks, gun barrels split like celery', a job as a staff camouflage officer kept Douglas out of the front line. Instead, his observations were of the flora and fauna of Cairo's corrupt society. In October 1942, as the British went over on to the offensive at El Alamein, Douglas disobeyed orders and re-joined his regiment. Having already lost a number of officers in battle, they welcomed this strictly irregular replacement. Douglas was given a tank, and took part in the pursuit of Rommel's forces as far as Bu Ngem, when the regiment was badly mauled and Douglas was wounded. After three months of hospital and convalescence, he rejoined outside Enfidaville, but the North African campaign ended with the German surrender a week later. His account of his part in the campaign, *Alamein to Zem Zem*, was published in 1946. It is a firm and straightforward record of the strengths and weaknesses of himself and his fellow officers, 'direct and simple', as he intended his poetry to be.

'I never tried to write about war (that is battles and things, not London can Take it), with the exception of a satiric picture of some soldiers frozen to death, until I had experienced it. Now I will write of it, and perhaps one day lyric and cynic will meet and make me a balanced style.' This is Douglas writing to a former Oxford friend, the poet John Hall, in August 1943. In May he had written an essay on why: 'In the fourth year of this war we have not a single poet who seems likely to be an impressive commentator on it', arguing that the poets of the Great War had already described the battlefield so impressively that: 'Almost all that a modern poet on active service is inspired to write, would be tautological.' But his experience had given him that 'authority' which Lewis had been seeking.

> Three weeks gone and the combatants gone,
> returning over the nightmare ground
> we found the place again, and found
> the soldier sprawling in the sun.

The description of the dead German anti-tank gunner in 'Vergissmeinicht' achieves the directness and simplicity he was aiming for:

> We see him almost with content
> abased, and seeming to have paid
> and mocked at by his own equipment
> that's hard and good when he's decayed.

'Vergissmeinicht' – forget-me-not – is the message on the photograph of the dead gunner's girlfriend found in the litter of the gunpit, and Douglas ends with a metaphysical conceit that – as Lewis had done – links love and death:

> For here the lover and killer are mingled
> who had one body and one heart.
> And death who had the soldier singled
> has done the lover mortal hurt.

In November 1943 Douglas's regiment embarked for England to prepare for the coming invasion of Europe. In the meantime his reputation had been growing, thanks to publication in *Eight Oxford Poets* and a joint volume with John Hall and Norman Nicholson, *Selected Poems*. Tambimuttu reprinted some of his poems from the Oxford and Cambridge magazine *Fords and Bridges* in *Poetry* (*London*) Nos 7 and 8, offering him a contract for a book while he was still in the Middle East. He had also contributed to *Citadel* in Cairo, and *Personal Landscape*. Back in England in December he signed a contract with Nicholson and Watson for a collection to be called *Bête Noire*, illustrated with his own drawings. Tambimuttu was happy to involve him in the life of the London pubs, but Douglas's biographer says he preferred the office, wanting to get his business settled. (Nothing was done about the collection until 1951, when John Waller and G.S. Fraser got Tambimuttu's permission to edit it.)

In England Douglas was fully occupied with training, and he seems to have been certain that in the next campaign he would be killed. His last complete poem 'On a Return from Egypt' begins, 'To stand here in the wings of Europe/disheartened', and concludes with the decision to go forward towards the lover/killer he must meet:

> The next month, then, is a window
> and with a crash I'll split the glass.
> Behind it stands one I must kiss,
> person of love or death
> a person or a wraith,
> I fear what I shall find.

Douglas landed in Normandy on D Day and was killed on 9 June.

Roy Fuller, happily, has survived, so that we are at least free from the distortion imposed by having to consider only a snapped-off career; Fuller has continued to develop as a poet and a novelist since 1945. Instead, there is the other distortion, that the poet's ideas now are not what they were then. Fuller is a different subject for consideration in other ways as well. He was older than Douglas, Keyes or Lewis, being twenty-seven when the war began; he was married and working as a solicitor, and his poetry had had time to mature in the immediately pre-war period. He had been a contributor to *New Verse*, and his first collection *Poems* was published in 1939. At that time he was considered to be a junior member of the Auden generation who had not quite found a distinctive voice. The war helped him to find it.

Associated with the 1930s, Fuller shared his contemporaries' commitment to Marxism, though, like C. Day Lewis, he had gradually withdrawn from active support. He has written: 'I was just as critically rigid in 1939 as I expect I was when I first discovered Marxist writings, but I had not been active in politics for more than three years.' Unlike some other members of his generation, he did not have any doubts as to whether the war was for a purified cause:

Many felt at the time that it was wrong to opt out of action. In my own case, it seemed unarguable in the very early years of the decade that the intellectual should join non-intellectuals in quite ordinary political activity on the left; and at the end of the decade there seemed no reason except personal cowardice for trying to opt out of service in the armed forces. On the contrary: one felt one ought to be on hand in the services to help to resolve on the right lines any crisis arising in the State, an eventuality that seemed, in 1939 and 1940, quite likely.

It was only later, after the war, that his view of his political obligations changed. In the event Fuller did not experience the physical aspects of action which confronted Douglas or Keyes – in his own words he had 'the disadvantages of noise and gregariousness without the stimulant of action' – but in many other ways his poetry reflects the themes of others in the services.

Fuller probably saw more violent destruction at first hand while still a civilian during the Blitz; his 'Soliloquy in an Air-Raid' states what was to become the central problem of his wartime work: how does the poet, by education sensitive to the values of civilization, and by conviction committed to political change, confront the necessary brutality of warfare without losing hold of the values which he embodies as a poet?

> Ordered this year:
> A billion tons of broken glass and rubble,
> Blockades of chaos, the other requisites
> For the reduction of Europe to a rabble.
> Who can observe this save as a frightened child
> Or careful diarist? And who can speak
> And still retain the tones of this civilization?

The question is at least partly answered further on in the 'Soliloquy', when Fuller accepts that willingly or not he must become an actor in the drama, and that a commitment is called for:

> It is goodbye
> To the social life which permitted melancholy
> And madness in the isolation of its writers,

One part of that commitment was to the poet as recorder – it is noticeable how many of Fuller's titles are chosen dates – as a man a participator, as a poet a recorder. Appropriately, 'Soliloquy in an Air-Raid' is followed almost immediately by 'ABC of a Naval Trainee', for in April 1941 Fuller was called up into the Royal Navy. The poem shows Fuller adapting to the laconic, self-protecting mood of service life:

A is the anger we hide with some danger,
Keeping it down like the twentieth beer.
B is the boredom we feel in this bedlam.
C is the cautious and supervised cheer.

In Fuller's case the self-protection includes self-protection as a
poet, the rejection of the role of war poet quoted earlier: 'This one
is remembered for a lyric./His place and period – nothing could be
duller.' The grandiose gesture towards the absolutes 'Freedom',
'Good' and 'Duty' that seems called for by the Chaplain in 'Spring
1942' is impossible in the face of the reality of the servicemen's life:

And we made no reply to that
Obscure, remote communication,
But only stared at where the flat
Meadow dissolved in vegetation.

And thought: O sick, insatiable
And constant lust; O death, our future;
O revolution in the whole
Of human use of man and nature!

Though it is the Chaplain's remarks that are described as obscure and
remote, the landscape of the poem suggests that it is the servicemen
(Fuller writes in the first person plural) who are cut off from the
world, their minds on lust and death, in that state of death-in-life
noted before.

Shortly after writing 'Spring 1942' Fuller was drafted to East
Africa, where he served as a radar technician for the Fleet Air Arm,
rising to the rank of Petty Officer. The move brings out strongly two
further themes of service poetry: the impact of travel, the loneliness
of separation. They appear together in 'In Africa', the opening poem
of his second wartime collection, appropriately titled *A Lost Season*
(1944). *The Middle of a War* had been published in 1942.

Just as the lives of lions now are made
Shabby with rifles,
This great geography shrinks into sad
And personal trifles.

For those who are in love and are exiled
Can never discover
How to be happy:

135

The theme of longing for his wife is reinforced in the following poem 'The photographs', in which pornographic pictures stimulate authentic memories, yet somehow empty them, leaving the unreal lust of the photographs. It concludes 'it seems to me/Our faces, bodies – both of us – are dead.'

The flora and fauna of Africa contribute fresh images to Fuller's poems, but at the same time they are seen at a distance (often literally so), and the landscape is reduced to an abstraction:

> Like small forked twigs or insects move
> Giraffes, upon the great map where they live.

Fuller does not, however, neglect his obligation to social commentary, specifically on the destructive effect of the West on African life, which is violent and superstitious, yet formerly sustained in a balance now upset. 'The Tribes' concludes:

> The most horrible things you can imagine are
> Happening in the towns and the most senseless:
> There are no kings or poison,
> Are laws but no more reason.

Fulfilling as he was two roles, as observer and participator, the effect of service life on Fuller was to narrow his poetic perception to a series of intense visions, so reducing the possibility of making a wider statement. 'October 1942' explores the difficulty of recording anything beyond momentary perceptions; 'Sadness, Glass, Theory' tries to break out:

> Cast up by war upon this freakishly
> Quiet and neutral shore I should deliver
> A statement, a summing up, an integration
> Of all the passion, boredom, history,
> Of all the suddenly important lives;

But the very neutrality of his geographical location is a figure for the location of the poet in time. The future is a theory, the past a sad memory, and the present is only an occasional brief intensity. And even then the role of participator is more significant than the recorder's:

> There is a time when on reality
> The vision fits, and sadness, glass and theory
> Fuse and, as easily as squadrons clear
> The sky, the mass directs its destiny.

> The integration is the action, I
> Can only scribble on the margin:

Lewis and Douglas sought their integration in action; the man as actor acquired authority on behalf of the man as poet. Excluded from action, Fuller tried to overcome the difficulty by confessing it. For the most part the serviceman's life is boredom, not history-making, in a world organized for destruction (see 'What is Terrible'), and the poet's experience is reduced, as in 'The Petty Officer's Mess', to 'small stabbing observations!'

The obligation to perceive and record, however, remains; and *A Lost Season* concludes with a heroic attempt to relate the roles of participator and observer. 'Winter in England' (later called 'Winter in Camp') is a sequence of nine sonnets written at a shore station after Fuller returned from East Africa in November 1943. (Fuller was made an officer and ended the war at the Admiralty.) The fact that they are nine short pieces emphasizes the restricted field available to the poet; the fact that they are a sequence shows that he is trying to build up a broader picture with small touches.

The first two sonnets are such individual moments of intense vision; the third opens the problem of relating these moments to the broader historical context:

> Beyond the word, the chosen images,
> Painful and moving as they are, I feel
> Unutterably the epoch's tragedies,
> Beside which this scene's cruelties are real
> But hopelessly inadequate; like the pities
> Of living airmen borne above smashed cities.

'Unutterably' is an important adverb, for Fuller goes on in the following sonnet to protest at the difficulty of making a judgment, plunged as he is in the middle of his subject, 'Nor can I think in discipline and slime'.

The war and the disciplines of war affect others besides himself, and Fuller turns to the subject of his fellow servicemen caught in the ambiguous crux: 'Now man must be political or die.' (Is this an answer to Auden's 'We must love one another or die'?) On the one hand man must organize himself politically, act *en masse*, yet politics as practised 'is an enormous lie'. Sonnets seven and eight counter with realities of political necessity:

> What does the robin whisper and the trees,
> Expressive of wind and winter, round this coast,
> The hanging coat which might contain a ghost?
> Only plain words like *oil* and *manganese*.

Finally the poet returns to his service companions, employed in a boring menial task. Fuller sees them as easily fooled, easily led, yet he identifies himself with them:

> Their weakness is the measure of
> My own; their guilt my own inactive past;
> Their stormy future mine, who wish that love
> Could melt the guns, expropriate a caste.
> How, when my only rank is consciousness,
> Can I despise them, far less pity, bless?

As in the case of 'Sadness, Glass, Theory', Fuller at least partly resolves the problem by describing it. He may conclude with a question about his right to judge his fellow-men who do not, it is clear, experience the 'small stabbing observations' of the poet, but the diffidence is a sign of compassion. He wishes to 'melt the guns, expropriate a caste', but perceives the difficulty of moving from consciousness to action. The sequence communicates the physical and mental impositions of service life and wartime, and manages to transcend them, so that we do find:

> A statement, a summing up, an integration
> Of all the passion, boredom, history,
> Of all the suddenly important lives;

Fuller had the advantage of greater maturity on his fellow service poets; further, though a figure of the 1930s, he did not lose his nerve.

Sidney Keyes was a youthful poet killed before he had time to register the impact of warfare; Alun Lewis registered the deadening effect of regimentation and the stimulus of travel, but left no record of the military action it seems it was his destiny to seek. Keith Douglas sought action, found it, recorded it and his fear of its consequences, before he too died. Roy Fuller was excluded by circumstance from action and was able, literally from a distance, to mark the changes that wartime forced on society and the enclosed microcosm of the services. Each is an individual experience, and it is because of the quality of their work that they are accepted as the chief poets of the Second World War. But it is appropriate that none of them wrote the *poem* of the Second World War. That was written by Henry Reed.

As Vernon Scannell has said, 'It is a curious fact that what is probably the most widely quoted and anthologized single poem written in the Second World War came from the pen of some one who served only a few months in the Army before being released to work at the Foreign Office.' A journalist before the war, Henry Reed was called up in 1941 and released in 1942. The three poems for which he is celebrated are collectively known as 'The Lessons of War', and they reflect that period of transition when the poet still has the sensibilities of a civilian, but is uncomfortably encased in the uniform of a soldier. The titles of the individual poems are taken from the vocabulary of Basic Training: 'Naming of Parts', 'Judging Distances', and 'Unarmed Combat'.

There are two voices in the poems, that of the professional soldier instructor, and that of the ex-civilian trainee. The civilian turns military language of description into a metaphor for the artist's perennial difficulty. 'Judging Distances' begins with the military/poetic problem:

> Not only how far away, but the way that you say it
> Is very important. Perhaps you may never get
> The knack of judging a distance, but at least you know
> How to report on a landscape:

In this case the landscape has to be interpreted in formal terms; the distance cannot be judged emotionally, the territory must be seen as a map. But in the trainee-soldier the surviving civilian persists in reading the topography with his own eyes:

> The still white dwellings are like a mirage in the heat,
> And under the swaying elms a man and a woman
> Lie gently together. Which is, perhaps, only to say
> That there is a row of houses to the left of arc,
> And that under some poplars a pair of what appear to be humans
> Appear to be loving.

Here we have the isolation of the soldiers who must survey the landscape impassively as a target, the alienation of the civilian cut off by the recitation of military ritual from the world of feeling.

The modulations between the harsh direct speech of the instructor and the interior eloquence of the trainee reflect the transition from peace of a generation called upon to fight a 'people's war'. Individuality has to be sacrificed to the needs of the military machine, the landscape reduced to the terms of tactical necessity, but some small item of personality could be retained – the observing eye of the poet. War, literally, imposed concrete imagery, so that the interplay had to be between things as they fiercely were and, with laconic humour, things as they might be. Thus Henry Reed achieves a rare fusion between soldier and poet of the Second World War in the conclusion to 'Unarmed Combat':

> Things may be the same again; and we must fight
> Not in the hope of winning but rather of keeping
> Something alive; so that when we meet our end,
> It may be said that we tackled wherever we could
> That battle-fit we lived, and though defeated,
> Not without glory fought.

There are, unfortunately, other reasons beside the positive ones that have been suggested, for saying that Henry Reed's is the poem of the Second World War. Though it expresses best the type of poem stimulated by the war, and thus is typical (in the proper sense) of all the others, it is untypical of the rest of Henry Reed's work. There are no other poems in his single volume *A Map of Verona* (1946) which attempt the synthesis of military and personal reference that makes 'The Lessons of War' such a distinctive achievement. And the fact that Henry Reed has published but one volume is also significant. Though not uncreative since the war (writing a series of radio plays, adaptations and translations), poetically he has been virtually silent. Typical in a less welcome way.

Others, of course, have not been silent, have found their voices since the war: Vernon Scannell, who fought in Normandy but seems to have turned back to his war experiences only in the 1950s; Gerry Wells, who also fought in the battle for France and Germany, but who did not publish *Obie's War* until 1975, and Alan Ross, who found fresh inspiration when he discovered an old notebook which had been tucked away in a drawer for twenty-five years. *Open Sea* (1975) collects poetry published in wartime, and material which he wanted to use then, 'but simply didn't know how'. *Open Sea* is a reminder that 'war poetry' and the experience of war do not end arbitrarily in 1945, and that the Second World War, like the First, haunts modern memory.

140

CHAPTER SEVEN

Our Time

*'What, then, has been the
distinctive cultural expression
of the English genius during
the years 1939 to 1941?...
The answer is "light music".'*

C.E.M. Joad

In 1939 writers were numbed with shock as the literary world col-
laped around them; painters seem to have been far less disturbed.
Conscription, shortages, uncertainty and the general disruption of
life affected them as much as anybody, but whereas the government
became interested in literature only in order to tax it, steps were taken
immediately to ensure that art should be the responsibility of an
official organization, the War Artists Advisory Committee, chaired
by the distinguished patron of contemporary art and Director of the
National Gallery, Sir Kenneth Clark. Writing in the 1943 jubilee
number of *The Studio*, the Director of the Tate Gallery, John
Rothenstein, argued that the war had done a service to English
painting:

British artists have been strongly affected by the spectacle of the present
war and official patronage has given them every occasion to express their
feelings and has even pointed the way to themes which have evoked in
them an earnest response. As a result many artists who might have seemed,
before the war, to have cultivated an esoteric vision, have found, in their
reactions to the war, a common ground of contact with the public, thus
narrowing the lamentable rift which had tended in the years between the
wars to place the artist, increasingly immersed in theory or the curiosity of
his personality, in a position of unprecedented isolation.

This was not simply the official view. The young left-wing painter Graham Bell commented in October 1940 that after war broke out 'English painting flourished as it had not done since the gay boom years of the Twenties. . . . For a time it seemed as though the golden age had come.' With the arrival of the Blitz the picture became grimmer but, excepting Christie's Sale Rooms, the art trade survived the winter of 1940–1 without major damage. In August 1942 *Time and Tide* reported 'There are almost as many pictures to be seen in London today as in peace-time.' Most of those pictures were contemporary. The country's art collections lay in vaults and mines, although Sir Kenneth Clark introduced the practice of bringing one old master to the National Gallery at a time, as a reminder of what could not be shown.

The rest of the empty rooms of the National Gallery were gradually filled with paintings bought by the War Artists Advisory Committee on behalf of the Ministry of Information. More than a hundred artists received commissions from the Committee, some two hundred had works bought in, and thirty artists had full-time salaries. It is a sign of the national character of the war that artists were sent to paint coal mines and factories as well as ships and Major-Generals. Naturally, government practice extended to the administration of the arts. John Armstrong's commission to paint the construction of Mosquito fighter-bombers included third-class rail travel, £1 a day for subsistence, and the stipulation that all sketches and the finished painting should be submitted for censorship. (The fee was thirty guineas.)

Official permission was needed in order to paint out of doors at all. In September 1940 Keith Vaughan was attracted by the visual possibilities of a tank trap outside Guildford. The officer in charge did not object to Vaughan setting up his easel, but the police took a different view. Vaughan was arrested, his mother's flat in London was raided at two a.m., and he spent eight days in prison waiting for trial. (Vaughan was a conscientious objector, which made his interest in landscape all the more suspicious.) The outcome was a fine of £25 and confiscation of the half-finished painting. It had been produced as evidence in court; Vaughan commented, 'the first picture of mine ever to be publicly exhibited'.

Although the practice of commissioning works and buying up others helped to keep painters going, the fact that this was 'official art' somehow crept into the pictures themselves. At first there was little of excitement to record, except such stirring images as *Auxiliary Firemen at Tea,* by the official ARP artist Robert Medley. Leonard Rosoman's *House Collapsing on Two Firemen, Shoe Lane* (Plate 20), bought by the War Artists Advisory Committee for £30 at 'The Firemen's Exhibition' at the Royal Academy in 1941, is a notable exception to the static quality of most official art.

Even when air-raid and battle-field had produced the necessary raw material, the resulting pictures continued to disappoint. The critic Jan Gordon commented when a further room of Ministry of Information pictures was opened at the National Gallery in October 1943:

> The pictures are capable and in many ways excellent, but as the collection grows, a conviction becomes increasingly strong that something is lacking from many of them, and that lack seems to be an expression of war consciousness. Every time one goes to the National Gallery saying to oneself: 'Have they yet discovered anybody new who can give us a real feeling that war is not just a sleek business which an artist can contemplate without his stomach turning within him?'

A more imaginative and successful scheme was sponsored at the beginning of the war by the American-funded Pilgrim Trust. Assuming that many artists would be immediately thrown out of work, the Pilgrim Trust began 'Recording Britain', a project to record as much as possible of Britain's architectural and natural beauties before war destroyed them. The scheme ran until 1943, and gave work to a wide variety of draughtsmen and water-colourists. In practice the work fell to those who wanted to do it and were good at it, while the unemployed proved to be so because they had insufficient talent. The invitation to reconsider the English countryside had its effect on more than one artist employed on the scheme.

There were, of course, exceptions to the general dullness of the official productions. John Piper was greatly influenced by his work for the 'Recording Britain' series. Between 1940 and 1945 Stanley Spencer produced a striking sequence of nine large paintings of ship-building at Port Glasgow on the Clyde, the most ambitious works commissioned by the War Artists Advisory Committee. In the early part of the war Paul Nash painted a series of zoomorphic pictures of aircraft for the RAF (predictably, there were objections to the liberties he took with their appearance). Graham Sutherland was employed as an official artist from 1940 until the end of the war, effectively recording the surreal destructiveness of the bombing (Plate 27). Moore made an immediate impression with his shelter drawings – but Moore's work is a case in point. The shelter drawings were begun spontaneously, only later were they taken up officially. A formal commission followed to draw in a coal mine at Castleford, and Moore has admitted that the latter are less successful. 'The shelter drawings came about after first being moved by the experience of them, whereas the coal-mine drawings were more in the nature of a commission coldly approached.' A later project to draw at the Bomb Museum was abandoned altogether.

London's tiny *avant garde* of painters was broken up and dispersed by the war, while at the same time England was cut off from the Continent, the energy-source of the modern movement. Refugee artists like Piet Mondrian moved on to America; others who stayed were interned for a time. Ben Nicholson and Barbara Hepworth, the chief exponents of abstract constructivism, moved to Cornwall, and the period of intense activity that had centred on the Mall Studios off Parkhill Road in Hampstead came to an end. Herbert Read, who also had a studio there, moved to Suffolk. Henry Moore took over Nicholson's studio at the beginning of the war, but worked mainly at Much Hadham in Hertfordshire, having been forced to give up his cottage in Surrey when it became part of a restricted area. In October the Mall Studios were damaged by bombing. Paul Nash moved to Oxford in 1939. Ivon Hitchens, bombed out in August 1940, moved to a caravan plunged in the middle of a thicket on land he owned at Lavington Common in Sussex – in Patrick Heron's phrase 'to paint the war out'. Stephen Bone, Richard Carline and Roland Penrose were among those who became involved in camouflage. Conscription gradually absorbed the younger artists into the services.

The effect of dispersal and isolation from the Continent was to turn British art back on itself, rather as poets and writers turned to introspection. In fact a reaction against the pervasive influence of French painting had already set in before the war began. In the 1930s the two strands of Continental modernism, Surrealism and Abstractionism, had been reflected in the loose and overlapping associations that had formed around the Seven and Five Group, Unit One (1933–4), the magazines *Axis* (1935–7) and *Circle* (1937) and the International Surrealist Exhibition in London in 1936. While Abstractionism and Surrealism continued to have influence, younger painters felt that they had been led into a *cul de sac*, and that the only way out was back. The early part of the war saw this reaction in the brief flowering of the Euston Road School.

The Euston Road School literally was a school, set up originally at 12 Fitzroy Street in 1937, and transferring to 316 Euston Road in 1938. Its prime movers, William Coldstream, Claude Rogers, Victor Pasmore and Graham Bell, had all experimented with abstract work (for instance the contributions to the 'Objective Abstraction' show organized by Robert Wellington at Zwemmers in 1934), but by 1936 they had swung back in favour of making a new start from the Impressionists and Cézanne. The precedent was there from 1911 and 1912, when a number of London painters led by Walter Sickert had allied themselves as the Camden Town Group, impressionist in style, but social realist in subject matter. Several of the group's former members were still painting at the end of the Thirties, principally Lucien Pissaro (died 1944), Augustus John, and Sickert himself (died 1942). Reviewing the state of British art for *The Studio* in 1940, Graham Bell described Sickert as Britain's 'greatest living artist', rivalled only by Augustus John, who by then had become more famous for his life-style as a Bohemian artist than for his creative achievements.

In the same article for *The Studio* Graham Bell described the direction that art was supposed to take. 'Five or six years ago all exhibitions were dominated by the abstract tendencies, today stunts have dwindled away.' Instead there was a small group of artists who considered themselves 'professional', concentrating on trying to record the object as it was. However, as in the case of the Camden Town Group, the choice of subject implied a social awareness. William Coldstream and Graham Bell stressed the social context of art, Bell in his pamphlet *The Artist and his Public* (1939): 'The rich have grown to hate art (as they hate all things) because it reminds them of their guilt.'

The ages, interests and experience of the Euston Road School match those of the *New Writing* circle, indeed Stephen Spender studied at the school in 1938. William Coldstream, forced by the Depression to give up painting for a while, worked on documentaries with the GPO Film Unit, where he met W.H. Auden. In 1937 he painted portraits of Auden, Spender and Christopher Isherwood. The School's political overtones were caught by Geoffrey Grigson, who quoted the remark 'a Coldstream group exhibition is like a double number of *Left Review*', and by Clive Bell, critic of the *New Statesman* and promoter of the Bloomsbury painters, his wife Vanessa and Duncan Grant. Bell attacked the author of *The Artist and his Public* for being 'a "scientific socialist", which, if one happens to be a painter in the Euston Road is called being a "social-realist", he has orders, down whatever road he chance to stray, to end at Moscow'.

The war meant that the school had to close, and the group held only one exclusive exhibition, and that at the Ashmolean Museum in Oxford in May 1941. The exhibitors were Claude Rogers, William Coldstream, Lawrence Gowing, Rodrigo Moyniham, Graham Bell and Victor Pasmore. Graham Bell was killed with the RAF in 1943, Moyniham and Coldstream became official War Artists.

The major figure of the group, Victor Pasmore, was the one least typical of it. Though he taught at the school, Pasmore's position was recognized as being different, in that he took no interest at all in its political aspects. Indeed, Pasmore was indifferent to most things outside the work of painting. William Townsend, a sympathetic associate of the group, recorded a conversation with Pasmore in March 1940:

> He is against taking any interest in the war, politics, etc. .... Against state patronage, official war artist appointments; and as usual vehemently. ... The war has made little if any difference to him. Outside events never did trouble him much and he doesn't propose they shall now.

Pasmore secured a discharge from the Army in 1942 as a conscientious objector. Living in Chiswick he concentrated his efforts on rediscovering the 'real tradition' of painting, represented to him then by Degas and the Impressionists, producing a series of Whistlerian studies of the riverside. In 1945 he told the painter and critic Robin Ironside that the ' "Euston Road School" has, or had, no collective critical significance whatever'.

Though the Euston Road School had no chance to develop because of the war, the political attitude of its members (excluding Pasmore) illustrates the left-wing tendency of most contemporary artists at that time. The channel for this radicalism was the Artists' International Association, founded in 1934. The Artists' International was a reflection of the Popular Front politics of the Thirties, containing Communists, Socialists and Liberals, and standing for 'unity of artists against Fascism and war and the suppression of culture', as an AIA pamphlet of 1939 put it. The Association had a very broad front: the advisory committee of 1944 had a wide selection of respectable names – James Bateman ARA, Vanessa Bell, Misha Black, Sir Muirhead Bone, Frank Dobson, Duncan Grant, Augustus John RA, E. McKnight-Kauffer, David Low, Henry Moore, Paul Nash, Lucien Pissaro and Ethel Walker ARA. The names show that there was no intention to create a particular style (nor, with some 700 members, including designers, teachers and students besides professional artists, would it have been possible to impose one). The purpose of the Association was to reassert the social importance of the artist.

During the war this took the form of propaganda aimed at closing the gap between the artist and society by 'democratizing' art. To this end exhibitions were held in such places as Charing Cross Underground Station (a show seen by 150,000 people) and the Morris works at Coventry; AIA exhibitions toured the British Restaurants that had been set up by the government to provide wholesome unrationed meals. In 1940 the AIA initiated 'Everyman Prints', selling specially commissioned lithographs for 1/- each in black and white or 1/6d in colour. Sir Kenneth Clark, an active supporter of the Association, welcomed the scheme as a solution to the problem of popular patronage for the arts, but though some 5,000 were sold the scheme foundered because of production difficulties in 1942.

The Association's biggest war effort was the 'For Liberty' exhibition sponsored by the *News Chronicle*, held in the basement air-raid shelter of John Lewis's bombed-out department store in Oxford Street in March 1943. The catalogue shows that the AIA was aware of the limitations of official art:

Here is a demonstration that artists feel that they can contribute more than is at present being asked of them; that the function of art in wartime is not only to record what is happening and to give pleasure and recreation but to stimulate and encourage by vividly showing what we are fighting for.

Accordingly, sixteen painters and sculptors, among them Augustus John, Kenneth Rowntree, Ruskin Spear, Fred Uhlmann, Julian Trevelyan and Oscar Kokoschka, contributed works on the theme of the four freedoms outlined in the Atlantic Charter: freedom of worship and speech, freedom from want and from fear. C. Day Lewis supplied a poem to bind the themes together. The 'For Liberty' exhibition was the outcome of a decision taken in 1942 to try to professionalize the role of painters by offering welfare benefits to members, in the manner of a Trades Union, and by organizing joint projects to produce socially conscious propaganda that would be more effective for change than the wooden efforts of the government. In August 1943 the AIA opened up its own cultural centre at 84 Charlotte Street, under the direction of the Marxist art critic F.D. Klingender.

British artists turned back to reconsider, not just the state of painting as it had been left by the French Impressionists, but the much earlier British landscape tradition. England was once more an island; its countryside offered plenty of new and old problems to be solved in an island manner. If (with the exception of Ben Nicholson and Barbara Hepworth) that meant turning away from Abstraction, the Surrealism that had been imported from the Continent still had something to offer. It was after all partly grafted on to an earlier tradition. As Herbert Read wrote in the catalogue to the International Surrealist Exhibition in 1936: 'A nation which has produced two such superrealists as William Blake and Lewis Carroll is to the manner born. Because our art and literature is the most romantic in the world, it is likely to become the most superrealistic.'

The reversion to a British romantic tradition was under way when the war began, and its effects were quickly noticed. Reviewing shows by John Piper and Katherine Church in March 1940, Raymond Mortimer commented on the increasing rejection of the doctrine of 'Significant Form' preached by Roger Fry:

Evidently it was impossible for the younger generation to follow their parents in the pursuit of 'Significant Form' or merely plastic values. In some cases the destined reaction has led artists to exploit the merely disquieting, in others to concentrate upon naturalism. The most interesting to me of our younger painters, Mr Graham Sutherland, has taken something from Samuel Palmer, something from Picasso, and is making personal and exciting pictures by metamorphosing natural scenery into landscapes that have the suggestive power of romantic poetry and music. Mr Piper, and less evidently, Miss Church, can roughly be classified with him. After most profitably going to school in France, English painting in the work of these three artists is reasserting national characteristics.

Surrealism was by no means abandoned. In June 1940 Zwemmers mounted a show by Henry Moore, Edward Burra, John Tunnard, John Banting and Paul Nash, and there was a new issue of the Surrealist *London Bulletin*. According to the *New Statesman*, soldiers back from Dunkirk saw the work in a new light after the battle. ' "This isn't strange to us", they said, "it's just like what we've been seeing over there." '

'Over there' was now inaccessible, there was social tension at home. In the *Listener* (also in June 1940), Geoffrey Grigson drew a parallel between the difficulties and disturbances in England between 1815 and 1848, and the tensions of 1940, arguing for a revival in interest in the British artists of that earlier period. The parallel is a good one, for following the isolation from Europe by the Napoleonic wars, painters like Palmer, Francis Danby and John Linnell had evolved their own romantic landscape tradition. In 1944 John Piper approvingly recalled Benjamin Haydon's remarks in 1816 about the benefit of war to English art and added:

During the art-blockade of war, British art does raise its head and become more perky. The English are better when they do not compete in the grand style, and when they do they are usually soon extinguished like Haydon: this is the reason that superior writers pretend that there is no British art. But during war, especially when insular artists are driven in on themselves, they make original and positive statements. . . . There is such a thing as the English vision, and war, luckily, is only one stimulus that affects it.

The 'English vision' has always had strong poetic and literary reference, hence the acceptability of Surrealism, whose imaginative exuberance or psychological gloom had a precedent in Blake, John Martin, Fuseli, Richard Dadd and the fantasies of the Gothick revival. The ground was prepared for a return to the picturesque, the mystical and the visionary – the 'Englishness' of Samuel Palmer. Here Geoffrey Grigson had an important influence, publishing a series of articles which were to culminate in his book *Samuel Palmer* in 1947. Grigson's anthology *The Poet's Eye* (1944) with lithographs by John Craxton underlines the poetic link in this revival; Craxton's *Poet in a Landscape* (1941) (Plate 24) makes the connection in a near pastiche of Palmer's style.

By 1942 the romantic revival had emerged as an independent force. Reviewing the London Museum's 1942 exhibition 'New Movements in Art – Contemporary Work in England', Raymond Mortimer noted the exclusion of Impressionists or the Euston Road School, 'not only disquieting but distressing' Surrealist work, 'puritanical and hygienic' contributions from the Constructivists, and 'what I tentatively call the Neo-Romantic' work by Frances Hodgkins, Graham Sutherland, Ivon Hitchens, Henry Moore and John Piper. 'The appeal of their art, I fancy, is to mystics and particularly to pantheists who feel a fraternity, or even a unity, with all living things, to those with the "sense sublime. Of something far more deeply interfused." '

In the same year John Piper brought out his book *English Romantic Artists*, reviewing landscape painting from William Gilpin and Richard Wilson through Turner and Constable, Blake, Fuseli, Palmer and Rossetti, up to the contemporary work of Frances Hodgkins, Graham Sutherland and Paul Nash. Piper's own work strongly reflects the heritage of the picturesque tradition, though up until 1938 he had been a committed abstract painter. He makes this comment on the experiments of the Twenties and Thirties:

> Post Impressionism was necessary. But in the long run it was applied with too much austerity by the more adventurous painters. The accent on design, form, structure, which they began to press home, and the suppression of literary interest and atmosphere, tended to squash all that was most natural to English painters and produced a new and artificial academicism.

Piper's work for the 'Recording Britain' project, his study of Blake and Palmer, reinforced his rejection of abstraction; the ruins caused by bombing became the picturesque ruins of Britain's Gothick past (Plate 22). Appropriately Geoffrey Grigson dedicated his 1942 anthology *The Romantics* to John Piper.

Paul Nash began the war as he had ended the last one, as an official war painter. In 1918 and 1919 his subject had been the shattered landscape of the Western Front, a genuinely surreal vision, had the term then been in existence. Landscape, and the mystical properties of landscape, continued to obsess him, though for a period in the Thirties exploration of its symbolism led him close to completely abstract designs. In 1933 he first encountered the prehistoric megaliths at Avebury, stones which gradually took on disturbing qualities as 'personages . . . the stones have a character influenced by the conditions of Dream'. Nash was evolving a distinctive mixture of English landscape and surrealist symbolism, suggesting life forms in inanimate objects, a transference that Nash continued in his paintings for the RAF, implicit in titles like *Wellington Bombers Watching the Skies, Whitleys at Play* or *Wellingtons Waiting*.

Nash stopped work for the RAF at the end of 1940 and transferred

20 Leonard Rosoman *House Collapsing on Two Firemen. Shoe Lane* 1941

21 Henry Moore *Grey Tube Shelter* 1940

22 John Piper *Council Chamber. House of Commons* 1941

23 Paul Nash *The Landscape of the Vernal Equinox* 1943

24 John Craxton *Poet in Landscape* 1941

25 Cecil Collins *The Sleeping Fool* 1943

26 Eric Kennington *The Heart of England* (Richard Hillary) 1943

27 Graham Sutherland *Devastation in the City: Twisted Girders against a background of Fire* 1941

28 Army Education: The artist Adrian Hill lecturing on 'The Art and Aims of Picasso' 1944

to the Ministry of Information; there the terms of employment were easier and he could follow his own interests. Nash's deteriorating health caused him many difficulties – one consequence of his asthma was that he never actually flew in a plane. The drive to penetrate and express the mystery of landscape, seasons and flowers became more urgent, and in 1941 he took up again the study of Rossetti, Palmer and Blake. Blake inspired the titles for *Tyger, Tyger* and his painting of the Battle of Britain, *The Defence of Albion*. In 1942 Nash began to explore the imagery of the Wittenham Clumps, two groups of trees he could just see from a friend's house on Boar's Hill, outside Oxford, a view he found 'transcendental'. At the same time old books on palaeontology peopled the landscape with prehistoric monsters, as the stones at Avebury had done before the war. The actual landscape is overlaid by myth (in the case of Nash's contemporary David Jones it disappears almost completely beneath the layers of symbolism), flowers and fungi are registered for their magic properties, while above reign the deities of sun and moon.

Nash's last symbolic sequence of sun and sunflower was incomplete when he died in July 1946. His note on *Landscape of the Vernal Equinox* (1943) (Plate 23) sums up the synthesis he was trying to make:

> Call it, if you like, a transcendental conception; a landscape of the imagination which has evolved in two ways: on the one hand through a personal interpretation of the phenomenon of the equinox, on the other through the inspiration derived from an actual place.

The same moulding of inner and outer vision can be seen in the work of Henry Moore and Graham Sutherland. In both cases the emotional nature of their subject matter formed a reconsideration of how they were communicating with their audience. In 1942 Sir Kenneth Clark defended the War Artists' Advisory Committee's decision to commission work from Sutherland and Moore: 'both artists, before the war, were producing work which departed very far from ordinary visual experience', but confronted by the human problems of the war they had found a way to register people's emotions. John Piper, Clark suggested, had possibly gone too far towards turning raw experiences into *objets d'art*.

The war forced a simple but sudden change in Moore's work, in that he was unable to make any sculpture until 1944. In consequence drawing, previously only a preliminary to sculpture, took on importance in its own right. But the confrontation with his subject matter was equally significant:

It humanized everything I had been doing. I knew at the time that what I was sketching represented an artistic turning point for me, though I didn't realize then that it was a professional turning point too.

Commissioned to paint tin mines and factories, Graham Sutherland found himself similarly confronted with human subject matter, something he had avoided in his pre-war landscapes – though like Nash his natural shapes seem somehow informed with life. Now figures appear, servants of the furnace, a monster that makes in order to continue the destruction of war.

Although almost everything militated against it, a small group of younger painters, as opposed to these more established figures, did manage to make the beginnings of their careers during the war years. Those who did largely had Peter Watson to thank. Peter Watson, the patron of *Horizon*, had lived in Paris before the war and had been friendly with the artists and writers there, particularly the Surrealists. He was therefore anxious to keep the flame of international modernism alive in England, and in the art pages of *Horizon* he was able to push the work of young men such as John Craxton, Lucian Freud, Jankel Adler and Robert Colquhoun while also giving them direct financial help.

It was with Peter Watson that the Glasgow-trained Colquhoun and Robert MacBryde first stayed when they arrived in London in 1941, after Colquhoun had been invalided out of the Royal Army Medical Corps. For a time they shared their studio in Campden Hill with the wealthy John Minton, himself invalided out of the Army in 1943. Minton had worked with Michael Ayrton on the scenery and costumes for John Gielgud's 1942 production of *Macbeth*, Ayrton having left the RAF in that year. Minton, Colquhoun and MacBryde shared a show at the Alex Reid and Lefevre Gallery in 1944, where Colquhoun had first shown in 1943. Minton introduced Keith Vaughan (then a clerk at a prisoner-of-war camp in Yorkshire) to the gallery, which showed a small collection of his drawings in December 1944.

These painters only established themselves post-war, at this early period they were no more than a group of friends, there was no group style, nor had they settled down individually. The influences of

Samuel Palmer, Picasso and Graham Sutherland interlace: Colquhoun and MacBryde were followers of Picasso, Jankel Adler helped to introduce the work of his compatriot Paul Klee; Craxton seems most influenced by the romantic reversion, though it was Michael Ayrton who argued that the isolation of wartime had been beneficial: 'The artists now nearing their thirties have been forced by circumstances to fall back not only upon British art but upon British landscape . . . and they have thus been forced into an aesthetic stock-taking which has given their work an individual and national character. British painting is alive today as it has not been for a hundred years.' Ayrton wrote this in 1946, by which time the national characteristics of British art were already fading once more.

The poetic element in wartime British art, romantic and essentially literary, had its correspondence in the poetry of the Apocalyptics and the New Romantics. Mervyn Peake's illustrations to Coleridge's *The Ancient Mariner* in *Poetry* (*London*) No. 10 have an Apocalyptic horror about them. (Peake was also a poet.) In 1940 Cecil Collins began his series of paintings *The Holy Fool*, which come closest to Apocalyptic intentions; indeed, when the series was first shown at the Lefevre Gallery in 1944 Stephen Spender found it 'natural to associate Collins with young poets like Treece and Hendry, rather than with painters like Henry Moore, John Piper and Graham Sutherland'. Collins was a contributor to *Transformation* No. 3 and his wartime essay explaining the intention of his pictures, published as *The Vision of the Fool* in 1947, has an Apocalyptic ring about its anti-mechanist and anarchic argument:

The crucifixion of the poetic imagination in man by the Machine Age, is a religious fact. And modern society has succeeded very well in rendering poetic imagination, Art, Religion, the three magical representatives of life, an heresy; and the living symbol of that heresy is the Fool. The Fool is the poetic imagination of life, as inexplicable as the essence of life itself.

Like the poetry of Treece and Hendry, Neo-Romanticism was a wartime phenomenon. In 1945 *Penguin New Writing* reported: 'at this moment Blake and Turner are in their zenith; in every other studio there is a painter reeling about intoxicated by one or other'. But the moment of intoxication was short-lived. Later that year the Victoria and Albert Museum put on the first post-war show of

Matisse and Picasso; isolation was over. One painter, Francis Bacon, had already struck out boldly on his own. His *Three Figures at the Base of a Crucifixion*, first shown in April 1945, is the one genuinely apocalyptic painting of the war.

Whether the revival of romanticism was a genuine attempt to communicate human experience on a higher level by transcending the harsh realities of wartime, or merely a refusal to come to terms with what was actually taking place – and in fact it was both – the appeal of romanticism was to the emotions, emotions most easily satisfied by music. In ballet, music and painting came together. Besides extending Neo-Romantic imagery into the theatre, designing sets and costumes was a practical way to earn a living. The choreographer Frederick Ashton chose Graham Sutherland to design *The Wanderer* (to music by Schubert) for Sadler's Wells in 1941, and in 1943, while on temporary release from the RAF, Ashton used John Piper for *The Quest* (to music by William Walton). Leslie Hurry made his reputation with his set for Robert Helpmann's *Hamlet* in 1942. The ballet itself – the plot of the play passing through Hamlet's mind in his dying minutes – exactly caught the emotions of the period. Sidney Keyes went to see it twice when the production was on tour in Edinburgh:

> I was able to accept the whole thing entirely without question. . . . Its total effect is one of great horror and pain – all the more so, because one can well imagine that the moment of death will take such a form.

Sadler's Wells had to carry most of the responsibility for keeping both ballet and opera alive during the war years. Their theatre closed by the Blitz, the company had no base in London until the New Theatre was taken over in 1943, followed by the Princes Theatre in 1944. Sadler's Wells Opera only just survived the winter of 1940 and '41 by mounting a tour of *The Marriage of Figaro* and *La Traviata*, using a company of twenty-six, which included the 'orchestra' of four. That at least preserved the nucleus of the organization, and with help from the Carnegie Trust and the Council for the Encouragement of Music and the Arts it was able to build up again. Certainly there was no shortage of demand for the company's work; by November 1942 the popularity of Sadler's Wells ballet was such that the *New Statesman* complained that the company was labouring 'under a number of disadvantages, of which not the least is the undiscriminating enthusiasm of the audience. The most by dancers whose technique is obviously immature gets acclaimed as if it were *Petrouchka* with Karsavina and Nijinsky.'

In the concert hall symphony orchestras had the advantage of a ready-made romantic repertoire from Beethoven, Brahms and Sibelius; provincial tours, factory concerts and radio broadcasts brought them to a new audience. The demand for music was seen as a healthy sign. In July 1943 Eve Kisch, a 'Music Traveller' for CEMA, argued:

Call it escapism if you like; but the present general urge to listen to Beethoven symphonies is very different from that ordinary ostrich mentality which sets night-clubs and music-halls booming all over a wartime world. Rather it is as if the ordinary person finds some kind of spiritual anchorage in witnessing a drama that bears no relation to the spatial world, but is played out between characters existing only in the dimensions of time and tune.

Others were less certain of the educative value of the boom in concert going. The 1943 *Annual Register* commented:

the musical experience brought to vast numbers of people by this war-time movement ranged little beyond a few symphonies headed by Beethoven's fifth and seventh, and a few concertos headed by Rachmaninov's in C minor and Tchaikovsky's in B flat minor for piano. The vogue of the last named work was carried to such a point that its title became a byword wherever musical affairs were responsibly discussed. To make matters worse, the standard of performance went down.

A notorious example of 'middlebrow' taste was the great popularity of Richard Addinsell's Warsaw Concerto, originally part of the score of the film *Dangerous Moonlight*, which came to be treated with the same reverence as the Tchaikovsky concerto it resembles. The BBC, however, did much to redress the balance of musical appreciation by presenting new works, and taking over the management of the Promenade Concerts, transferred to the Albert Hall. Between 1942 and 1944 the proportion of 'serious music' on records played by the BBC rose from 6% to 40% – although less than a third of that was by British composers.

Like all professional artists, musicians suffered as a result of the war, particularly in the early years. In 1939 the London Philharmonic Orchestra faced total dissolution, but the players formed themselves into a company, Musical Culture Ltd, and ran the orchestra themselves, working with guest conductors after Sir Thomas Beecham left for Australia. A second crisis in the autumn of 1940 was overcome when, at the instigation of J.B. Priestley, the impresario Jack Hylton presented a series of LPO concerts in provincial music-halls, where previously no serious musician had dared to tread. The orchestra began to visit regularly more than a hundred towns. In 1942 a London base was acquired by default when the lessee of the Orpheum, Golders Green – where they had been giving Sunday concerts – disappeared with the takings. The Philharmonic took over the lease and made the Orpheum into a genuine cultural centre, providing opera, ballet, theatre and exhibitions, besides music. Unfortunately the difficulties caused by location and transport prevented the Orpheum from becoming a paying proposition, and the project had to be abandoned after a year.

The LPO was not alone in exploiting the boom in concert going. The armed forces set up their own orchestras from conscripted players, and in 1943 a new National Symphony Orchestra was formed. In the same year the National Association of Symphony Orchestras was established in order to co-ordinate the activities of the six leading orchestras, and to regulate the often competing schedules of their tours.

Wartime must be the hardest time of all to get new work performed, though Alan Bush, Edmund Rubbra, Alan Rawsthorne, Lennox Berkeley, Elisabeth Lutyens, Michael Tippett, Ernest Moeran and Benjamin Britten were among those who succeeded. Britten, who had been in America from 1939 until 1942, made an immediate impression when his Sinfonia da Requiem was first performed in England. Edward Sackville-West's review shows the emotional release music could give:

> Our reactions to the idea of death become simpler in times when that event tends to be a sudden matter rather than gradual. Feelings become less mixed, love and admiration remain whole, self pity shows for the self-indulgence it is. This astringency makes for the kind of single-pointed attitude which results in considerable works of art. At the Albert Hall, on July 22 [1942] many among the audience must have felt that the fact underlying the experiences of the last three years had at last been given a satisfying form.

Britten's Serenade for tenor, horn and strings, given its first performance in 1943, with its settings of poems by Blake, Tennyson and Keats, complements the romantic mood in poetry and painting. (Similarly,

Alan Rawsthorne wrote a setting of Coleridge's 'Kubla Khan' for soloists, chorus and orchestra.) Michael Tippett's oratorio *A Child of Our Time*, first performed in 1944, and Britten's opera *Peter Grimes*, which reopened Sadler's Wells Theatre in June 1945, marked the 'arrival' of two major composers.

The orchestras, opera and ballet would not have survived had it not been for the Council for the Encouragement of Music and the Arts. Eve Kisch has described the meeting on 14 December 1939 between the Minister of Information, Lord Macmillan, and Lord De La Warr, President of the Board of Education, which led to CEMA's formation:

> Lord De La Warr was enthusiastic. He had Venetian visions of a post-war Lord Mayor's Show on the Thames as the Board of Education led the Arts in Triumph from Whitehall to Greenwich in magnificent barges and gorgeous gondolas; orchestras, madrigal singers, Shakespeare from the Old Vic, ballet from Sadler's Wells, stirring canvases from the Royal Academy, folk-dancers from village greens – in fact, Merrie England. Lord Macmillan's grave judicial calm collapsed suddenly and completely. At the moment he was responsible for the national morale, and in the President's dream he saw employment for actors, singers and painters, and refreshment for the multitude of war-workers for the duration. Supply and Demand kissed. Would £25,000 be of any use?

It took a little time for the government to take full responsibility for CEMA, but government grants rose from £100,000 in 1942 to £235,000 in 1945, when CEMA became the Arts Council of Great Britain. Fulfilment of Lord De La Warr's vision of post-war celebration had to wait until the Festival of Britain in 1951.

The operations of CEMA changed as its responsibilities increased. Originally its purpose was to provide entertainment in the provinces, particularly by encouraging amateur efforts. Hence the creation of Music Travellers, who were sent round the country sponsoring local music-making groups. Support for art was limited to grants to the Institute for Adult Education, which had been running 'Art for the People' shows since 1935. By mid-1942 museums had begun to open up again, and CEMA began buying up new works as a circulating collection. In September 1943 it was estimated that half a million people had been to the thirty shows organized by CEMA and 'Art for the People' in the previous eighteen months.

The change in CEMA's policy began in April 1942 when Lord

Keynes took over as chairman. Himself married to a former professional ballet dancer, Keynes did much to professionalize the Council. The directorates of the various departments became salaried posts, and the Council's expanding budget was devoted to supporting professional performers. In 1943 CEMA took over the Carnegie Trust's guarantees to the London Philharmonic Orchestra, the London Symphony Orchestra, the Hallé, Liverpool Philharmonic, Northern Philharmonic, Bournemouth Municipal and Scottish Symphony Orchestras. CEMA held 4,449 concerts in 1943, in 1944 concerts and recitals were taking place at the rate of seventy a week in factories, and thirty a week in churches and village halls. In 1943 Sadler's Wells Opera and Ballet came in under CEMA's wing, the Ballet Joos was reconstituted and the Ballet Rambert reorganized as a small company to tour factories and hostels. Small touring drama companies were set up, and besides re-opening the Liverpool Playhouse and the Lyric Hammersmith, CEMA saved the Theatre Royal, Bristol, from demolition.

CEMA was not the only institution contributing to the preservation of cultural life. The British Council, promoting the British image abroad, sponsored recordings of British composers. Though ENSA's principal product was light entertainment, it put on nearly four hundred full-scale symphony concerts between 1943 and 1946, and commissioned work from contemporary composers. As an employer and promoter the BBC covered the whole field of artistic activity, directly commissioning music and plays, employing actors, writers and musicians, publishing the *Listener*, and with talks and poetry readings providing the freelance work which is an essential part of the humus needed by cultural life in order to thrive.

In general, the commercial theatre was more imaginative than it had been during the First War, but predictably, musicals and revues dominated. In December 1941 the *Evening Standard* reported: 'New nude is in town. Dinora, who stands undraped in seven tableaux to represent "the plight of Poland" is now in *Glamour Serenade* (Prince of Wales)', which sums up one aspect of the commercial theatre's activity. By 1942 business had rallied after the collapse of 1940–41; the difficulty then became that once a play had become established it was kept on for a very long run. John Lehmann commented in September 1942: 'One begins to wonder whether the English theatre, caught in the slow strangulation of anti-cultural profiteering, and struggling for years against the competition of Hollywood cinema, is alive at all.'

In an attempt to raise the intellectual content of the West End theatre, CEMA encouraged managements to take advantage of the concession that non-profit-making organizations like Sadler's Wells were exempt from entertainment tax. H.M. Tennent, one of the major West End promoters, formed Tennent Plays Ltd to operate on a non-profit basis, backing a number of successful productions including John Gielgud's *Macbeth*, Priestley's *They Came to a City*, and John Steinbeck's *The Moon is Down*. In 1942 Alec Clunes set up the Arts Theatre Group of Actors, run, according to Clunes, on 'amateur-socialist' lines. Half the money from each performance went to pay production expenses, the rest was shared between the actors and the staff. Peter Ustinov's first play, *The House of Regrets*, was put on in this way.

Commercial managements did have a few respectable successes that did not try to take people's minds off the war. Terence Rattigan's *Flarepath*, directed by Anthony Asquith, was a hit in 1942. In 1943 Robert Sherwood's *There Shall Be No Night* arrived in London. The play had already run for two and a half years on Broadway, but went through a curious change during the journey across the Atlantic. When they opened on Broadway in 1940 Alfred Lunt and his wife Lynn Fontanne had been starring in a play set during the Russian invasion of Finland. By 1943 Russia had become an ally, so, by subtle adjustments, the setting was changed to Italy's invasion of Greece, without losing any of the drama.

The West End theatre remained almost impenetrable to new-comers. In 1944, of the thirty-four theatres in central London four-teen were putting on musicals, three had plays that had started their run in 1942 or '43 (including Noel Coward's *Blithe Spirit*), four more were doing revivals, and of the thirteen remaining, seven had plays by established writers, two had inconsequential farces, and two had American hits, leaving the tiny Arts Theatre and St Martin's where actors' companies were also doing old plays. The only comfort was that business was good.

The shortage of both new plays and theatres in which to perform them was matched by a shortage of actors. *Penguin New Writing* reported at the end of 1943:

people left out of the machinery of war organization, for health or other reasons, are coming into the theatre to pick up what is, owing to the limited supply and increased demand, an easy living. More and more frequently one hears of cases of new actors proving totally incapable of doing even an average job, and of productions shelved for want of a cast.

Something was done to correct this in 1944 when Ralph Richardson and Laurence Olivier were released from the Fleet Air Arm. With Tyrone Guthrie and Sybil Thorndike they established the Old Vic Repertory Company at the New Theatre, putting on *Richard III*, Ibsen's *Peer Gynt* and Shaw's *Arms and the Man*. *Time and Tide* greeted the decision to do repertory in the West End as 'a theatrical revolution'. The experiment was sufficiently successful for Tennent Plays to start repertory at the Haymarket with *Hamlet*, Somerset Maugham's *The Circle* and Congreve's *Love for Love*.

It would be easy to overestimate the richness of the national diet of symphony orchestras and Shakespeare – C.E.M. Joad's complaint at the head of this chapter has some justification. The BBC had more influence on popular culture with the comedy of Tommy Handley's *It's That Man Again* than with Louis MacNeice's play *Christopher Columbus*. But the diffusion of music and drama, above all the dispersal from London at the beginning of the war and during the Blitz, undoubtedly had an educational effect. The government's recognition that the arts *are* important, even in wartime, was a vital decision for the future.

In December 1944 *Time and Tide*'s theatre critic, Philip Hope-Wallace, decided to review not the play but the audience. It turned out to be a new one, 'unselective, Penguin-educated', but not to be ignored, for it was responsible for 'a genuine and spontaneous, if a little muddled' revival of the theatre. It was an audience that was prepared to work for its enjoyment, not to sit back and be fed. Robert Speaight took the same view:

although we may seem to see only indecision in the temper of our drama-tists, the war years have brought about a profound change in that other party in the production of drama – the audience. This change may produce the climate in society which the dramatist so badly needs. We have long suffered from a divorce of the artist from society, and in the theatre there were times between the two wars when the creative imagination seemed altogether to have deserted the theatre.

Whatever the indecisions of playwrights (which match those of other writers), the performers responded to the enthusiasm of the new audience. Michael Redgrave wrote in 1943: 'I see in the theatre considerable signs that actors, directors and designers of all generations are determined that the future shall be better than the past, if it lies in their power to make it so.' Since the war that determination has borne fruit.

A new young audience also filled the concert halls and art galleries. Edward Sackville-West reported in April 1943: 'at no time in the pre-war years was there so large and varied a public for good literature, pictures, plays and music, as there is at present. In fact the demand hugely exceeds the supply.' In March 1945 Mollie Panter-Downes noticed the same discrepancy:

During the war years, more and more Londoners have taken to reading poetry, listening to music, and going to art exhibitions, although there is less of all three in this shabby, weary capital. Most of the poets are too personally involved in the war to have attained that state of impersonal tranquility which generates good poetry. . . . The output of good poetry is small, but the public hunger for it is pathetically great. The demand for music is probably not much greater now than it was in peacetime, but it looks greater because the supply of concert halls and orchestras is sadly limited. . . . People line up at the National Gallery every day for the lunchtime concerts organized by Myra Hess.

The provision of recreation for the war workers in the huge factories up and down the country was educational in a very direct way. Many workers, often young women conscripted for National Service, lived in hostels on isolated sites, so that entertainment had to come to them. The Royal Ordnance hostels for munitions workers had their own specially built theatres. Eric White's history of the Arts Council notes that:

It is a startling fact that, at the beginning, only about two per cent of these hostel audiences had ever seen a stage play before. In the early days many of them did not know how to behave before live players. . . . Gradually they acquired a theatre etiquette and ceased to talk, walk about and drink tea during the performances.

These hostel tours were new experiences for the actors as well. Because the factories were working twenty-four hours a day, *Hedda Gabler* might be performed between seven and nine in the morning or at half-past eleven at night. Half-hour music recitals were a regular feature of meal breaks in factory canteens: since some factories covered several square miles, musicians found themselves putting on fifteen separate performances between 9.15 a.m. and 3.15 the following morning, to cover one site.

Factories were only part of the picture; mining villages, parish halls, remote gun-sites and aerodromes received their quota. Ivor Brown has described a performance of *Macbeth* with Sybil Thorndike in Burnley:

> The theatre was packed with people who, as I suddenly realized, were not just waiting to see what a famous player would do with a familiar speech. They were gripped with curiosity, wanting to know what happened and how it ended. They were the counterparts of Shakespeare's own audience.

Of course, not all entertainment was intended as moral uplift, yet J.B. Priestley's description of two desperately bad ENSA comedians, 'Dolly and Dan', hints at deeper qualities:

> A fat middle-aged woman, most unsuitably dressed and raddled, and an elderly painted buffoon, shouting and posturing, yelling in coarse accents their stale old jokes, busy vulgarizing the sex instinct, performing without grace or wit. Gaping at the tiny stage, staring and nudging, guffawing and screaming, there are the thousands of workers of all ages, making what seem animal noises that yet no animal has ever made and seeming all mindless eyes and ears, wide loud mouths and clapping hands. A strange and no doubt a deplorable scene. Yet there was about it an air of release and innocent happiness; a kind of struggling goodness in it; a mysterious promise, not mentioned, not tried for, not even understood, but there somewhere all the time, of man's ultimate deliverance and freedom, a whisper of his home-coming among the stars.

The Army found itself drawn willy-nilly into the educational process. At the beginning of the war the Army Education Corps was disbanded, but after Dunkirk, faced with a long period of training and relatively little military activity, the War Office ordered all units to appoint an Education Officer, who would co-operate with the local Adult Education Committees. Civilian lecturers from the Workers' Education Association were brought in to talk to the troops, and the Army Education Corps was reformed. In June 1941 the Army Bureau of Current Affairs was brought into being under the direction of the enthusiastic adult educationalist W.E. Williams. In 1942 three hours a week were taken away from military training ('Judging Distances', 'Unarmed Combat') for educational purposes. A recipient of the ABCA's material was G.S. Fraser:

Headquarters had two attitudes – that lectures and debates were better than drinking and whoring, or that it was all crypto-communism and would only produce 'army lawyers'. But there was a general feeling that soldiers should be provided with more than coffee and buns and civilian ladies being kind to them over counters.

The political results of inviting soldiers to debate such questions as 'What are we fighting for?' has been discussed by Paul Addison in *The Road to 1945*; he concludes that Army Education was not the left-wing menace that some Conservatives still believe it to be. The cultural influence is hard to quantify, though there were practical benefits in that conscripted intellectuals could find moderately congenial work in the Education Corps, and lecturing to the troops was a useful source of income for literary civilians (Plate 28). In 1943 the ABCA set up its own Theatre Group, directed by Michael MacOwen, in order to present drama-documentaries that would provoke discussion among the soldiers. A sympathetic commanding officer allowed the novelist Jack Lindsay to be transferred to the unit as a script writer. Lindsay described himself in an interview as the only Private in the War Office. He had an office to himself because there was no one of low enough rank to share it with him.

ABCA Theatre dramatized such issues as *LendLease*, *The Japanese Way* (to prepare for the invasion of Japan), and *Where Do We Go From Here?*, on the post-war future. After seeing an ABCA performance, J.B. Priestley wrote *Desert Highway* and presented it to the group, following it up with a comedy for performance overseas *How Are They At Home?*, in both cases waiving his royalties. As with the Education Corps, the ABCA was a compromise between the needs of the Army and the interests of culture, but it seemed to work. This is an account of a performance of *Where Do We Go From Here?*:

> The audience was as bad as it could be: it consisted largely of men recently called up who had had to march to the theatre through some miles of pouring rain, had to sit in their drenched raincoats, were not allowed to smoke, and wanted no part of any play, least of all a propaganda play that told them of years more in the Army and years more of 'direction' afterwards. Yet within a short time they were as responsive as any audience I have seen, they laughed at all the right moments, stopped coughing, applauded for a long time at the end of the performance.

The growth of Britain's cultural renaissance was enthusiastically welcomed by the small group of Communists and left-wingers centred on the magazine *Our Time*. The magazine had begun life as *Poetry and the People*, a small cyclostyled pamphlet from the poetry section of the Left Book Club. In 1941 it changed its name and format, introducing photographs and illustrations that make *Our Time*, by wartime standards, a glossy magazine. The editorial board saw frequent changes, but the actress Beatrix Lehmann, the painter John Banting, the composer Alan Bush, the art critic F. D. Klingender, and the writers and poets Sylvia Townsend Warner, Randall Swingler, and Montagu Slater all had a hand. In 1944 the poet Edgell Rickword, former editor of *The Calendar of Modern Letters* in the Twenties, and *The Left Review* in the Thirties, took over direction.

In 1942, under the editorship of Alan Sharp, *Our Time* announced its intention to concentrate on 'a stocktaking of the cultural activities taking place at the present time. Far more is happening in the country than many of us suspect.' *Our Time* saw itself 'becoming the conscious voice of all efforts to build a national people's culture, which at this moment will be a vivifying force in the effort to victory, and which will later become the rallying point for rebuilding in peace'. To this end the magazine publicized and supported the work of the British Drama League, the National Book League, CEMA, the London Philharmonic Orchestra, PEN, union action by Equity and the film makers, the Artists' International Association, the Workers' Music Association, the Workers' Film Association, Toynbee Hall, Morley College, the Unity Theatre and the City Literary Institute. (This is not a complete list.) *Our Time* believed that a 'cultural upsurge' had taken place in wartime, and in the bleak aftermath of war did what it could to keep the impetus going. *Our Time* folded in 1949.

Inevitably, there were protests at the wartime handling of cultural affairs, from both Left and Right. A CEMA violinist complained in *Our Time* that: 'Music was being ladled out, like soup in the canteen, and was regarded with no more interest, if even as much, as was accorded to the hot dishwater given that name.' Thinking ahead to *Nineteen Eighty Four* George Orwell was worried by the political dangers of state intervention:

When you see what has happened to the arts in the totalitarian countries, and when you see the same thing happening here in a more veiled way through the Ministry of Information and the BBC and the film companies – organizations which not only buy up promising young writers and geld them and set them to work like cab horses, but manage to rob literary creation of its individual character and turn it into a sort of conveyor-belt process – the prospects are not encouraging.

Yet it was the disorganized nature of Britain's cultural life that Philip Hope-Wallace welcomed: 'I am an enemy of mass, state organized culture: muddling-through to art, as to other things, seems to me the good way; the touch of CEMA, the cautious benevolence of commercial managers and the integrity of critics will play their part.'

Right-wingers complained of waste of public funds and political dangers. A question in the House of Commons about the 'debasing effects' of CEMA's art shows in February 1944 won approval from a group who wrote a letter to *The Times*:

For the most part the exhibitions comprise paintings devised to carry on the baleful influence of what is known as 'modernistic' art. This is a subversive movement which, with its several 'isms', has been for many years endeavouring to undermine the traditional glories of painting and sculpture, thus to lower the standards of artistic ideas and technical performance.

Replying to the letter, Lord Keynes pointed out that only six of the twenty-five shows circulated by CEMA had been of contemporary art – and two of those had been selections from the Royal Academy summer shows. Shortly after signing the letter of protest to *The Times* the painter Sir Alfred Munnings became President of the Royal Academy.

It was Cyril Connolly, critical as ever, who pointed out the weakness that the cultural renaissance, genuine as it was, affected only the performing arts:

We are becoming a nation of culture-diffusionists. Culture-diffusion is not art. We are not making a true art. The appreciation of art is spreading everywhere, education has taken wings, we are at last getting a well-informed inquisitive public. But war-artists are not art, the Brains Trust is not art, journalism is not art, the BBC is not art, all the CEMA shows, all the ABCA lectures, all the discussion groups and MOI films and pamphlets will avail nothing if we deny independence, leisure and privacy to the artist himself. We are turning all our writers into commentators until one day there will be nothing left for them to comment on.

Nonetheless, there were benefits to literature as well, if only writers could rise to the occasion. Stanley Unwin recalled:

Young people were buying books, and not merely books, but good books. They wanted the best. The war created a new reading public. Many acquired the reading habit who had never turned to books before, and there is much comfort in the realization that they did so for the acquisition of knowledge and the enjoyment of good literature, and not merely as an escape from the war.

The concerts which Dame Myra Hess began on her own initiative in the National Gallery in 1939, and which continued throughout the war, have become a symbol of Britain's cultural resistance – and have been satirized as such. Yet there is something very moving about Stephen Spender's description of the audience's behaviour when a bomb went off during the performance of a Beethoven string quartet in the Gallery's shelter:

In the middle of the minuet there was a tremendous explosion. A delayed-action bomb had gone off in Trafalgar Square. In the trio of the minuet which they were playing, the musicians did not lift the bows from their strings. A few of the audience, who had been listening with heads bowed, straightened themselves for an instant and then resumed their posture.

CHAPTER EIGHT

There is no such thing as Culture in Wartime

'It did not at once become clear
. . . but the end of the war was
a disaster for many writers.'

Dan Davin

In January 1944 the long lull of the middle passage was broken by a
series of sharp and noisy night raids, a reprise, as it were, of the
bombing of London in 1940. Alerts, accidents, and sneak attacks had
ensured that the lull had never softened into calm; the Black-Out,
Air Raid Precautions and the Home Guard had all been fully maintained; and now Londoners found themselves in 'the Little Blitz'.
Although superficially this was a replay of 1940, Charles Graves
noted the profound psychological difference between the two:

It was, of course, nothing like as heavy as what we had in 1940, but one
is four years older and all this wishful thinking of the past eighteen months
has led one to believe that air raids on a heavy scale over this country were
a thing of the past.

The features of 1940 reappeared. The queues reformed outside the
Tube stations, people reverted to sleeping in their Anderson shelters,
the theatres brought their evening performances further forward
from six to five o'clock, and London became once more silent and
empty at night. Mrs Robert Henrey recalled: 'This mantle of silence
was one of the strangest phenomena. One could hear it, yes, actually
hear it. On several occasions when I was at home with the curtains
drawn, this sudden blanketing fell upon my ears and made me aware
that it was now officially night.'

167

The only consolation was that the Russians had shifted the balance of the war decisively against the Germans, Allied troops were fighting their way up the Italian mainland, and there was a feeling of certainty that 1944 would at last see an invasion across the Channel. For civilians that certainty was confirmed when a ten-mile deep strip of coastline running from Land's End to the Wash was placed out of bounds from 1 April. In April the Little Blitz faded out – but the talk now was of secret weapons. In May London began to empty of the multifarious uniforms of the Allied fighting services; the dense population of American soldiers in Mayfair thinned out. Londoners noticed that it was possible to get a taxi again. Theatre and cinema receipts slumped. On 6 June the landings in Normandy took place. London was silent all day, waiting for the news.

A week later the quiet was interrupted by the arrival of the first flying bombs, the V.1s launched from the Pas de Calais; they began to arrive erratically over London by day and night, announcing themselves with the sound of their engines, which many people compared to the spluttering of an unsilenced motor-cycle. It was quickly learned that when the engine stopped it was time to take cover. George Stonier, author of 'Shaving Through the Blitz', sharpened his wit once more:

Never can a secret weapon have become so immediately public; English conversation, switched from the weather, developed suddenly a high-pitched buzz. On roof-tops and in pubs one heard of nothing else; it called for drinks, it put off dinner hours, it brought out the theoretician and the bogey man. And while the knots of talkers were still speculating, another of the assailants would come bumbling over ('hardly human, though, are they?'), the guns would crack, the drone would suddenly cease, and for a few instants sickening uncertainty took the place of gossip.

With British and American troops in France and the Luftwaffe virtually defeated, there was something absurd about this persistent deadly sniping. The sirens went so frequently that people became increasingly confused between the Alert and the All Clear. At the beginning of July Inez Holden wrote in her journal:

There is an old 1940 tradition of avoiding the subject of bombardment, and yet they think about it all the time. Things seem the same. The department stores take the same interest in their customers, the taxis still go speeding by like arrows, American soldiers walk to the Valet Services carrying their pants to be pressed, the pubs are full, in the Ministries they are having as many conferences as ever; yet the shadow of these fascist-zombies falls across our waking and our sleeping hours like a troubled conscience or the presence in the house of an unsound relative. . . . It is generally admitted 'It's not nearly as bad as 1940.' Already the Battle of Britain has become a legend for those who were in it, and a myth for those who missed it.

Unlike 1940, there was nothing particularly heroic about carrying on with one's job in London. Militarily the bombs were merely a nuisance – but a vicious nuisance whose blast wrecked streets and killed and maimed with flying glass. George Orwell reported to the *Partisan Review*:

> After the wail of the siren comes the zoom-zoom-zoom of the bomb, and as it draws nearer you get up from your table and squeeze yourself into some corner that flying glass is not likely to reach. Then BOOM! the windows rattle in their sockets, and you go back to work. There are disgusting scenes in the Tube stations at night.

The psychological strain was increased by the sheer futility of being killed in London at this stage of the war; there was also something unpleasant about the anonymity of pilotless rockets. It was suggested in the *New Statesman* that someone should invent automatic guns and leave the two weapons to fight it out. Others thought the flying bombs were steered by the ghosts of dead Luftwaffe pilots.

The barrage took its toll of London's cultural life. *Time and Tide*'s theatre critic Philip Hope-Wallace was at the opening of a feeble sex comedy at St James's Theatre when a V.1 was heard approaching. As he and the rest of the audience ducked beneath their seats he thought: 'How squalid to be killed at this disgusting little farce.' Several shows were forced to close, including the Lunts in *There Shall be No Night*. Public performances of the Promenade Concerts were stopped, and the series continued only as broadcasts from the BBC music studios in Bedford. This was the fiftieth season of the Proms and their ailing founder Sir Henry Wood was bitterly disappointed by their interruption. He died just before the last concert was broadcast.

Social life also saw changes. Lunching at the Hungaria in Lower Regent Street, Charles Graves noticed: 'This restaurant seems to have taken the place of the Savoy Grill in popularity. Flanagan and Allen, Will Hay, Jack Hylton, Sir Miles Thomas, and other celebrities whom one would have expected to see at the Savoy were there. Possibly it is because the Savoy is on the vulnerable side of the Thames.'

This caution seemed justified in December, when a V.2 crashed into the Thames just in front of the Savoy, and the restaurant windows were smashed for the seventh time. In the autumn John Lehmann attended a poetry reading given by Edith, Osbert and Sacheverell Sitwell in front of a glittering gathering at the Allied Forces' Churchill Club:

> As Edith got up to read, and began with her poem about the air-raids in 1940, 'Still Falls the Rain', the warning whistle was sounded in the Club. She had, I believe, never experienced a doodle-bug raid before; but she seemed quite unperturbed. As she reached the passage:
> Still falls the Rain –
> Still falls the blood from the Starved Man's wounded Side:
> He bears in His Heart all wounds –
> the rattle grew to ominous proportions, and it was impossible not to think that the monstrous engine of destruction was poised directly overhead. . . . Edith merely lifted her eyes to the ceiling for a moment, and, giving her voice a little more volume to counter the racket in the sky, read on. . . . Not a soul moved, and at the end, when the doodle-bug had exploded far away, the applause was deafening.

The liberation of Paris on 25 August was an occasion for relief and small celebration, but it was galling to know that Paris was liberated while London was still under aerial siege. Mrs Robert Henrey noted that although London wine merchants were suddenly eager to sell previously hoarded French wines:

> The coffee we used to buy now crosses the Channel to swell the Parisian 'black market', and the foreign women who used to walk our streets now wear foreign uniforms and travel between London and Paris, where they sell the golden sovereigns they have concealed about their persons for ten thousand francs apiece. The 'black market', which used to be local, has now an international flavour.

The first V.2 hit London on 8 September. Since these flew faster than sound there was no warning at all, simply a devastating explosion. In September's *Horizon* Cyril Connolly betrayed the effect of the flying-bomb campaign on his morale:

they have made London more dirty, more unsociable, more plague-stricken than ever. The civilians who remain grow more and more hunted and disagreeable, like toads each sweating and palpitating under his particular stone. Social life is non-existent, and those few and petty amenities which are the salt of civilian life – friendship, manners, conversation, mutual esteem – seem now extinct for ever. Never in the whole war has the lot of the civilian been more abject, or his status so low.

There were other, more cheerful signs. To begin with, in spite of the deaths and destruction, the V.1s and V.2s did not alter the course of the war. On 17 September the Black-Out was officially replaced by a Dim-Out, in December the Home Guard was stood down. Captain Simon Fine's *With the Home Guard* was advertised as just the right gift for Christmas 1944, 'a perfect souvenir'. 1940 seemed a very long way away.

All was by no means over, however. The attempt to break into Germany through Holland by dropping parachute troops failed in September. On 16 December the Germans counter-attacked in the Ardennes. While the Russians pushed on towards Berlin through East Prussia the Rhine was not crossed from the West until March 1945. On 27 March the last high explosive to fall on London killed 137 people in Stepney. In April the concentration camps were over-run, and on 30 April Hitler committed suicide. On 7 May came the final surrender in Europe, though the war with Japan was expected to go on for at least two more years. After atom bombs were dropped on Hiroshima and Nagasaki the Japanese surrendered on 14 August. Already there had been a general election in England, and a Labour government was in power.

After nearly six years of war, there was little energy left for rejoicing, and little left to celebrate with. The poet Henry Treece recorded the depressing sense of anti-climax after the singing and fireworks of Victory-in-Europe night:

As I walk on, I cannot help thinking that before the Japanese are defeated, war will have taken perhaps eight years of my life. Maybe I can just afford to lose eight years; there are many thousands who can't though. As I turn into my road, I pass a soldier staggering along with his girl. She is wearing a comical coloured cardboard hat, bearing the words: YOU'VE HAD IT, BIG BOY! I can't help feeling how very true these foolish words are for so many of us.

The bombing of Hiroshima and Nagasaki spared Treece from another two years in the RAF, but the Atom Bomb was yet another horror to pile on the horrors of war. In a sense the last six months of the war blotted out everything that had gone before. The novelist William Golding has written:

The experiences of Hamburg and Belsen, Hiroshima and Dachau cannot
be imagined. We have gone to war and beggared description all over again.
These experiences are like the black holes in space. Nothing can get out to
let us know what it was like inside. It was like what it was like and on the
other hand it was like nothing else whatsoever. We stand before a gap in
history. We have discovered a limit to literature.

The literary world shared the general exhaustion and depression, and
was overcome by a mood of irritation and petulance. In January 1945
the editor of *Life and Letters Today*, Robert Herring, saw no signs of
the much heralded brave new world: 'Instead I see in all fields, from
international relationships to literary politics, the familiar jockeying
into position whose selfishness results in dissipation of energy and
halted achievement.' Wrey Gardiner's *Poetry Quarterly* chimed in:

It is disturbing . . . to look around us and see the same sordid picture of
ignorance, corruption, and collusion, editors of reliable periodicals print-
ing verse as a fill-up of blank space who have no qualifications for choosing
poetry at all, and literary editors who give books of poems to reviewers
who are themselves failures as poets, and who merely use the space at their
disposal to project their own sense of frustration into their silly remarks,
or, which is perhaps more an act of prostitution, lending their pens to
please influential persons in rival literary gangs.

Cyril Connolly made *Horizon*'s birthday into an occasion to hold a
wake over the dead body of the arts:

Horizon's first five years have witnessed a decline in all the arts, together
with a belated recognition by the State of their importance. The State now
sits by the bedside of literature like a policeman watching for a would-be
suicide to recover consciousness, who will do anything for the patient
except allow him the leisure, privacy and freedom from which art is produced. Books are becoming as bad as they are ugly; newspapers continue
to be as dull with four pages as they were with forty; reviewing has sunk to
polite blurb-quoting; nothing original is produced: journalists grow
sloppier, vainer, more ignorantly omniscient than ever; the BBC pumps
religion and patriotism into all its programmes; mediocrity triumphs.

Orwell was equally gloomy: 'I am startled and frightened by the lack
of talent and vitality. The crowd who are grouped about *New Road*,
Now and *Poetry London* – and I suppose these are "the movement" in
so far as there is one – give me the impression of fleas hopping among
the ruins of a civilization.'

Constantine Fitzgibbon has summed up the mood of those last, frayed days of the war:

The atmosphere might be described as one of exhaustion shot through with violence and hatred. We read about the concentration camps, and we wondered which pub would have beer tonight. We were horrified by Hiroshima, which seemed to make it all meaningless, and we wanted out.

During the Blitz of autumn 1940, George Orwell wrote *The Lion and the Unicorn*, an attempt to define the nature of British civilization: 'a family with the wrong members in control'. He predicted: 'We cannot win the war without introducing Socialism, nor establish Socialism without winning the war.' In July 1945 the Labour Party won a sweeping victory, and in theory at least, both parts of Orwell's predictions were proved correct. The war had seen the planning of the National Health Service, Social Insurance, and the reform of education. Industries had been under national direction, with the end of the war the Labour government was able to bring in its schemes for nationalization – not 'Socialism' as Orwell had used the term in 1940, but a socialist government was indeed one result of winning the war. It is ironic that after all the political struggles and defeats of the Thirties the general election meant very little to the intelligentsia, if anything at all. Orwell himself predicted a narrow Conservative win.

In his political history of the war years *The Road to 1945*, Paul Addison has shown how events conspired to assist the Labour Party in 1945: the débâcle of 1940 after a long period of Conservative rule, admiration for the military achievements of Russia, the increase of radical influence in newspapers, the emphasis on post-war reconstruction, the educational influence of permitting political discussion in the services – but his conclusion about the role of the intellectuals is cautious: 'Perhaps left-wing ideas, popularized and translated into stock phrases by the press, ABCA and so forth, carried the day indirectly. After 1945 the radical intelligentsia claimed to have won the election for Labour: but we shall never know whether their influence was great or small.'

Writing in the *New Statesman* in September 1944, V.S. Pritchett shows how diffuse the radical feeling was – but makes no particular claim for the influence of literature:

At one period, at the time of Dunkirk, the blitz and the total call up of men and women, the word revolution was even fashionable. The most eminent people have welcomed the revolutionary character of the war. We have felt that our war is a war to defend civilization, even when we are not reading official propaganda; and we have felt this not because we are especially clear about what our civilization is, but because we have thought that this war and the kind of society that produced it, was a conspiracy against man. And whereas in the last war the social ideas of the Left were totally swallowed by nationalism, in this war they have been only partly swallowed. All classes went into this war with a developed social conscience, and the social legislation that has been enacted – modest as it is – has been enacted because it is part of the equipment we have used against the Fascist idea.

Certainly books played their part in developing the nation's social conscience – beginning in 1940 with *Guilty Men*. Allen Lane's Penguin Specials, *Christianity and the Social Order* for instance, by the radical Archbishop of Canterbury William Temple, and more campaigning books from Gollancz, *The Trial of Mussolini* (1943) by Michael Foot as 'Cassius', and *Your M.P.* (1944) by Tom Wintringham as 'Gracchus', helped to maintain the drive against the old order that had begun with the Blitz, but the articulate left-wing pressure came from journalists rather than writers or poets. J.B. Priestley was the only major writer on the 1941 Committee, and dropped out of the political arena after the Committee merged with Sir William Acland's forces to form the progressive Common Wealth Party in 1942. (Priestley did, however, campaign for Labour in 1945.) It is consistent with the general disillusion with the political commitments of the Thirties that writers and poets – with the exception of the Communists – should, while in general preferring a progressive government to a reactionary one, ignore the political situation. In June 1945 Cyril Connolly announced in *Horizon* that he would vote Labour – but he pointed out that those who had done most for the arts were Conservative.

In 1945 the political concern of writers was not with the pre-war conflict between Communism and Fascism, but with the post-war conflict between the individual artist and totalitarianism of any kind. Their views of the present can be deduced from their predictions of the future. George Woodcock, the editor of *Now*, as an anarchist and pacifist an outsider to both Right and Left, expected his difficulties to continue, while:

Only two possible alternatives seem to face the writers who have collaborated. Either, as has indeed been rumoured, some kind of State-subsidized culture service will be set up, to maintain subservient and persecute recalcitrant authors and artists. . . . The independent artist, the daring thinker, will have to work in the shadows, clinging to the edge of existence and continually in danger of suppression. . . . Alternatively, the State may decide that it can no longer find work for this large body of literary gentlemen. If this happens, there will be a great and pathetic exodus from the cosy Government offices to the chilly bread-lines of post-war Bloomsbury.

George Orwell had seen the way things were going in 1943: 'More and more the channels of production are under control of bureaucrats, whose aim is to destroy the artist or at least to castrate him.' Then Orwell was able to console himself with the fact that in spite of trying to ignore it, the government had been forced to give employment to the intelligentsia, and the need for an intelligentsia would ensure its preservation. But by the time he came to write *Nineteen Eighty Four* in 1948, the intelligentsia are reduced to frightened functionaries in the Ministry of Truth, whose looming architecture and endless corridors are a parody of the Ministry of Information and the BBC.

Over on the right wing, the patrician Osbert Sitwell was saying many things that Orwell found profound. His pamphlet *A Letter To My Son* (1944, a revised version of a *Horizon* article) forecast a difficult future for a young man with ambitions to be a writer. Sitwell attacks critics and politicians alike, but these traditional enemies were nothing to the new threat to art, and Sitwell's mockery becomes near-hysterical:

Above all, do not under-estimate the amount and intensity of the genuine ill-will that people will feel for you. . . . And here I must first make special mention of the civil servant as enemy. Throughout your career your liveliness will provoke his particular attention, and so you will suffer the continued passive obstruction that his resistant softness opposes to the will of the artist towards whom he bears an inborn loathing. . . . At best you will be ground down between the small but powerful authoritarian minority of art directors, museum racketeers, the chic, giggling modistes who write on art and literature, publishers, journalists and dons (who will, to do them justice, try to help you if you write as they tell you) – and the enormous remainder, who would not mind, who would indeed, be pleased, if they saw you starve.

John Lehmann, also worried by the growth of bureaucratic control, saw a warning for England in the 'withering disease of conformity, of literature with a State axe to grind' which he found in contemporary Russian novels. By contrast Lehmann celebrated the fact that writers in England had evaded government pressures, and chosen to be, if they wished, irrelevant:

Within the fairly wide bounds prescribed by security needs and the law about 'incitement to disaffection', we have held passionately to our right to be critical, to be antinomian, to be gloomy when we should have been enthusiastic, to write about the rambler rose against the garden wall and the kingfisher on the willow branch, the sensual charms of our mistress, the monster-minute dramas of our childhood and school-days, and everything else that has no immediate connection with the war – though it may have a permanent significance in human life.

Lehmann has a point, but it is difficult to reconcile the rambler rose against the garden wall with Keith Douglas's dead anti-tank gunner in his pit.

Stephen Spender was able to give a reason why the future of literature seemed so bleak:

A certain discouragement haunts sensitive people today because they envisage the possibility of a society organized in such a way that it is completely independent of the values which are maintained by art. There seems to be the possibility of a self-sufficient, materially successful kind of world, an organization of machinery producing other machinery which could dispense altogether with what we call culture.

Even those who, like Julian Symons, still believed that there was a necessary connection between art and politics, could see no hope for the future:

The arts, like European society, are disintegrating. A symptom of this disintegration is the rapid advance of kitsch, and its penetration into the previously sacrosanct area of highbrow art. . . . As art becomes more and more identifiable with kitsch it becomes more nearly true that its objective is to divert attention from the class struggle. The conflicts that prompted the great European literature of the last few hundred years have gone, and nothing has replaced them. It can practically be said that we are today *men without art*.

The thought of a future world bureaucratically organized, closely managed, authoritarian, technologically efficient and spiritually dead produced a response that was remarkably similar from all shades of the political spectrum. Whatever political complexion society would have, it was bound to be philistine: the answer was to assert the rights of the individual. E.M. Forster had warned writers at the PEN Conference in London in 1941 that all talk of a 'New Order' was futile. There never was an Old Order, what was needed was a New Disorder more favourable to the artist, who *should* be a Bohemian, an outsider, even a rat, but better a swimming rat than a sinking ship. 'To me, the best chance for future society lies through apathy, uninventiveness and inertia. If this war is followed – as it may be – by universal exhaustion, we may get the Change of Heart which is at present so briskly recommended from a thousand pulpits.'

Exhaustion did follow, and the change of heart turned out to be a refusal to engage with society at all. Pacifists took the most extreme view. Alex Comfort explained:

politically we regard ourselves as absolved. The State has consistently shown itself to be evil, insofar as we are able to understand evil. It has absolved us by rejecting individuality, to which as artists we are obliged to cling, even though in retaining it we are forced to face the reality of personal death, the bitterest thought that any interpretative can face. We now accept no responsibility to any group, only individuals.

This is the political background to the wave of Neo-Romantic and Apocalyptic poetry of the war years. The critical works of the movement like Paul Bloomfield's *The Many and the Few* (1942) or D.S. Savage's *The Personal Principle* (1944) assert that the writer has no responsibility at all, that instead of seeking to change the world he must withdraw from it, and that only those writers who do *not* share the values of society have any hope of creative achievement. Instead of social values there must be 'personal values':

the outlook for the creative writer . . . is identical with the outlook for the values of personal creativeness in general – with the outlook for the human being as such. We have reached a point in the progress of civilization in which those values have been almost completely exiled from the world of social relationships. Civilization's apotheosis, totalitarianism, which is everywhere becoming an actuality, represents the final displacement of personal values within society. This is signified by the status of art and religion within the totalitarian structure. Henceforth the personal values have no official sanction at all. Officialdom, which has always been the enemy of creativeness, is at last victorious.

When we turn to the Apocalyptics' most consistent critic, Stephen Spender, we find that, whatever he thought of their poetry, he took a similar view of the value of the individual:

The creative writer, ignoring the depersonalized assumptions and generalizations of the State, expressing only his own relationship with the universe, expresses the experience of the whole humanity which consists not of a social mass but of a plurality of individuals each with his individual relationship with the external world.

Only the handful of committed Communists contributing to *Our Time* retained their faith in the writer's direct political role.

On the day before war broke out the *New Statesman* had published John Lehmann's observation that political disillusionment was general among writers, and that 'a withdrawal is necessary in self-defence'. The assertion of the value of the individual is the correlative of the Strategic Retreat of the Left. The difficulty was that the emotional upheaval caused by this change of direction made it very difficult to write at all. In the summer of 1942 Lehmann reported: 'the book that everyone is waiting for is still to come', and went on to explain why. He could now see that while there had been social and literary quality in the Marxist writings of the Thirties, 'a hint of discomfort was constantly appearing, a sense of the partial inhibition of human sympathy which they implied. This suggestion of discomfort began to develop into a strong sense of revulsion very soon after the war broke out.' Now, after three years of war, Lehmann could describe the effect that revulsion had had:

There was, in fact, a change in the fundamental attitude to life, which was bound to show itself sooner or later in a new kind of writing. The desire to control the outer world waned rather sharply – if one can judge by the declarations authors made in articles and reviews – and with it the confidence that the formula for Utopia was within everyone's grasp, and that it needed a simple act of the will to realize it. . . . There was a feeling that a great deal had been left out, that the trouble went far deeper than had been suspected, and that values needed to be thoroughly overhauled before one could hope to make a success of refashioning the world.

Or, one might add, refashioning literature.

In 1942 the new literature had not emerged, as far as Lehmann could see, though he forecast that it would be 'a new attempt to find poetic symbols for human experiences'. Ironically, Lehmann was right, for he was describing precisely what the Apocalyptics tried to do – and of that Lehmann strongly disapproved. The books 'that everyone is waiting for', if they emerged at all, turned out to be

Elizabeth Bowen's collections of short stories, or Rosamond Lehmann's *The Ballad and the Source*, books which cast back in search of some explanation of how everything had gone wrong.

The change of direction explains why it was not just the physical difficulties of wartime that caused so few novels to be written. The poet Norman Nicholson noted in 1943:

> Many writers find that the economic-social-intellectual framework around which they constructed their philosophy of life is now inadequate. They have nothing to put in its place, but they have glimpses and hints of the personal values and of the religious aspect of Man. These hints are not yet formulated, often they are not fully understood or acknowledged. They could not be used for the structure of a novel, but they do find natural expression in poems, stories and sketches.

But few of these short stories or poems did more than convey the pervading feeling of loneliness and despair; they do not describe what was to replace it. Poets and prose-writers retreated into themselves, into reminiscence, self-contemplation, or silence.

There were some attempts to define the new ethic for literature that would result from the revaluation taking place, and again it is the Apocalyptics who present it in its most extreme form. In order to combat the life-destroying forces of the totalitarian State-machine the writer must assert his individuality, an individuality which Henry Treece defined as 'his own organic myth'. Poetry will depend

> not on the writer's selectivity, but rather on his ability to combine, to fuse into a justifiable whole, his several sets of experience, in such a way as to recreate a forgotten truth, and to erect for public recognition those fundamental myths and ideologies which will germinate naturally and inevitably as the soil is turned and fertilized.

The difficulty of the Apocalyptics' argument is that they never satisfactorily define what these fundamental myths and ideologies *are*. As Alex Comfort wrote, 'we accept an *emotional* analysis of history in preference to an intellectual one', it would appear that the myth had to remain so individual that to explain it was to risk its becoming hardened into an instrument of State propaganda.

Yet the search for a myth, individual or collective, something that would act as an image of oneself and society and be the source of a common set of values, was the purpose of the revaluation or change of direction that took place in the war years. In 1944 John Lehmann noted the 'division and loneliness' expressed by service contributors to *Penguin New Writing*. In explaining their isolation he showed both that something was being looked for – and that it had not been found:

It is from the absence of a generally accepted myth or system of beliefs that it arises; a myth whose wholeness would heal the wound between war and peace-time occupation, between the past and present, between one class and another; a myth which we in England felt we were about to recapture for one moment of astonishing intensity in 1940, when everything seemed to be falling into place.

Connolly's *The Unquiet Grave* encapsulates the problem: he writes not a novel but a journal, and tries to become a creative writer by writing about the difficulty of being a creative writer. 'Three requisites for a work of art: validity of the myth, vigour of belief, intensity of vocation. . . . The belief in a myth whose validity is diminishing will not produce such great art as the belief in one which is valid, and none are valid today.'

'Decadence of the myth' is a theme of *The Unquiet Grave*, the absence of a sustaining myth is one of the causes of the book's failure.

The demoralization of writers was so complete that not only were they unable to define the organic myth that they had lost, they were unable to explain how they had lost it. Edwin Muir's essay 'The Natural Man and the Political Man' (*New Writing and Daylight*, 1942) is the most successful attempt. Muir argued that man's image of himself had changed as a result of materialist theories of history and Darwinian theories of evolution. Man was no longer a spiritual or even a humanistic being whose identity was formed by confronting a series of moral choices; instead he had become a mechanical object governed by his material environment, and, like his environment, capable of improvement along scientific lines. Hence the totalitarian policies of Communism and Fascism, where the State manipulated the individual for whatever purposes the State considered to be right. Life ceased to be thought of in terms of a continuous struggle between the conflicting forces of good and evil within the individual, but as a logical, inevitable process: 'man developing within an environment in a calculable way, without any effective inward struggle, or a permanent conception of a desirable life, or any personal striving to realize it'.

Muir's idea of 'a permanent conception of a desirable life' is the nearest he gets to defining Lehmann's healing myth – but he does explain how the absence of myth was damaging to literature. Life had become a matter of controlling *things*, not living people; in literature human beings were reduced to creatures that were mechanical, sentimental, primitive, anti-social. The result was an impoverishment of literature itself:

Human life thus became a thing completely contained in an environment, and therefore a thing to which the writer could give no ultimate significance, since there was not in it even the pretence of choice, even the day-dream of freedom. If the life of the individual is a development, then that development is simple and inevitable. If the life of the individual is a conflict, then that conflict implies a choice, and the choice, complexity, and complexity, the existence of more in human life than can be compressed into a formula.

And – though Muir does not say this – since the secret of human life cannot be compressed into a formula, there is no definition of the absent myth.

In 'The Yogi and the Commissar' (*Horizon*, also 1942), Arthur Koestler offered a different explanation for the change of heart experienced by writers, though he uses the same oppositions of materialism and religion, Marxism and mysticism. He presents a philosophical model of social behaviour in terms of a spectrum that ranges from the infra-red, totally materialist and determinist Commissar at one end, to the ultra-violet super-spiritual Yogi at the other (with most people somewhere in between). The oppositions of the ends of the spectrum are permanent, and irreconcilable. A consequence of this is a periodic shift of emphasis along the spectrum, a pendulum swing which Marxist thought, with its own model of progression by a series of dialectical syntheses, is unable to comprehend. One may or may not accept Koestler's theory; what is important is that he detected a shift towards the irrational Yogi end of the spectrum – and this was most evident among the 'pink' artists:

Turning to the more muddled, intermediary bands of the spectrum we find that their reactions to the mystic current are of a revealing nature. In the pink regions the reaction first manifests itself by an intense consciousness of the Left's serial defeats, of disgust with the old parties, disgust with their worn-out leaders, with plans and promises, ideas and ideals, and most of all with one's own foolish and frustrated hopes. This pink hangover is the emotional starting point.

Koestler has brought us back also to our own starting point, the disillusion and revulsion that Lehmann noted on 2 September 1939. As – to borrow from Auden – the clever hopes expired of a low, dishonest decade, English literary life fell into a state of shock from which it found little cause to recover during the war years. Samuel Hynes concludes of *The Auden Generation*:

For the writers *as writers*, the appropriate response to the end of the 'thirties was silence, or a retrospective brooding over what had happened. Some of them would fight in the war, or support the war in various other ways, but they would not write much about it; it was not really their war, and when it overtook their lives it came not as a cause, but as a consequence of a cause that had already been lost.

This explains the departure of Auden and Isherwood to America, and the demoralization of those who stayed behind – and demoralization is infectious. Literature became non-combatant. In a phrase which echoes the public-school background of the Thirties radicals, Alan Ross commented in an interview: 'It was as though all the prefects had suddenly disappeared.'

There was a real sense of regret that the older generation did not engage more directly in the war. It was all very well to be in the Ministry of Information writing about the war, but somehow these people were not of the war. If some of them had been in the services they might have written differently.

The argument over the attitude writers should take to the war goes back to 1940, and Connolly's statement that 'War is the enemy of creative activity, and writers and painters are right and wise to ignore it'. Goronwy Rees, a writer already in uniform, sent a 'Letter from a Soldier' in reply. Rees pointed out that Connolly did not take his own advice, in fact he referred to the war obsessively: 'The war will not be ignored: it is your guilty conscience, and your obsession is an unconscious profession of disbelief in the view you profess to hold.' Rees did not mean that the only thing a writer could do in wartime was to take up arms:

Yet the soldier has the right, in return for his blood and his life and his despair, for the crimes he must take on himself, to ask that those most qualified, by their sensibility, by their more lucid perception of values, by their release from belligerence, should comprehend, analyse, illuminate, commemorate, his sacrifice and his suffering and the horror to which he is condemned, to understand and reveal that even in war he is a human being and not a brute too ignoble for the artist's notice.

Connolly's answer was that by creating more 'culture' he was giving the soldiers something worthwhile to defend, but it was an uneasy solution. It was the civilian writer who found himself in no-man's-land. Every option open to him meant a curtailment of his creative potential, potential already severely limited by the physical constraints of wartime existence. A writer might choose pacifism, accept whatever physical penalties were imposed, and preserve his literary independence. But the act of rejection that implied – of society by the artist, of the artist by society – set the writer in such isolation that he no longer cared about communication and indulged in egotistical fantasies. Hence the fundamental feebleness of so much Neo-Romantic poetry. Another option open to the writer was to join the Ministry of Information or the BBC and become a civil servant of letters, but here too there were penalties in the loss of creative freedom and the absorption of creative energy, as so many examples quoted have shown. Writers seem to have been so numbed that they could do little more than protest at their condition. C. Day Lewis, at the Ministry of Information, produced a wry justification for their creative silence:

> Where are the War Poets?
> They who in folly or mere greed
> Enslaved religion, markets, laws,
> Borrow our language now and bid
> Us to speak up in freedom's cause.
>
> It is the logic of our times,
> No subject for immortal verse –
> That we who lived by honest dreams
> Defend the bad against the worse.

The uneasiness and guilt felt by writers shows most acutely in attitudes to what was happening to literature on the Continent. Both pacifists and those who supported the war seemed to have had a nostalgia for defeat, for the reality of occupation and the threat of death. There was passionate interest in the works of Aragon, Gide and Vercors, which seemed to be enhanced by their being smuggled out of occupied France. English men of letters suffered from an inferiority complex when it came to French literature, and Cyril Connolly more than most. He wrote in December 1944:

In France there was no total war, but the Germans were directly in command. Instead of the State becoming the enemy (for Vichy was too weak for that) there was a military tyranny to be opposed. The attitude of writers therefore was not one of anarchic sulking but of fraternal conspiracy against the enemy. And in the case of writers their liberty was not interfered with. . . . We on the other hand who have neither starved nor been tortured, have never had our liberation, our moment of glory.

This tells us more about Connolly's guilty conscience than the reality of literary life under the Germans, where writers' responses were as various, from collaboration to resistance, as in England, as André Halimi's *Chantons Sous l'Occupation* (1976) goes some way to showing.

The final option open to civilian writers was to take up arms. That was assuming that one's age and health were acceptable to military requirements; it probably meant that writing itself would become virtually impossible during the war years – if one survived them. Of all the options, the immediate penalties were the severest; membership of the armed forces was no guarantee of integration with military society, as, again, many examples quoted have shown. But, to refer to the case of Alun Lewis, it was consistent with his desire to be a writer that he should seek the authority that experience of war gave him, 'the true story and the proper ending'. It was with the authority of someone who had both served in the Forces and continued to write that Roy Fuller stated in 1945:

In my view the two most important factors determining the character of English poetry during the late war are: first, the absence of a clear and consistent political attitude towards the war from English intellectuals as a whole; and secondly, the mass withdrawal of poets from active participation in the war.

Yet even the experience of war could be disillusioning. In 1939 Evelyn Waugh considered the options before him of military service or the Ministry of Information. He decided, correctly, that the novels could wait, a decision justified by the *Sword of Honour* trilogy. But Waugh's high hopes of the Army were bitterly disappointed; instead of comradeship and valour he found place-seeking and muddle, and all for the sake of a post-war world for which he felt a passionate hostility.

If the closing pages of this book are depressing, it is because the times they describe are depressing. There are positive achievements to be celebrated: the State's recognition that the arts are important and worthy of support; the educational effect of the wide diffusion of culture; the genuine enthusiasm many people felt for books, music, art and the theatre. The *Daily Express*'s claim that there was no such thing as culture in wartime was roundly disproved. But for the most part writers, in their inner emigration, felt alienated from the history that was being made around them. Even when they drew towards each other, in the Bohemia of Fitzrovia, it was in opposition to the outside world, and that enclosed society proved nihilistic, alcoholic and self-destructive.

Yet, if the end of the war was a depressing time, the next years were to be worse. Living conditions were even more harsh, and lacked the social discipline of war. Koestler forecast: 'The interregnum of the next decades will be a time of distress and of gnashing of teeth. We shall live in the hollow of the historical wave.' V.S. Pritchett summed up the years in the hollow in his autobiography:

English writing did not vanish, but for years the experience exhausted us mentally and physically. And then there is nothing as dead as a dead war and, as the pace quickens, the latest war kills the one before it quickly. One is ridiculous to be still alive and the best thing is to keep one's mouth shut. Looking back at the war egotistically from a writer's point of view, it was a feverish dispersal and waste of one's life. It is often said that this was a good time, when all private defences gave way, especially the defence of class differences, and that we all came together for once; and one hears regrets that after the war this revolution spent itself and that we went back to our old privacy. We did; though not to the old kind.

Even those who did not spend a demoralizing war in London, who returned full of energy and experience, eager to take advantage of the still buoyant book market, somehow were unable to settle down. G.S. Fraser remembers: 'I knew dozens of people who said they were going to write a great novel about their experiences in the desert – and of course they never did. We talked away the rest of the 1940s, instead of writing our great novels.'

Both *Horizon* and *Penguin New Writing* folded in 1950. Looking back in 1961 Alan Ross reflected: 'The left-wing idealism of the thirties under whose honourable, if battered, banner both these reviews were launched, had disintegrated in the threadbare bureaucracies of the Welfare State, the excitement of social revolution been deflated by fulfilment, as well as by the drab realities of post-war life.'

The idealism of the Thirties had been supplanted by the frozen academicism of the Cold War.

Fitzrovia continued into the post-war period but the camaraderie was gradually diluted as writers dispersed abroad, to the universities, into advertising, to television – or succumbed to drink and despair. As competition increased from easier forms of entertainment, books themselves lost the advantages they had had during the war. Julian Maclaren-Ross, the first and greatest memorialist of this now lost Bohemia, considered the Fifties 'a decade which I could well have done without'. His friend Dan Davin knew why:

when the writers formed and clustered again it was about the knees of the BBC, in the Stag's Head, in the Whore's Lament, in the George. And Julian, in the Wheatsheaf, was asking querulously where everyone had gone.

Notes on Sources

I refer here only to material that has been quoted in the text. Where the context is clear in the text itself I have not repeated the reference here. One source, though not quoted anywhere in the text, which requires a major acknowledgment, is Angus Calder's *The People's War: Britain 1939–45* published by Cape in 1969. This is a key study of all aspects of the Home Front, and has a useful section on the Arts.

PROLOGUE

The epigraph is from an article by E.M. Forster in the *Listener* 11 January 1940. Connolly's *Enemies of Promise* was published first in 1938 by Routledge and in a revised edition in 1949; a Penguin edition was published in 1961. Jason Gurney's *Crusade in Spain* was published by Faber and Faber in 1974. Julian Symons is quoted from his book *The Thirties*, published in a revised edition by Faber and Faber in 1975. 'Today was a beautiful day . . .' comes from Louis MacNeice's *Autumn Journal*, in his *Collected Poems*, Faber and Faber 1966 and Oxford University Press (New York). George Orwell is quoted from Volume One of *The Collected Essays, Journalism and Letters of George Orwell* edited by Sonia Orwell and Ian Angus, 4 volumes, Secker and Warburg 1968 and Harcourt, Brace Jovanovitch (New York). I refer to this from now on as *The Collected Essays, etc.*

CHAPTER ONE

The epigraph is from MacNeice's *Autumn Journal. The Fate of Homo Sapiens* was published by Secker and Warburg in 1939; *The Idea of a Christian Society* was published by Faber and Faber in 1939 and Harcourt, Brace Jovanovitch (New York); *Between the Acts* was published by the Hogarth Press in 1941, *Barbarians at the Gate* by Gollancz in 1939. Lehmann is quoted from the *New Statesman* 2 September 1939. Jack Lindsay's comment was made in an interview with the author. Richard Crossman was writing in *Time and Tide* 9 December 1939. Connolly made his comment on Auden and Isherwood in *Horizon* February 1940; Louis MacNeice made his in *Horizon* for January 1941. John Lehmann made his comment in an interview with the author.

Herbert Read was writing in *New Verse* No. 31, Basil Dean in his memoir of ENSA, *The Theatre at War*, published by Harrap in 1956. Sir Kenneth Clark and Stanley Unwin are quoted from Rom Landau's *Love for a Country*, published by Nicholson and Watson in 1939. Geoffrey Faber was writing in the *Spectator* for 15 September 1939. Patrick Hamilton's *Hangover Square* was published by Constable in 1941. Henry Green's *Party Going* was published by the Hogarth Press in 1939 and by the Viking Press (New York).

The evacuation of the National Gallery is described in Kenneth Clark's *Another Part of the Wood*, John Murray 1974. For general information about the 'phoney war' I have drawn on R. Seth's *The Day War Broke Out*, Neville Spearman 1963, and E.S. Turner's *The Phoney War on the Home Front*, published by Michael Joseph 1961; Mass Observation's *War Begins at Home*, Gollancz 1940, is invaluable. Richmal Crompton's *William and A.R.P.* was published by George Newnes in May 1939. The *New Statesman*'s comment is from the 3 September 1939 issue, Merle Oberon is quoted from the *Spectator* 3 November 1939. Dylan Thomas is quoted from *Selected Letters of Dylan Thomas*, edited by Constantine Fitzgibbon, published by Dent in 1966 and by New Directions Inc. (New York). Stephen Spender's 'September Journal' began in *Horizon* February 1940. Connolly's article is in the *New Statesman* for 7 October 1939.

Time and Tide's comment on music is in the issue for 14 October 1939, the comment on the theatre is in the *Listener* for 18 January 1940. John Piper's comment on the Royal Academy is in the *Spectator* for 29 December 1939. Victor Cazalet's biography by Robert Rhodes James was published by Hamish Hamilton in 1976. Evelyn Waugh's *Men at Arms* was published by Chapman and Hall in 1952, Graham Greene's story 'Men at Work' was published in *Penguin New Writing* No. 9. The files on the Authors' Committee and related matters in the Public Record Office are numbers INF/1/229, INF/1/32, and INF/1/39. Asa Briggs's official history of the BBC,

Notes on Sources

Volume Three, *The War of Words*, Oxford University Press 1970, describes the evacuation and emergency plans. Geoffrey Grigson's *The Crest on the Silver*, Cresset Press 1950, and Gilbert Harding's *Along My Line*, Putnam 1953, describe the atmosphere at Evesham. Mollie Panter-Downes is quoted from her *London War Notes*, edited by William Shawn, published by Longman in 1972 and Farrar, Straus Giroux Inc. (New York). The *Notes* originally appeared in the *New Yorker*.

London during the phoney war is described by Mrs Robert Henrey in *The Siege of London*, Dent 1946. The *New Statesman* article is in the 20 April 1940 number. Orwell's diary is in *The Collected Essays, etc.*, Volume Two. Vera Brittain's diary was reprinted as *England's Hour*, Macmillan 1941. Mass Observation's analysis of paintings was made in its short-lived magazine *Us*, which ran from February to May 1940. The prostitute appears in Henry Green's *Caught*, published by the Hogarth Press in 1943 and the Viking Press (New York). Stanley Unwin's battles with the authorities are recorded in his *Publishing in Peace and War*, Allen and Unwin 1944, and *The Truth about a Publisher*, Allen and Unwin 1960, and R.R. Bowker (New York). Ivor Brown's article is in the *New Statesman* for 14 December 1940. The plight of internees is described in François Lafitte's Penguin Special *The Internment of Aliens* 1940. The artists' protest is in a letter to the *New Statesman* 20 August 1940. *Garrison Theatre* is described in the *New Statesman* 18 May 1940. Peter Opie's story 'It was a defeat' was published in *Bugle Blast* No. 2, edited by Jack Aistrop and Reginald Moore, Allen and Unwin, 1944. Priestley's comment on the writer's role is in the *New Statesman* for 13 July 1940.

CHAPTER TWO

The story of the Blitz comes from many sources, but I have used in particular two accounts – Constantine Fitzgibbon's *The Blitz*, published by Allan Wingate 1957, and William Sansom's *Westminster in War*, Faber and Faber 1947. The best short account of the Blitz is in Chapter Four of Angus Calder's *The People's War*, Cape 1969. Since the completion of this chapter Tom Harrisson's *Living Through the Blitz* has been published by Collins, 1976. The epigraph for Chapter Two comes from 'The Aftermyth of War' from the revue *Beyond the Fringe*, published by the Souvenir Press © 1963 Alan Bennett, Peter Cook, Jonathan Miller and Dudley Moore.

Cecil Beaton's *The Years Between: Diaries 1939–45* was published by Weidenfeld and Nicolson in 1965. Norman Demuth's description of the Proms is in *Transformation* No. 1, Gollancz 1943. Eric Newton was writing in the *New Statesman* 28 June 1941. The night-life crisis is described in Basil Woon's *Hell Came to London*, Peter Davis 1941. Ritchie Calder's comments on the Blitz are in *The Lesson of London*, Secker and Warburg 1941. Harold Nicolson's *Letters and Diaries* Volume Two 1939–45, was published by Collins in 1967 and the Atheneum Press (New York). Vera Brittain's diary of the Blitz was published as *England's Hour* by Macmillan in 1941. Connolly's complaint is in *Horizon* for December 1940. Leonard Woolf's *The Journey Not the Arrival Matters*, autobiography 1939–69, was published by the Hogarth Press in 1969 and Harcourt, Brace Jovanovitch (New York). Charles Graves's diary *Off the Record* was published by Hutchinsons in 1941. Herbert Mason's comment is quoted from Constantine Fitzgibbon's *The Blitz*, Allan Wingate 1957.

Negley Farson's comment on the Communist campaign is in his *Bombers' Moon*, published by Gollancz in 1941. The criticism of ENSA is in the *New Statesman* of 14 December 1940. Ralph Ingersoll's *Report on England* was published by the Bodley Head in 1941. The gossip columns are reported in Basil Woon's *Hell Came to London*. Charles Graves tells the story of the Café de Paris in *Off the Record*; a full account of the incident is in Constantine Fitzgibbon's *The Blitz*.

Complaints about censorship are in Mollie Panter-Downes's *London War Notes*, edited by William Shawn and published by Longman in 1972 and Farrar, Straus Giroux Inc. (New York), and in Maurice Richardson's *London's Burning*, published by Robert Hale 1941. Tom Harrisson's comment on memories of the Blitz is in the *New Statesman* 19 September 1975. Louis MacNeice's comment on American reporting is in *Penguin New Writing* No. 5. Charles Graves's *The Thin Blue Line* was published by Heinemann in 1941. Tom Harrisson's article on war books is in *Horizon* for December 1941. Henry Moore's notes on the Tilbury food store shelter (which is depicted in the jacket illustration), are transcribed from an illustration of his unpublished sketchbooks in Constantine Fitzgibbon's *The Blitz*. George Stonier's 'Shaving Through the Blitz' (under the pseudonym 'Fanfarlo') appeared in *Penguin New Writing* and was published by Cape in 1943.

The Lesson of London was published by Secker and Warburg in

1941, Orwell's review of *Home Guard for Victory* is in *Horizon* for March 1941, (it appears to have been omitted from *The Collected Essays, etc.*). Strachey's *Post D* and *A Faith to Fight For* were both published by Gollancz in 1941. Priestley's comment on his 'Post-scripts' is in his *Margin Released*, Heinemann 1962 and Harper and Row (New York). Harold Nicolson is quoted from the second volume of his *Letters and Diaries*, published by Collins in 1967 and the Atheneum Press (New York). 'William Whitebait's' review of *Mrs Miniver* is in the *New Statesman* for 18 July 1942; Marie Scott-James's comment on war books is in *Time and Tide* 14 August 1943.

Graham Greene's *Ministry of Fear* was published by Heinemann in 1943, Rex Warner's *The Aerodrome* by The Bodley Head in 1941; they also published his *Why Was I Killed?* in 1943. Henry Green's *Caught* was published by the Hogarth Press in 1943 and the Viking Press (New York). William Sansom gave the account of his start with *Horizon* in an interview with the author. Faber and Faber published James Hanley's *No Directions* in 1943; Andre Deutsch published *A Dream Journey* in 1976. Dent published Robert Greenwood's *The Squad Goes Out* in 1943. 'Ceremony After a Fire Raid' was not published until 1944, but its quotation is valid here. It appears in *The Collected Poems of Dylan Thomas*, published by Dent and New Directions Inc. (New York). Eliot's encounter with the ghost of Yeats appears in 'Little Gidding' in *Four Quartets*, published by Faber and Faber and Harcourt, Brace Jovanovitch (New York).

Richard Hillary's *The Last Enemy* was published by Macmillan in 1942; Koestler's essay 'The Birth of a Myth' first appeared in *Horizon* for April 1943 and was reprinted in *The Yogi and the Commissar*, Cape 1945. Lovat Dickson's biography *Richard Hillary* was published by Macmillan in 1950. John Lehmann's comment on 1940 is in *Penguin New Writing* No. 19. Elizabeth Bowen's *In the Heat of the Day* was published by Cape in 1949 and Alfred Knopf (New York).

Stephen Spender's autobiography *World Within World* was published by Hamish Hamilton in 1951. Virginia Woolf's 'Thoughts on Peace during an Air Raid' is in Volume Four of her *Collected Essays*, published by the Hogarth Press and Harcourt, Brace Jovanovitch (New York). Lehmann's optimism is expressed in his editorial for *Penguin New Writing* No. 5, C. Day Lewis's autobiography *The Buried Day* was published by Chatto and Windus in 1960. Francis

Scarfe's *Auden and After* was published by Routledge in 1942. Alun Lewis's comment comes from *In the Green Tree*, published by Allen and Unwin 1948. John Lehmann sees the consciousness stirring in *Penguin New Writing* No. 4. Orwell's diary is in Volume Two of his *Collected Essays, etc.*

CHAPTER THREE

Nearly every book and magazine of the period contributes something to our knowledge of the social geography of London; I have also drawn on a wide range of personal reminiscences. Fitzrovia's particular chronicler was Julian Maclaren-Ross, whose unfinished *Memoirs of the Forties* were published by Alan Ross in 1965. His stories *Nine Men of Soho*, published by Allan Wingate in 1946, also convey the flavour of the period. Julian Maclaren-Ross and other leading characters are themselves recalled in Dan Davin's *Closing Times*, published by the Oxford University Press in 1975. John Lehmann's autobiography *I am my Brother*, Longman 1960, spans the social distance between the Fitzroy and Emerald Cunard's salon at the Dorchester. The epigraph is from Elizabeth Bowen's *In the Heat of the Day*, Cape 1949 and Alfred Knopf (New York).

Joseph Grigg's comparison between London and Berlin is in the *Spectator* for 26 June 1942, William Sansom's comment on the Lull is in *Westminster In War*, Faber and Faber 1947. George Stonier's comment is in a book review for the *New Statesman* 4 April 1942. John Lehmann's editorial protest is in *Penguin New Writing* No. 12.

The description of London's social geography, as I said, comes from many sources. Very useful is the map at the beginning of *Fitzrovia and the Road to the York Minster*, the catalogue to an exhibition at the Michael Parkin Gallery 1973, with an introduction by Ruthven Todd. John Lehmann's novel *In the Purely Pagan Sense* was published by Blond and Briggs in 1976. Heath-Stubbs's 'Lament for the Old Swan, Notting Hill Gate' is in his *Selected Poems*, Oxford University Press 1965. Rayner Heppenstall's *The Lesser Infortune* was published by Cape in 1953; see also his novel *Saturnine* published by Secker and Warburg in 1943 for the immediate pre-war period. Harold Nicolson's and Cecil Beaton's comments on Sybil Colefax are in their respective published diaries. Goronwy Rees recalls the wartime *ménage* of Guy Burgess in *A Chapter of Accidents*, Chatto and Windus 1972. William Sansom's recipe for red wine comes from an interview with the author. Charles Graves followed up his diary *Off the Record* (1941) with *Londoner's Life*, also with Hutchinson, in 1942.

John Heath-Stubbs is quoted from an interview with the author. The *Goncourt Journals* are published in four volumes by Fasquelle and Flamarion, Paris 1956. Louis MacNeice is quoted from *Springboard: Poems 1941–44*, Faber and Faber 1944 and Random House (New York). 'Alcohol' first appeared in *Horizon* January 1943. Paul Potts's *Dante Called You Beatrice* was published by Eyre and Spottiswoode in 1960. Dan Davin's encounter with Maclaren-Ross is recalled in *Closing Times*, Oxford University Press 1975.

Constantine Fitzgibbon's phrase 'inner emigration' is in his *Life of Dylan Thomas*, Dent 1965 and Little, Brown and Co. (Boston). George Orwell's 'London Letters' to the *Partisan Review* are reprinted in Volume Two of his *Collected Essays, etc.*, 'My Country Right or Left' in Volume One. The Searchlight Book series of which Stephen Spender's *Life and the Poet* is one, were published by Secker and Warburg. John Lehmann was writing in *Folios of New Writing* No. 4, Connolly's comment is in his editorial for *Horizon* May 1942.

The *Times Literary Supplement* editorial attacking intellectuals was published on 20 April 1940, *The Times* fourth leader on 25 March 1941. Jenni Calder's *Chronicles of Conscience*, which concentrates on Orwell and Koestler, was published by Secker and Warburg in 1968. *Horizon*'s 'Why Not War Writers?' was in the October 1941 number.

Alan Ross's epitaph for Fitzrovia is in *The London Magazine*, December 1942.

CHAPTER FOUR

The problems of publishing in wartime are described in John Brophy's *Britain Needs Books* published by the National Book Council in 1942, Sir Stanley Unwin's *Publishing in Peace and War*, Allen and Unwin 1944, and his autobiography *The Truth about a Publisher*, Allen and Unwin 1960 and R.R. Bowker (New York). The epigraph comes from Lord Elton's speech in the House of Lords debate on 23 October 1941. The Ministry of Information's file on paper rationing is in the Public Record Office, INF/1/238, the Ministry of Supply's file on Paper Control is SUPP/14/726. Orwell's comment on censorship is from his 'As I Please' column for *Tribune*, reprinted in *The Collected Essays, etc.*, his comment on the quality of paper is in a 'London Letter' for the *Partisan Review*, reprinted in Volume Two. Statistics on books published are taken from the annual volumes of *Whitaker's Cumulative Book List*. Sir Stanley Unwin's protest about mushroom firms was published in *The Times* for 11 October 1943.

Rupert Hart-Davis's fiction review is in the *Spectator* for 8 March 1940. Maurice Grindea tells his story in *Adam* Nos 385–90, a special Cyril Connolly number. Denys Val Baker's *Little Reviews* was published by Allen and Unwin in 1943, he is quoted from an article in *Transformation* No. 3, Lindsay Drummond 1943. The *Time and Tide* reviewer was Frances Meres writing in the number for 2 December 1944. Maclaren-Ross is quoted from his *Memoirs of the Forties*.

For a discussion of wartime tastes in reading see Henry Reed's *The Novel Since 1939*, British Council/Phoenix Press 1949. Seán Jennett's article 'The Price of Books' was published in *Life and Letters Today* for January 1945. Arthur Koestler's fears are expressed in his essay 'The Intelligentsia', *Horizon* March 1944, reprinted in *The Yogi and the Commissar*, Cape 1945. Stephen Spender's letter to the *Times Literary Supplement* was published 20 February 1943. William Walton was writing in *Time and Tide* 30 December 1944. George Orwell's comment on the BBC is in a letter reprinted in Volume One of *The Collected Essays, etc.*, on wartime bureaucrats in an 'As I Please' article in Volume Three.

Alun Lewis's comment on his life in India is quoted in the introduction to *Ha! Ha! Among the Trumpets*, Allen and Unwin 1945. John Sommerfield's stories were collected in *The Survivors*, published by John Lehmann Ltd in 1947. Connolly's view of service writing is in *Horizon* June 1944, John Lehmann's in *Penguin New Writing* No. 19. Nigel Balchin's novels were published by Collins. William Sansom's journal is reprinted in *Leaves in the Storm*, edited by Stefan Schimanski and Henry Treece, Lindsay Drummond 1947. Elizabeth Bowen was writing in the *New Statesman* 23 May 1942, Raymond Mortimer in the *New Statesman* 30 September 1944. H.E. Bates's *The Modern Short Story* was published by Nelson in 1941.

John Hampson was writing in the *Spectator* for 30 July 1943. Elizabeth Bowen's collections of short stories *Look at all those Roses*, 1941, and *The Demon Lover*, 1945, were published by Cape and Alfred Knopf (New York). Rosamond Lehmann's *The Ballad and the Source* was published by Collins in 1944. Ivy Compton-Burnett's novels were published by Gollancz, Joyce Cary's by Michael Joseph. Evelyn Waugh's *Work Suspended* was published by Chapman Hall, who also published *Brideshead Revisited* in 1945, and a revised edition, with an introduction, in 1960. *The Unquiet Grave* was published by Hamish Hamilton in 1944, who reprinted it with an introduction from Connolly in their twenty-first birthday volume *Majority* in 1952, from which I quote. The jaundiced critic is Philip Toynbee in *Penguin New Writing* No. 23.

CHAPTER FIVE

The epigraph is from Cyril Connolly's *The Unquiet Grave*, Hamish Hamilton 1944. There are a number of studies of twentieth-century English verse, but few give more than a chapter to the Forties. Of the more sympathetic studies there are John Wain's contribution on poetry to *The Twentieth Century Mind*, edited by C.B. Cox and A.E. Dyson and published by Oxford University Press 1972, and G.S. Fraser's *The Modern Writer and his World*, published by Derek Verschoyle in 1953 (where he corrects his earlier view of Apocalypticism). Ian Hamilton wrote a series of articles for *The London Magazine* in April, June and August 1964. John Press's *A Map of English Verse*, Oxford University Press 1969, is both criticism and anthology; Robin Skelton's anthology *Poetry of the Forties*, Penguin 1968, is best read in conjunction with Kenneth Allott's *Penguin Book of Contemporary Verse* (revised 1962) which has useful biographical and bibliographical information. Stephen Spender's *Poetry Since 1939*, British Council/Phoenix House 1948, constitutes the 'official history' of the poetry of the period, and is a very fair account. Two recent books help set the war years in context – Samuel Hynes's *The Auden Generation, Literature and Politics in England in the 1930s*, The Bodley Head 1976 and the Viking Press (New York), and Paul Fussell's *The Great War and Modern Memory*, Oxford University Press 1975.

Douglas's comment comes from his poem 'Desert Flowers' in *The Collected Poems of Keith Douglas*, Faber and Faber 1966; John Heath-Stubbs was taking part in Michell Raper's BBC radio programme on Fitzrovia and the war, reprinted in the *Listener* 3 October 1974. Roy Fuller's 'The Middle of a War' is the title poem for his collection published by the Hogarth Press in 1942. Herbert Read's 'Ode Without Rhetoric' was first published in *Kingdom Come*, Autumn 1940, and is reprinted in his *Collected Poems*, Faber and Faber 1966 and the Horizon Press (New York). Graves's 'The Persian Version' is in his *Collected Poems 1914–47*, Cassell 1948.

Connolly was writing in *Horizon* January 1941, George Stonier in the *New Statesman* 16 August 1941. Connolly's complaint about poetry fever is in *Horizon* June 1940.

Charles Hamblett's anthology *I Burn For England* was published by Leslie Frewin in 1966. Keidrych Rhys edited *Poems from the Forces* for Routledge in 1941, and *More Poems from the Forces* for the same publishers in 1943. Dylan Thomas was writing on poetry editors to Tambimuttu, see *Selected Letters of Dylan Thomas*, edited by Constantine Fitzgibbon, Dent 1966 and New Directions Inc. (New York). Naomi Ryde Smith was writing in *Time and Tide* for 26 September 1942. Alun Lewis's *Ha! Ha! Among the Trumpets* was published by Allen and Unwin in 1945.

Stephen Spender was writing in *Horizon* for June 1942; I then quote his *Poetry Since 1939*, British Council/Phoenix Press 1948. Auden's collection *Another Time* was published by Faber and Faber in 1940 and by Random House (New York), who both published his *New Year Letter* in 1941. John Lehmann made the comment on Auden in *New Writing and Daylight* 1944. C. Day Lewis's dedicatory poem to the *Georgics* was published in *Horizon* September 1940, *Word Over All* by Cape in 1943 and the Transatlantic Press (New York). Spender's *The Still Centre* was published by Faber and Faber in 1939, *Ruins and Visions* by them in 1942. George Barker's sonnet on Spender is in his *Eros in Dogma*, Faber and Faber 1944. *The Strings Are False, An Unfinished Autobiography*, edited by E. R.Dodds was published by Faber and Faber in 1965. T.S. Eliot's interview with Donald Hall is in the Spring/Summer 1959 number of *The Paris Review*. *Four Quartets* are published by Faber and Faber and Harcourt, Brace Jovanovitch (New York).

'John Weaver' makes his appearance in *Horizon* for November 1941. Kenneth Allott's *Collected Poems*, with an introduction by Roy Fuller, were published by Secker and Warburg in 1975. Edith Sitwell's *Street Songs* were published by Macmillan in 1942, her autobiography *Taken Care Of* by Hutchinson in 1965. David Gascoyne appears in *Poets of Tomorrow, Third Selection*, Hogarth Press 1942, his *Poems 1937–42* were published by Editions Poetry London in 1943. I quote from 'The Fortress' and 'A Wartime Dawn'. George Barker is quoted from *Eros in Dogma*, published by Faber and Faber 1944. Dylan Thomas's 'I See The Boys Of Summer . . .' and 'A Refusal to Mourn . . .' are quoted from *Dylan Thomas: The Poems*, edited by Daniel Jones, published by Dent in 1971. Thomas's poems are published in America by New Directions Inc. *Deaths and Entrances* was published by Dent.

George Woodcock reviewed *Poets of Tomorrow* in *Poetry (London)* No. 8, Keidrych Rhys was writing in his anthology *Poems from the Forces*, Routledge 1941. *The New Apocalypse*, edited by Henry Treece was published by the Fortune Press; *The White Horseman*, edited by Henry Treece and J.F. Hendry, was published by Routledge; *The Crown and the Sickle*, edited by Treece and Hendry, was published by King and Staples; *Lyra* was published by The Grey Walls Press. Thomas's refusal to Treece is in *Selected Letters of Dylan Thomas*, Dent 1966 and New Directions Inc. (New York). *How I See Apocalypse* was published by Lindsay Drummond in 1946. I quote Treece's 'The Lying Word' from his *Invitation and Warning*, published by Faber and Faber in 1942, and J.F. Hendry's 'Apocalypse' from *The New Apocalypse*. The comment on regimentation in poetry is from G.S. Fraser's article in *The White Horseman*, Herbert Read's comment is in his introduction to *Lyra*, Alex Comfort's in *Now* (new series) No. 2 1944, followed by a quotation from *Lyra*. D.S. Savage's *The Personal Principle, Studies in Modern Poetry* was published by Routledge in 1944; John Lehmann was writing in *New Writing and Daylight* 1942/3.

CHAPTER SIX

The most recent study of Second World War poets is Vernon Scannell's *Not Without Glory*, the Woburn Press 1976, which includes commentary on the American service poets. Very useful is Ian Hamilton's anthology *The Poetry of War*, Alan Ross 1965, for it includes some brief comments by poets who survived. Ronald Blythe's anthology *The Components of the Scene*, Penguin Books 1966, and Charles Hamblett's *I Burn for England*, Leslie Frewin 1966, contain a wide range of war poetry. R.N. Currey wrote a brief but perceptive survey for the British Council in 1960, *Poets of the 1939–45 War*. With R.V. Gibson, Currey edited *Poems from India*, Oxford University Press 1946 (first published India 1945). The epigraph to Chapter Six comes from Roy Fuller's poem 'Sadness, Glass, Theory' in *A Lost Season*, Hogarth Press 1944.

Poems from the Desert and *Poems from Italy* were published by Harrap in 1944 and 1945. *Air Force Poetry*, edited by John Pudney and Henry Treece, was published by John Lane in 1944. *Poems from the Forces* and *More Poems from the Forces* were published by

Routledge in 1941 and 1943. Alan Rook is quoted from *Wartime Harvest*, edited by Stefan Schimanski and Henry Treece, John Bale and Staples 1943. Clifford Dyment was writing in *Time and Tide* for 2 January 1943. G.S. Fraser's description of army life is in *Transformation* No. 1, Gollancz 1943. Laurence Little's 'Tram Ride' is in *Poets of Tomorrow, Third Selection*, Hogarth Press 1942; Alan Ross's 'Messdeck' and 'Radar' are in Ian Hamilton's *The Poetry of War*, as is Norman Hampson's 'Assault Convoy'. Timothy Corsellis's 'Drill' is in *Air Force Poetry*; Uys Krige's 'Midwinter' was first published in *Horizon* December 1942. Barry Amiel's 'Death is a Matter of Mathematics' is in *Poems from India*. Bernard Gutteridge's *Traveller's Eye* was published by Routledge in 1947, Norman Cameron's 'Green, Green is El Aghir' is in *The Collected Poems of Norman Cameron*, Hogarth Press 1957. Robert Medley's 'Egypt' appeared in *Penguin New Writing* No. 24. Trooper Morris is quoted from *Poems from Italy*.

Olivia Manning's defence of the Cairo and Alexandria exiles is in *Horizon* October 1944. Jocelyn Brooke is quoted from *Bugle Blast* No. 1, edited by Jack Aistrop and Reginald Moore, Allen and Unwin 1943, Roy Fuller from *The Middle of a War*, Hogarth Press 1942. Gavin Ewart's 'When a Beau Goes In' is in Ian Hamilton's *The Poetry of War*, Alan Ross 1965. Donald Bain's 'War Poet' appeared in *Penguin New Writing* No. 21. Keith Douglas is quoted from *Poetry (London)* No. 10.

The life of Sidney Keyes is told in John Guenther's *Sidney Keyes: A Biographical Enquiry*, London Magazine Editions 1967. *The Collected Poems of Sidney Keyes*, with an introduction by Michael Meyer, was published by Routledge in 1945, who published *The Iron Laurel* in 1942 and *The Cruel Solstice* in 1944. They also published *Eight Oxford Poets* in 1941 and John Heath-Stubbs's *Wounded Thammuz* in 1942. Drummond Allison's *The Yellow Night* was published by The Fortune Press in 1944.

Ian Hamilton gives an account of Alun Lewis's life in his introduction to *The Selected Poetry and Prose of Alun Lewis*, Allen and Unwin 1966, who also published *In the Green Tree* (letters and stories), in 1948, *Ha! Ha! Among the Trumpets* in 1945, and *Raider's Dawn* in 1942. *Poetry Wales* Volume Ten No. 3, 1975, is a special Alun Lewis number.

Desmond Graham's full-length biography *Keith Douglas* was published by the Oxford University Press in 1946, his *Collected Poems* in

1951, and republished by Faber and Faber in 1966. Roy Fuller's *The Middle of a War*, 1942, and *A Lost Season*, 1944, were published by the Hogarth Press; I also quote a review he wrote for the *New Review* in July 1976.

Vernon Scannell is quoted from *Not Without Glory*, published by the Woburn Press 1976. Henry Reed's 'The Lessons of War' comes from his *A Map of Verona*, published by Cape in 1946 and Reynal and Hitchcock (New York). Gerry Wells's *Obie's War* was published by Lincolnshire and Humberside Arts in 1975, Alan Ross's *Open Sea* by London Magazine Editions 1975.

CHAPTER SEVEN

The epigraph is from an article by Joad in the *New Statesman* 11 October 1941. The main source of biographical details of artists working in this period are the brief entries in the many catalogues to exhibitions held then and since. They have not been listed individually. The main study of twentieth-century English painting is Sir John Rothenstein's *Modern English Painters*, in three volumes, published in a revised edition by Macdonald and Jane's 1976, although this is in fact a series of accounts of individual painters. Robin Ironside's *Painting Since 1939*, British Council/Phoenix House 1948, favours the Neo-Romantics, but is useful.

John Rothenstein was writing in *The Studio* April/May 1943, Graham Bell in *The Studio*, October 1940. The *Time and Tide* report was for 15 August 1942. Keith Vaughan tells the story of his arrest in his *Journal and Drawings 1939–1965*, published by Alan Ross in 1966. Jan Gordon was writing in *The Studio* November 1943. Henry Moore's comments are quoted from the catalogue to his show 'War Drawings' at the Imperial War Museum in 1975.

The catalogue to the Camden Arts Centre exhibition 'Hampstead in the Thirties', edited by Michael Collins, has much useful information about the *avant garde*. Patrick Heron is quoted by T.G. Rosenthal in *Ivon Hitchens*, edited by Alan Bowness, published by Lund Humphries in 1973. The story of the Camden Town Group is told in Wendy Baron's catalogue *Camden Town Recalled*, The Fine Art Society 1976. Graham Bell's pamphlet *The Artist and his Public* was published by the Hogarth Press in 1939. Geoffrey Grigson's comment on the Euston Road School is in *New Verse* January 1939, Clive Bell's on *The Artist and his Public* in the *New Statesman* for 18 November 1939. *The Townsend Journals*, edited by Andrew Forge, were published by the Tate Gallery in 1976. Victor Pasmore's comment is in *Horizon* March 1945.

Raymond Mortimer's review is in the *New Statesman* for 9 March 1940, the soldiers' comments in the *New Statesman* for 29 June 1940. John Piper's comment is in the *Listener* for 21 December 1944. Geoffrey Grigson's *The Poet's Eye* was published by Frederick Muller in 1944. Raymond Mortimer's review of 'New Movements in Art' is in the *New Statesman* for 28 March 1942. John Piper's *British Romantic Artists* was published in the 'Britain in Pictures' series by Collins in 1942. Grigson's anthology *The Romantics* was published by Routledge in 1942. The quotations from Paul Nash are from the catalogue to the Tate Gallery's 1975 exhibition *Paul Nash: Paintings and Watercolours*. Sir Kenneth Clark's comments are from the January 1942 number of *The Studio*.

Peter Watson's role as patron is recorded in the Cyril Connolly number of *Adam* (Nos 385–90 1974/5). Michael Ayrton's comment on British painting is in the December 1946 number of *The Studio*. Spender's comment on Cecil Collins is in *Horizon* February 1944; Collins's *The Vision of the Fool* was published by the Grey Walls Press in 1947. The comment on Turner and Palmer comes from 'A Painter's Notebook' in *Penguin New Writing* No. 25.

The story of ballet in wartime is told by Arnold Haskell in *Ballet Since 1939*, British Council/Phoenix House 1948. Keyes's comment on *Hamlet* is in *Sidney Keyes: A Biographical Enquiry* by John Guenther, London Magazine Editions 1967. The *New Statesman* comment on the audience for Sadler's Wells is in the number for 28 November 1942. The story of music is told by Rollo Myers in *Music Since 1939*, British Council/Phoenix House 1948. Eve Kisch was writing in *Our Time* July 1943. Statistics on BBC output come from Alan Peacock and Roland Weir's *The Composer in the Market Place*, Faber Music 1975. The story of the London Philharmonic Orchestra is told by Thomas Russell in *Philharmonic Decade*, Hutchinson 1945. Edward Sackville-West's review of Britten's Sinfonia da Requiem is in the *New Statesman* for 1 August 1942.

Eve Kisch gave her account of the foundation of CEMA in *Our Time*, July 1943. Eric White's history *The Arts Council of Great Britain* was published by Davis Poynter in 1975. John Lehmann's comment on the state of the theatre is in *Penguin New Writing* No. 14. The comment on the shortage of actors is in *Penguin New Writing* No. 19. *Time and Tide*'s comment on West End repertory is in the issue for 27 May 1944. Robert Speaight is quoted from his *Theatre Since 1939,* British Council/Phoenix House 1948. Michael Redgrave's comment is in the *New Statesman* for 4 September 1943. Mollie Panter-Downes is quoted from her *London War Notes,* Longman 1972 and Farrar, Straus and Giroux (New York). Ivor Brown is quoted by Eric White in his *The Arts Council of Great Britain.* J.B. Priestley's description of ENSA comes from his novel *Daylight on Saturday,* Heinemann 1943.

G.S. Fraser's comment on ABCA was made in an interview with the author, as were Jack Lindsay's on ABCA theatre. The description of a performance was made by Ernst Sigler in *Poetry Quarterly,* Summer 1945. *Our Time* editorials are quoted from the October and November 1942 numbers. The comment on CEMA comes from *Our Time* September 1941. George Orwell's comment comes from his 'As I Please' column in *Tribune,* reprinted in Volume Three of *The Collected Essays, etc.,* Philip Hope-Wallace's comes from his review of the audience for *Time and Tide* for 11 March 1944. Connolly's comment comes from *Horizon* December 1942. Stanley Unwin is quoted from *The Truth about a Publisher,* Allen and Unwin 1960 and R.R. Bowker (New York). Spender's autobiography *World Within World* was published by Hamish Hamilton in 1951.

CHAPTER EIGHT

The epigraph is from Dan Davin's *Closing Times,* Oxford University Press 1975. The comparison with 1940 is from Charles Graves's diary *Pride of the Morning,* Hutchinson 1945; the silence is recalled by Mrs Robert Henrey in her *The Siege of London,* published by Dent in 1946. George Stonier was writing in the *New Statesman* 24 June 1944, Inez Holden's diary is quoted from *Leaves in the Storm,* edited by Stefan Schimanski and Henry Treece, published by Lindsay Drummond in 1947; Orwell is quoted from *The Collected Essays, etc.,* Volume Three. Philip Hope-Wallace's memory of the V.1 comes from an interview with the author. Charles Graves is quoted from *Pride in the Morning.* John Lehmann is quoted from his autobiography *I am my Brother,* Longman 1960. Connolly was writing in *Horizon* 1944.

Henry Treece is quoted from *Leaves in the Storm,* Lindsay Drummond 1947. William Golding is quoted from a review of Paul Fussell's *The Great War and Modern Memory* in the *Guardian* 20 November 1975. Robert Herring is quoted from his editorial to the

January 1945 number of *Life and Letters Today*, Wrey Gardiner from his for the Winter 1944 number of *Poetry Quarterly*. Connolly was writing in the December 1944 issue of *Horizon*. Orwell was reporting to the *Partisan Review*, see Volume Three of *The Collected Essays, etc.*, Constantine Fitzgibbon is quoted from *The Life of Dylan Thomas*, Dent 1965 and Little, Brown and Company (Boston).

The Lion and the Unicorn is reprinted in *The Collected Essays, etc.*, Volume Two. Addison's *The Road to 1945* was published by Cape in 1975. V.S. Pritchett was writing in the 2 September 1944 issue of the *New Statesman*. George Woodcock was writing in *Now* (new series) No. 2 1944. Orwell is quoted from his essay 'Poetry and the Microphone', reprinted in Volume Two of *The Collected Essays, etc.* Osbert Sitwell's *A Letter to My Son* was published by Home and Van Thal in 1944; Lehmann and Spender are quoted from *Penguin New Writing* No. 24. Julian Symons was writing in *Now* (new series) No. 5 1944. Alex Comfort was writing in *Now* (new series) No. 2 1944. Routledge published Paul Bloomfield's *The Many and the Few* in 1942, and D.S. Savage's *The Personal Principle* in 1944. Spender is quoted from *Penguin New Writing* No. 24.

John Lehmann is quoted from the first of his series 'The Armoured Writer', which began with *New Writing and Daylight* No. 1 in 1942. Norman Nicholson is quoted from a review for *Time and Tide* 17 July 1943, Henry Treece from *How I See Apocalypse*, Lindsay Drummond 1946. John Lehmann was writing in *Penguin New Writing* No. 19. 'The Yogi and the Commissar' first appeared in the June 1942 number of *Horizon*, and became the title essay for his collection of wartime writings published by Cape in 1945.

Alan Ross is quoted from an interview with the author. Goronwy Rees's 'Letter from a Soldier', in reply to Connolly's editorial of the May 1940 number of *Horizon* appeared in the July 1940 number. C. Day Lewis's 'Where Are The War Poets?' is in his *Word Over All*, Faber and Faber 1943 and the Transatlantic Press (New York). Connolly was writing in *Horizon* December 1944. André Halimi's *Chantons Sous L'Occupation* was published in Paris by Olivier Orban in 1946. Roy Fuller is quoted from *Our Time*, October 1945.

Arthur Koestler is quoted from 'The Fraternity of Pessimists', reprinted in *The Yogi and the Commissar*, Cape 1945. V.S. Pritchett's *Midnight Oil* was published by Chatto and Windus in 1971. Alan Ross was writing in the April 1961 number of *The London Magazine*. Dan Davin is quoted from *Closing Times*, Oxford University Press 1975.

Acknowledgments

Details of the author, source and publisher of all quotations are given in the notes, and I gratefully acknowledge the permissions that have been granted by copyright holders to make them. Unfortunately it has not been possible in a number of cases to trace the present copyright holder, where the publication, publisher, or regrettably the author, is now defunct. Nor has it been possible to give the name of the American publisher of a number of works quoted. I hope that copyright holders will accept the acknowledgment made in the notes. Special acknowledgments are made:

For *The Modern Short Story* to the Estate of the late H.E. Bates; the quotations from *England's Hour* by Vera Brittain are included with the permission of Sir George Catlin and Paul Berry, her literary executors; quotations from *The Unquiet Grave* by Cyril Connolly © 1944 by Cyril Connolly are by permission of Hamish Hamilton Ltd, London, and Harper and Row, Publishers, Inc. (New York); from *Enemies of Promise* by permission of Andre Deutsch; acknowledgment is made to the Estate of the late Cyril Connolly for permission to quote from these works and Connolly's contributions to *Horizon*. Extracts from *Poems from India* (ed. R.N. Currey 1945) and from *Closing Times* by Dan Davin 1975 are quoted by permission of the Oxford University Press. Acknowledgment is made to the Estate of the late C. Day Lewis and to the Hogarth Press and Jonathan Cape Ltd for quotations from *Collected Poems*, 1954, and to Chatto and Windus Ltd for *The Buried Day*. Quotations from the writings of Keith Douglas are by permission of Marie J. Douglas and J.C. Hall. Extracts from T.S. Eliot's 'Little Gidding' are reprinted by permission of Faber and Faber Ltd, from *Four Quartets* by T.S. Eliot, pub-

Acknowledgments

Jovanovitch (New York); quotations from *The Collected Essays of Virginia Woolf* are by permission of the literary estate of Virginia Woolf, the Hogarth Press and Harcourt, Brace Jovanovitch (New York). Quotations from Richard Hillary's *The Last Enemy* are made by permission of Lovat Dickson and the Hillary Estate.

SOURCE OF ILLUSTRATIONS

The author and publishers would like to thank the following for kind permission to reproduce the photographs and illustrations: By courtesy of Sir Osbert Lancaster and John Murray (Publishers) Ltd, 1 (from *Horizon* January 1942); Fox Photos Ltd, 2; Radio Times Hulton Picture Library, 3, 4, 6, 12; The British Council, 5 (from *Prose Literature Since 1939* by John Hayward), 7, 10, 15 (from *Poetry Since 1939* by Stephen Spender); Alfred A. Knopf, 8; Syndication International, 9; by courtesy of the National Film Archive, 11 (Crown copyright, from Humphrey Jennings's film *Fires Were Started*); Alan Ross, 13 (photo: Thea Umlauff); Bill Brandt, 14, 18; J.C. Hall and Marie J. Douglas, 16; Roy Fuller, 17; *The Times*, 19 (from *British Achievement in Art and Music* by Jack Lindsay); the Trustees of the Imperial War Museum, 20, 27; The Tate Gallery, London, 21, 25; by permission of the Speaker of the House of Commons, 22; reproduced by gracious permission of Her Majesty Queen Elizabeth The Queen Mother, 23; from *Horizon* March 1942, 24; Studio International, 26 (from *The Studio* July 1943), 28 (from *The Studio* August 1944).

Index

207

Index

Carroll, Lewis, 148

Cary, Joyce: *Charley is My Darling*, 90; *A House of Children*, 90; *Herself Surprised*, 91; *The Horse's Mouth*, 91–2; *To Be a Pilgrim*, 91

Cazalet, Victor, AA Battery of, 15–16

CEMA (Council for the Encouragement of Music and the Arts), 34, 154, 155, 157–9, 164, 165; formation of (1939–40), 23, 157

censorship, 13, 16, 78, 142

Cézanne, Paul, 145

Chamberlain, Neville, 5, 9, 17, 24, 41

Chappell, William: 'Words from a Stranger', 85

Christian News-Letter, The, 12

Christianity, 12, 38, 47, 107, 109, 174

Christie's Sale Rooms, 142

Church, Katherine, 148

Churchill, Winston S., 24, 43, 74

Churchill Club, 170

Circle, 144

Citadel, 122, 132

Clark, Sir Kenneth, 8, 14; and AIA, 147; and National Gallery, 142; and WAAC, 141, 151

Clough, Prunella, 61

Clunes, Alec, 159

Coffee An', the, 57, 60

Coldstream, William, 145, 146

Colefax, Sybil, 63

Coleridge, Samuel Taylor: *The Ancient Mariner*, 153; 'Kubla Khan', 156–7

Colindale Library, 29

Collins, Cecil: *The Holy Fool*, 153; *The Sleeping Fool, Plate 25*; *The Vision and the Fool*, 153

Collins, publishers, 32

Colquhoun, Robert, 61, 66, 152–3

Comfort, Alex, 177, 179; 'On Interpreting the War', 69; (ed.) *Lyra*, 111, 114

Common Wealth, 80

Common Wealth Party, 80, 174

Communism: and AIA, 146; attraction of for British intellectuals, 72–3; Muir on, 180–81; and Russo-German Pact, 6–7; and Spanish Civil War, 2–3, 6; *and see* Communist Party, British; Marxism

Communist Party, British, 42, 51, 86, 174; and culture, 163–4, 178; magazines of, 81, 163–4; *and see*

Our Time; and the war, 6–7, 34, 35, 42, 69; *and see* Our Time, Unity Theatre

Compton-Burnett, Ivy, 63, 91

concentration camps, 171, 172

Conscientious Objectors, 15, 63, 142, 146

Congreve, William: *Love for Love*, 160

Connolly, Cyril, 45, 56, 63; on Auden and Isherwood, 7; on contributions from armed forces, 86–7; on culture-diffusion, 165; on flying bombs, 170–71; guilty conscience of, 183–4; on *Horizon*'s fifth birthday, 172; launches *Horizon*, 11–12; and 'John Weaver', 106; on myth, 180; and politics, 1–2, 3, 174; and 'new romanticism', 106, 109, 112–13; on war and the arts, 11–12, 31, 50, 72, 74–5, 89–90, 97, 182–3; wide influence of, 110; works referred to: *Enemies of Promise*, 1–3, 7; 'Ivory Shelter', 11; *The Unquiet Grave*, 93, 180; *Plate 3*

Conservative Party, 17, 173, 174; and coalition government, 2

Constructivists, 149

Contemporary Prose and Verse, 15

Cooke, Dorian, 121

Cornhill Magazine, 11

Corsellis, Timothy: 'Drill', 120

Council for the Encouragement of Music and the Arts *see* CEMA

Coward, Noel: *Blithe Spirit*, 159

Craxton, John, 61, 152–3; *Poet in a Landscape*, 149, *Plate 24*

Criterion, 11

Criterion Theatre, 29

Crompton, Richmal: *William and A.R.P.*, 9

Crossman, Richard, 7

Crowley, Aleister, 62

Crown and the Sickle, The, 111

Crusader, 117

Cunard, Lady Emerald, 63

Czechoslovakia, 2, 4, 5, 24

Dadd, Richard, 149

Daily Express, 23, 24, 185

Daily Herald, 30

Daily Mail, 24

Daily Sketch, 24

Daladier, Edouard, 5, 6